Welcome to Allez 1

KU-418-511

Corinne Dzuilka-Heywood
Yvonne Kennedy
Katie Smith

with Geneviève Talon

Meet Diakouba, Jules, Noura, Clarisse, Basile, Zaied and friends. Find out more about them in this book and on the *Allez 1* video.

Symbols and headings you will find in the book: what do they mean?

 A video activity

 A listening activity

 A speaking activity

 A reading activity

 A writing activity

 Work with a group

 Grammar explanation

Important words and phrases

 Language skills and strategies

 A plenary activity to review learning

 A bronze medal activity for further reinforcement

 A silver medal activity for core task support

 A gold medal activity for further extension

 Use your literacy skills

Extra Star / Plus Reinforcement and extension activities

Labo-langue Grammar, language learning strategies and pronunciation

Lire Reading pages

Vidéo Video pages

Test Test yourself

Vocabulaire Unit vocabulary list

Grammaire Grammar reference

Glossaire Glossary

 Use your numeracy skills

---

 kerboodle

Further resources available on *Allez 1 Kerboodle*

 An interactive activity

 An audio file

 A video clip

 A grammar presentation

OXFORD
UNIVERSITY PRESS

Table des matières

Table des matières

1.1 Le monde et moi

- Vocabulary: introduce yourself; say where you live, what languages you speak and your nationality
- Grammar: say that you live *in* a place; use *le/la/l'/les*
- Skills: answer questions

 1 **Lis le texte. Recopie et complète la grille. Fais la liste des pays et des nationalités.**
Read the text. Copy and complete the grid. Make a list of the countries and the nationalities.

Exemple:

pays	country	*nationalité*	nationality
la France	France	*française*	French

Je m'appelle Lara. J'habite en Écosse.

Je m'appelle Mackenzie. J'habite en Angleterre.

Je m'appelle Catrin. J'habite au pays de Galles.

Je m'appelle Declan. J'habite en Irlande.

Comment t'appelles-tu?

Où habites-tu?

l'Écosse
l'Irlande
le pays de Galles
l'Angleterre
la Belgique
l'Allemagne
la France
la Suisse
le Portugal
l'Espagne
l'Italie

Je m'appelle Jonas. J'habite en Belgique.

Je m'appelle Ferkan. J'habite en Allemagne.

Je m'appelle Morgane. J'habite en France.

Je m'appelle Cristina. J'habite en Espagne.

 **Make up phrases for the other countries on the map:** *Je m'appelle … J'habite en/au …*

🧍 Je suis anglais.	🧍 Je suis anglaise.
Je suis français.	Je suis française.
Je suis espagnol.	Je suis espagnole.
Je suis irlandais.	Je suis irlandaise.
Je suis écossais.	Je suis écossaise.
Je suis gallois.	Je suis galloise.
Je suis allemand.	Je suis allemande.
Je suis belge.	Je suis belge.

⚙ Grammaire
p. 166
WB p.5

How to say 'the' in French
All nouns (naming words) in French are either *masculine* or *feminine*.

le	masculine noun	**le** pays de Galles
la	feminine noun	**la** France
l'	noun beginning with vowel or (silent) *h*	**l'**Angleterre
les	plural noun	**les** continents

2 **Écoute, recopie et complète la grille.**
C'est quel pays? C'est quelle langue?
Listen, copy and complete the table with the
correct country and language.

nom	pays	langue
Mackenzie	*l'Angleterre*	*anglais*
Morgane		
Declan		
Lara		
Ferkan		
Catrin		

 **Which English-speaking person speaks
two languages? Where do they live?**

3 **Choisis une personne. Fais des dialogues. A↔B.**
Think of a person from activity 1. Your partner guesses
who it is.
Exemple: **A** J'habite en Écosse. Je parle anglais.
B C'est Morgane?
A Non, ce n'est pas Morgane!
B C'est Lara?
A Oui, c'est Lara!

4 **Écris des phrases.**
Write sentences for the pictures below.

Exemple: 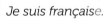 Je suis française.

a **b**

c **d**

e **f**

5 **Réponds aux questions.**
Write answers to the questions.
Exemple: Comment t'appelles-tu? – Je m'appelle …
Où habites-tu? – J'habite en/au …
Quelle langue parles-tu? – Je parle …

Quelle langue parles-tu?
What language do you speak?
je suis   *I am*
j'habite   *I live*
je parle (anglais/français/espagnol/
gallois/allemand)   *I speak (English/
French/Spanish/Welsh/German)*

Answering questions
You will hear an 'echo' of the
question in your answer.
*Comment t'**appelle**s-tu? –*
What is your **name**?
*Je m'**appelle** Mackenzie. –*
My **name** is Mackenzie.
*Où **habite**s-tu? –*
Where do you **live**?
*J'**habite** en Angleterre. –*
I **live** in England.

Grammaire p. 167

How to say 'in' + a country
*J'habite **en** France* (*la* France, feminine noun)
*J'habite **au** pays de Galles* (*le* pays de Galles,
masculine noun)
*J'habite **en** Angleterre* (*l'*Angleterre, noun
starting with a vowel)

Plenary

⭐ Say your name and what
country you live in.
◎ Add what nationality you
are.
➕ Add what language you
speak.
Think about <u>what</u> you have
learnt and <u>how</u>. Discuss the use
of *en/au* with your partner. Do
you both know the difference
between *anglais* and *anglaise*?

1.2 Quelle est la date ...?

- Vocabulary: learn numbers and the months of the year
- Grammar: learn how to say dates
- Skills: use strategies to learn new words

 1 Recopie les mois dans le bon ordre.
Copy the months of the year in the correct order.
Exemple: janvier, ...

décembre	avril	**février**	**juin**
septembre	**août**	octobre	janvier
mars	mai	juillet	*novembre*

 2 Écoute. Vérifie tes réponses.
Listen. Check your answers.

 3 Écoute et lis.
 See page 15 for strategies on how to remember new words.

1	un	11	onze	21	vingt et un	31	trente et un
2	deux	12	douze	22	vingt-deux		
3	trois	13	treize	23	vingt-trois		
4	quatre	14	quatorze	24	vingt-quatre		
5	cinq	15	quinze	25	vingt-cinq		
6	six	16	seize	26	vingt-six		
7	sept	17	dix-sept	27	vingt-sept		
8	huit	18	dix-huit	28	vingt-huit		
9	neuf	19	dix-neuf	29	vingt-neuf		
10	dix	20	vingt	30	trente		

 4 Sondage: 'Quel âge as-tu?'
Class survey. Ask 'How old are you?'

Quel âge as-tu?   *How old are you?*
J'ai douze ans.   *I am 12 years old.*

 5 Quel âge as-tu? Écris les réponses.
Write answers for each of the cards a–f.
Exemple: **a** *J'ai cinq ans.*

a C'est ton anniversaire! 5 ans

b Joyeux anniversaire! 11 ANS

c C'EST TON ANNIVERSAIRE! 19 ans

d Bon anniversaire! 21 ans

e Joyeux anniversaire! 26 ans

f Bon anniversaire! 30 ans

Quel âge as-tu?

Memorisation strategies
How are you going to remember the months and the numbers? See page 15 for some strategies.

Écoute (1–6). Écris les anniversaires en anglais.
Listen. Write the birthdays in English.
Exemple: **1** *April 9th*

 Note the speakers' ages.

Demande à ton groupe. A↔B.
Ask your group.
Exemple: **A** *Quelle est la date de ton anniversaire?*
      B *Mon anniversaire, c'est le (quatre juin). Et toi?*

Recopie et remplis la grille en anglais.
Copy and complete the table in English.

> Quelle est la date de ton anniversaire?
> Mon anniversaire, c'est le neuf avril.

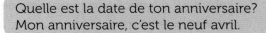

> **Grammaire** p. 170
>
> **Saying dates**
> To say dates, use:
> C'est + le + number + month:
> *C'est le quatre octobre.*
> The <u>first</u> day of the month is different.
> You have to use *premier* (first):
> *C'est le premier janvier.*

> Bonjour! **Je m'appelle** Saïd Zoltan. **Je suis** footballeur. **Mon anniversaire, c'est le** dix-huit août. **J'ai** dix-neuf **ans. Je suis** français (d'origine tunisienne).

> Bonjour! **Je m'appelle** Claudia Moreau. **Je suis** actrice. **Mon anniversaire, c'est le** neuf août. **J'ai** trente et un **ans. Je suis** française (d'origine belge).

> Salut! **Je m'appelle** Jamel Bizzou. **Je suis** acteur. **Mon anniversaire, c'est le** dix-huit juin. **J'ai** trente **ans. Je suis** français (d'origine marocaine).

nom	anniversaire	âge	nationalité	autres informations
Saïd	*18th August*	*19*	*French*	*Footballer; Tunisian origin*
Claudia				
Jamel				

Imagine que tu es célèbre.
Écris un petit texte.
Imagine you are a celebrity.
Using the phrases in **bold** in activity 9, write a short text.

> **Plenary**
>
> ★ Say your age.
> ◎ Add when your birthday is.
> ✚ Ask someone for their age and birthday.
>
> Discuss the meaning of 'conversation' in pairs. Is it important to ask as well as answer questions? Why/Why not?

1.3 Mon autoportrait

- Vocabulary: describe your appearance and that of another person
- Grammar: use present tense of *avoir*; apply adjectives
- Skills: use sound strategies to memorise new words

 Écoute (1–5) et lis. C'est quelle image?
Listen, read and match the description to the picture.
Exemple: **1** *b*

1 J'ai les yeux bleus.
2 J'ai les yeux marron.
3 J'ai les yeux gris.
4 J'ai les yeux noisette.
5 J'ai les yeux verts.

 Écoute, lis et mets dans le bon ordre.
Listen, read and put in the correct order.
Exemple: c, ...

J'ai les cheveux noirs et nattés.	J'ai les cheveux roux et bouclés.	J'ai les cheveux longs et bruns.	J'ai les cheveux courts et blonds.	Je n'ai pas de cheveux.	J'ai les cheveux blonds, mi-longs et raides.

 Décris-toi. Tu es comment? Prends des notes. A↔B.
In turns (i) describe yourself to your partner (ii) listen to your partner and note down what they say.
Exemple: **A** C'est à moi! **J'ai** les yeux verts et j'ai les cheveux courts et bruns.
B **Tu as** les yeux verts ... et les cheveux courts et bruns.
A Oui, c'est ça. C'est à toi maintenant.
B Alors, moi, j'ai ...

➕ **If your partner gets it wrong, tell them so and repeat your description:** *Non, ce n'est pas ça. Je répète. J'ai ...*

Grammaire p. 166

Adjectives

Adjectives are **describing** words. They describe nouns (naming words).
Here *les yeux* (eyes) is the noun and the colours are the adjectives.

You add an -*s* to adjectives describing plural nouns: *J'ai les yeux vert**s** et les cheveux long**s** et blond**s**.*

Some adjectives of colour never change: *J'ai les yeux noisette, j'ai les yeux marron.*

Grammaire p. 169
WB p.6

The verb *avoir* (to have)

j'**ai**	I **have**
tu **as**	you **have**
il/elle **a**	he/she **has**
on **a**	we **have**

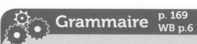

et   *and*
C'est à qui?   *Whose turn is it?*
C'est à moi.   *It's my turn.*
C'est à toi.   *It's your turn.*

 LIRE 4 **Lis les textes. C'est qui?**
Read the texts and look at the pictures. Who is it?
Exemple: **1** *e*

foncé *dark*   clair *light*

a   b   c   d   e

1 Voici mon copain Bruno. Il a les yeux bleus et les cheveux blonds, mi-longs.

2 Voici ma copine Caroline. Elle a les yeux verts et les cheveux roux, longs et raides.

3 Voici ma copine Axelle. Elle a les cheveux noirs, nattés et de grands yeux marron.

4 Voici mon ami Jamel. Il a les cheveux brun foncé, très courts, et les yeux noisette.

5 Voici ma meilleure amie, Élise. Elle a les yeux bleu clair. Elle a les cheveux noirs. Élise et moi, on a les cheveux bouclés.

 PARLER 5 **Décris un(e) camarade de classe. A↔B.**
In turns, describe a classmate.
Exemple: **A** *Il/Elle a les yeux … et les cheveux …*
  B *C'est [name]?*
  A *Oui, c'est ça. C'est à toi, maintenant.*
  B *Alors, il/elle a …*

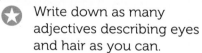 **If your partner gets it wrong, tell them so and repeat your description:**
Non, ce n'est pas ça. Je répète. Il/Elle a …

 ÉCRIRE 6 **Tu es comment? Et ton ami(e)? Écris un mail.**
Write an email to your pen-pal describing yourself and a friend.

	les yeux	bleus/verts/gris/ marron/noisette/ bleu foncé/bleu clair		
J'ai Il/Elle a	les cheveux	blonds bruns roux noirs	et	longs mi-longs courts bouclés nattés raides
Je n'ai pas Il/Elle n'a pas	de cheveux.			

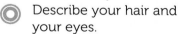
Sound strategies

How are you going to remember how to pronounce and write the words in the grid above?

• **Use what you know.** If you remember how to pronounce *je suis*, how do you say *gris*?

• Spot the other **'secret' letters** – the ones that are not pronounced unless they have *-es* at the end, like *g* in *longs* or *t* in *courts*.

• **Use your senses**. Say the word with an English accent, then read it again sounding as French as you can. For example, hold your nose to say *brun*.

• Listen to the word and **visualise** how it is spelt.

• **Split the word up**: *noi/sette*.

1.4 Mon objet préféré

- Vocabulary: name and describe your favourite object
- Grammar: use *un/une/des*; recognise and use *c'est, il est, c'est quoi?*
- Skills: ask questions using correct intonation

ÉCOUTER 1

Écoute et choisis le bon objet (1–6).
Listen and choose the correct object.
Exemple: **1** e

une peluche

une tablette

une console
(de jeux vidéo)

une collection
de BD

un portable

une petite
voiture

PARLER 2

Choisis un objet. Fais des dialogues. A ↔ B.
Choose an object from the list in activity 1.
Get your partner to guess it.
Exemple: **A** *J'ai choisi. Mon objet préféré, c'est quoi?*
   B *C'est une peluche?*
   A *Non, ce n'est pas ça.*
   B *C'est un portable?*
   A *Oui, c'est ça!*

Intonation
When you ask a question, your voice goes up at the end. This is the verbal equivalent of a question mark. When you answer a question, your voice stays even or goes down.

LIRE 3

Recopie et remplis la grille.

 Copy and complete the table with words from the list. See page 15 for memorisation strategies.

matière	forme
C'est en ...	C'est ...
... plastique.	... un rectangle.

Grammaire p. 166 WB p.4

How to say 'a'
French has two words for 'a'.

masculine noun	feminine noun
un portable a mobile phone	**une** peluche a cuddly toy

Use **des** for any plural noun:
des BD – (some) comics

Grammaire WB p.10

High-frequency structure: *c'est*

C'est means 'It is' or 'It's' in French. It can be used in lots of different ways:

C'est mon objet préféré. – It's my favourite object.
C'est quoi? – What is it?
C'est ça. – That's it./That's right.
Ce n'est pas ça. – That isn't it./That isn't right.

plastique   un rectangle   un rond
métal   une sphère   un carré   velours
un triangle   coton   un ovale
céramique   bois   papier   tissu

  Lis et regarde l'activité 1. C'est quel objet?

 Read and look at activity 1. Which object is it?
See page 15 for strategy advice.

Exemple: **1** *e*

1 Mon objet préféré? Il est en plastique. Il est vert.
C'est un rectangle.
2 Mon objet favori? Il est en velours. Il est marron.
C'est un chien.
3 Il est en métal. C'est un véhicule. Il est multicolore. Voilà
mon objet préféré!
4 Il est en papier. C'est un rectangle. J'en ai une grande
collection … ce sont mes objets préférés.
5 Mon objet (ou mon gadget) préféré, il est noir … c'est un
rectangle … non, un carré … il est en plastique et en métal.
6 C'est quoi, mon objet préféré? C'est un rectangle. Il est bleu.
Voilà, c'est tout!

Écoute et regarde l'activité 1. Recopie et
complète la grille. C'est quel objet?
Listen and look at activity 1. Copy and
complete the table. What is their
favourite object?

nom	
Julie	*b*
Léo	
Océane	
Samuel	
le professeur	

**Can you note (i) one detail for each item,
in English? (ii) Two details? (iii) More?**

Lis le mail de Bastien. Écris une réponse.
Read Bastien's email. Write a reply.
Change the text in italics.

**Can you include some adjectives of
your own?**
C'est … cool!

Sujet: Mon objet préféré

Salut!
Merci pour ton mail.
Voici une photo de mon objet préféré.
Il est en *métal*.
Il est *assez petit*.
Il est *rond*.
Mon objet préféré,
c'est *une médaille de
foot*.

Et toi? Quel est ton
objet préféré?
Il est comment?
Écris-moi bientôt!

Bastien

Plenary

 Say what your favourite object is.

 Add what material it is made from.

 Add what shape it is.

In pairs, consider how your listening skills have
improved. Can you predict what topic you will
be learning about next?

1.5 Le monde francophone

- Vocabulary: name some French-speaking parts of the world
- Grammar: use prepositions with countries
- Skills: recognise and apply French sound patterns

LIRE 1

Relie les mots et les images.
Match the words to the pictures.
Exemple: **a** *l'Amérique*
1 *le Canada/le Québec*

Le monde francophone

l'Afrique	l'Amérique
l'Asie	l'Europe	l'Océanie

l'Algérie	la Belgique	le Cameroun	le Canada/le Québec
le Sénégal	Tahiti	la Tunisie	le Vietnam

ÉCOUTER 2

Écoute (1–5). Note les continents.
Listen. In which continents is
French spoken?
Exemple: **1** *l'Europe*

PARLER 3

Fais des dialogues. A ↔ B.
In pairs, create new dialogues.
Exemple: **A** *On parle français en Algérie.*
B *Et on parle français au Vietnam.*

➕ **Use *c'est vrai* and *c'est faux* to say whether you agree or not with your partner's answer.**
Exemple: **A** *L'Algérie ... c'est en Amérique.*
B *Non, c'est faux! C'est en Afrique!*
A *Oui, c'est vrai!*

Écoute et répète.

In French, letters represent sounds, but not always the same sounds as in English. Listen and repeat.

Practise saying these words with a partner.

i Makes a long 'ee' sound, like 'ch**ee**se' in English: **I**talie, Belg**i**que, Afr**i**que, cont**i**nent, avr**i**l

ç The tail which appears sometimes under the letter *c* is called a cedilla and it changes the sound to an 's' sound: fran**ç**ais, **ç**a

é Sounds like 'ay' in English (but shorter): boucl**é**, natt**é**, v**é**hicule, pr**é**f**é**r**é**, f**é**vrier

e The letter *e* on the end of a word is mute (silent), but you can hear the consonant before (*t*, *g*): Afriqu**e**, Belgiqu**e**, Angleterr**e**, Franc**e** cour**te**, lon**gue**

oi Work together to make a 'wah' sound: tr**oi**s, m**oi**, n**oi**r, qu**oi**

eu Work together to make a 'euh' sound: d**eu**x, chev**eu**x, y**eu**x, bl**eu**

ui Work together to make a 'wee' sound: h**ui**t, S**ui**sse

ou Work together to make an 'oo' sound: r**ou**x, t**ou**t, c**ou**rt

gn Work together to make a 'nyuh' sound (as in 'onion'): Espa**gn**e, Allema**gn**e

au Work together to make an 'oh' sound: **au**, **au**jourd'hui

in Work together to make an 'an' sound (as in the middle of 'hand'): c**in**q, qu**in**ze, cop**ain**, ju**in** **5**

en/an Work together to make a sound like 'on' in English (but very nasal, high in the nose, and you can't hear the *n*): **en**, Fr**an**ce, contin**en**t, tr**en**te, j**an**vier **30**

qu Work together to make a 'kuh' sound like in 'king' (*not* 'kwuh' as in 'queen'): **qu**atre, **qu**inze, **Qu**ébec, **qu**and, **qu**oi **15**

Final silent consonants Most consonants on the ends of words in French are not sounded: deu**x**, cheveu**x**, yeu**x**, troi**s**, continen**t**, alleman**d**. The exceptions are **c**, **r**, **f**, **l**. Remember these as CaReFuL consonants.

 Crée un glossaire sonore.
Create a sound glossary. List words in groups according to a sound they have in common.

ui	oi	an/en
la Suisse	moi	la France
…	…	…

○ **Go back through the unit and create more sound groups.**

Plenary

★ Name at least five Francophone countries.

◎ Name the continents they are in.

✚ Say what country (and continent) you live in and what language(s) are spoken there, using *on*.

Look carefully through all the vocabulary and structures you have learnt in this unit. Analyse your progress so far. Colour-code in green five words that you can pronounce and spell easily, in orange three words that you can almost do, and in red two words you still need to work on. See page 15 for memorisation strategies. How can you learn the red words?

1.6 Labo-langue

Nouns and articles

1 **Rewrite the nouns below putting *le/la/les* and *un/une/des* in front.**

Exemple: **a** *le pays, un pays*

a pays *m*
b console *f*
c nationalités *fpl*
d véhicules *mpl*
e peluche *f*
f yeux *mpl*

A **noun** is a naming word. All nouns have a **gender** in French. Different **articles** (the words for 'a' and 'the') are used for masculine and feminine nouns.

	masculine singular	feminine singular	masculine/ feminine plural
the	**le**	la	les
a/ some	**un**	une	des

Le or *la* in front of a vowel loses a letter:

~~la~~ Europe – *l'Europe*   ~~le~~ anglais – *l'anglais*

Adjectives of nationality

2 **Write sentences.**

Exemple: **a** *Je suis anglais.* or *Je suis anglaise.*

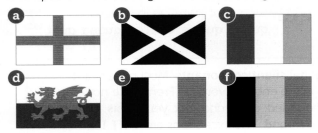

The sound and spelling of nationalities change according to whether the person is male or female. The feminine version adds an *-e*.

masculine	feminine
anglais	anglaise
français	française
irlandais	irlandaise
écossais	écossaise
gallois	galloise
Some nationalities do not change:	
belge	belge

3 **Translate the sentences into French.**

Exemple: **a** *Je suis écossaise.*

a I am Scottish. *f*
b I am Belgian. *m*
c I am French. *m*
d I am Belgian. *f*
e I am Welsh. *m*
f I am Irish. *f*
g I am English. *m*

Avoir

4 **Translate the sentences.**

Exemple: **a** *I am 11 years old.*

a J'ai onze ans.
b Tu as quel âge?
c J'ai raison.
d Tu as tort.
e Il a dix ans.
f Elle a quel âge?

The verb *avoir* means *to have.*

j'**ai**	I **have**
tu **as**	you **have**
il/elle **a** on **a**	he/she **has** we **have**

How to say 'in' a country

5 Complete the sentences.

a J'habite _en_ Angleterre.
b J'habite ▦▦ pays de Galles.
c J'habite ▦▦ Espagne.

d J'habite ▦▦ Italie.
e J'habite ▦▦ Sénégal.
f J'habite ▦▦ Écosse.

	masculine	feminine
in	**au**	en

le Canada – *J'habite au Canada.*
la France – *J'habite* en *France.*

En is used for all country names starting with a vowel.

Memorisation strategies

Use these strategies with activity 3, page 10 and Plenary, page 13.

Which of the words in this unit did you find easiest to remember and why?

How are you going to remember the hard words? Here are some ideas.

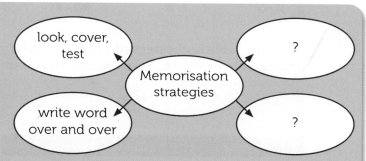

- Write down **three ways** you know of remembering words. For example, maybe you write the words down when you are given vocabulary to learn for homework. Perhaps then you even **cover them up** and **test yourself**? These kind of learning tools are called 'strategies'.
- Now take three minutes to compare your list with your partner's. Are your strategies the same?
- What about the whole class? You could copy the spidergram of all the strategies the class suggests.
- Try these three strategies:
  1 *Rond* may be easy because it's a bit **like English**. Words like that are called cognates and they help you to **use what you know already**.

2 But what about *carré*? **Use images.** **Associate** it with an English word and **visualise** it. For example, think of **carrying** a square suitcase 🧳. For *triangle*, think of the shape of a Christmas tree 🎄.

3 **Use your senses.** For *rond*, make a round shape with your mouth. It will also help you say it correctly. Make other shapes with your hands or put the colours to the tune of 'I can sing a rainbow'.

- Now work with your partner and practise these three strategies with the following words: *cylindre, étoile, croissant.* Discuss if the strategies help or not. Can you guess what the words mean?

Pronunciation: silent letters

6 Listen to the nationalities (1–8). Are they masculine or feminine?

Exemple: **1** *masculine*

Remember that most consonants on the ends of words in French are not sounded.

- Vocabulary: practise using vocabulary from the unit
- Grammar: recognise and respond to question words
- Skills: use knowledge to work out meaning; apply literacy and numeracy skills

 Write out the numbers in order from smallest to largest. What is the next number in the series?

Exemple: cinq, ...

trente   quinze   dix   vingt-cinq   cinq   vingt

 Write out the dates in words.

Exemple: **a** *le onze juin*

a 11/6   b 1/2   c **10/3**   d 31/10   e 4/7   f 22/8

 Copy the table and categorise the vocabulary under the appropriate headings. Some words can go under both.

bleus   blonds   bouclés   bruns   courts   gris   longs   marron
mi-longs   nattés   noirs   noisette   raides   roux   verts

J'ai les yeux ...	J'ai les cheveux ...
bleus	raides

 Match the questions and answers and write out the dialogue.

Exemple: **a** *Comment t'appelles-tu?*
           2 *Je m'appelle Moussa Barry.*

a Comment t'appelles-tu?
b Où habites-tu?
c Quel âge as-tu?
d De quelle nationalité es-tu?
e Tu parles quelle(s) langue(s)?
f Quelle est la date de ton anniversaire?

1 C'est le premier octobre.
2 Je m'appelle Moussa Barry.
3 J'ai vingt-neuf ans.
4 Je parle français et wolof (une langue sénégalaise).
5 J'habite en France et au Sénégal.
6 Je suis français (d'origine sénégalaise).

 Write your own answers to the questions above.
Exemple: **a** *Je m'appelle ...*

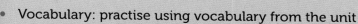

- Vocabulary: practise using vocabulary from the unit
- Grammar: practise verb forms *j'ai, je suis, j'habite, je parle*
- Skills: use knowledge to work out meaning; apply numeracy and literacy skills

Fais les calculs.
Do the sums. Write them out in words.
Exemple: **a** *dix + cinq = quinze*

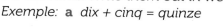

a 10 + 5 =
b 10 + 9 =
c 31 − 10 =
d 30 − 8 =
e 21 ÷ 3 =
f 9 × 3 =

Recopie et complète le texte.
You are putting three special objects in a time capsule. Copy and complete the text.
Exemple: L'objet numéro un, c'est **un portable**. *C'est un* **rectangle** *en* **plastique** *et en* **métal**.

Voici mes trois objets préférés pour ma capsule témoin.

L'objet numéro un, c'est . C'est un(e) *[shape]* en *[material]*.

L'objet numéro deux, c'est . C'est un(e) *[shape]* en *[material]*.

L'objet numéro trois, c'est . C'est un(e) *[shape]* en *[material]*.

Lis le texte. Vrai ou faux?
Read the text. True or false?
Exemple: **a** *vrai*

a Doria is an actress.
b Doria lives in Tunisia.
c Doria's birthday is on February 27th.
d She only speaks French.
e Her mother is Tunisian.
f She is thirty-two.

> Je m'appelle Doria Harzan. Je suis actrice. J'habite en France. Je suis française mais mon père est tunisien et ma mère est algérienne. Je parle français et arabe. J'ai vingt-cinq ans. Mon anniversaire, c'est le dix-huit janvier.

mais   *but*

Écris une autobiographie.
Imagine you are someone famous writing an autobiography. Write a paragraph.
Exemple: Je m'appelle Rachel Rayment. Je suis scientifique ...

Je m'appelle ...
Je suis ...
J'habite ...
Je parle ...
Mon anniversaire, c'est ...
J'ai ... ans.

scientifique	
artiste	
cycliste	
athlète	
acteur	actrice
footballeur	footballeuse
musicien	musicienne

Pour dessiner un bonhomme

Deux petits ronds dans un grand rond.
Pour le nez, un trait droit et long.
Une courbe dessous, la bouche.
Et pour chaque oreille, une boucle.

Sous le beau rond, un autre rond
Plus grand encore et plus oblong.
On peut y mettre des boutons:
Quelques gros points y suffiront.

Deux traits vers le haut pour les bras
Grands ouverts en signe de joie,
Et puis deux jambes, dans le bas,
Qu'il puisse aller où il voudra.

Et voici un joli bonhomme
Rond et dodu comme une pomme
Qui rit d'être si vite né
Et de danser sur mon papier.

Maurice Carême, 1899–1978
Fleurs de soleil
© Fondation Maurice Carême

un bonhomme	*man*	vers le haut	*going up*
dessous	*underneath*	dans le bas	*at the bottom*
des boutons	*buttons*		

This is a poem by a Belgian writer, Maurice Carême. You don't have to understand every word to make sense of it:

• Focus on the words you know, not the ones you don't know
• Use the context – here, the illustration.

1 **The poem describes a child's picture of a little man.**
Read the poem and find:
• the French words for the following parts of the body (they are highlighted in yellow)
  – arms *les bras*　　　– ear　　　– legs
  – mouth　　　　　　　– nose
• the French words for these shapes (they are highlighted in pink)
  – circle　　　　　　　　– a curve　　　– dots
  – a long straight line　– a loop　　　– oval

2 **Match the lines in the last two verses with these lines.**
Exemple: **a** *Et de danser sur mon papier*

a And dancing on my sheet of paper
b And here is a nice little man
c And then two legs, at the bottom
d Round and chubby like an apple

e So that he can go where he pleases
f Two lines going up for the arms
g Who enjoys having so quickly appeared
h Wide open to show he's happy

1.8 Vidéo

La capsule témoin

 Regarde l'épisode 1. Réponds aux questions en anglais.
Watch episode 1. Answer the questions in English.

a What town are the group in?
b What is the group discussing?
c Name two items they mention that can be put in the time capsule.
d Who are they going to make the time capsule for?
e Whose idea is it to make one?
f What topics are the reports going to be on?

 Relie l'objet et la personne.
Match the object and the person.

Exemple: **a** *Clarisse*

a un chat
b une peluche
c une tablette
d une photo
e une console de jeux vidéo
f une voiture

Diakouba | Jules | Noura

Clarisse | Basile | Zaied

 Qui est-ce?
Who is it?

Exemple: **a** *Zaied*

a
Âge: 13 ans
Anniversaire: 11 juillet

b
Âge: 14 ans
Anniversaire: 4 février

c
Âge: 14 ans
Anniversaire: 31 juillet

d
Âge: 14 ans
Anniversaire: 16 avril

e
Âge: 14 ans
Anniversaire: 11 mars

 Les jeunes parlent quelles langues? Recopie et complète la grille.
What languages do they speak? Copy and complete the table.

	français	anglais	arabe	espagnol
Zaied	✔			
Basile				

 Quel objet mets-tu dans la capsule témoin?
What object would you put in the time capsule?

Exemple: Moi, je mets une petite voiture – ma première voiture!

Listening strategies: Finding clues

Watch the video several times. Each time, you will understand a little more. Remember you don't have to get every single word. Instead, look out for:

• visual clues (Jules's laptop, for example, or the photo of Clarisse's cat)

• the speakers' tone of voice

• facial expressions

1.9 Test

(See pages 4–11.)

1 Listen (1–6). What are they talking about? (See pages 4–11.)

Exemple: **1** *d*

a the country they live in
b their age
c their nationality

d the languages they speak
e their appearance
f their favourite object

2 Answer the questions (your answers can be real or imagined). (See pages 4–11.)

a Comment t'appelles-tu?
b Quel âge as-tu?
c Quelle est la date de ton anniversaire?
d C'est quoi, ta nationalité?
e Où habites-tu?
f Quelle(s) langue(s) parles tu?
g Tu es comment?
h C'est quoi, ton objet préféré?

Je m'appelle …
J'ai … ans.
Mon anniversaire, c'est le …
Je suis …
J'habite …
Je parle …
J'ai les yeux … et les cheveux …
Mon objet préféré, c'est mon/ma/mes …

3 Read the text opposite and answer the questions in English. (See pages 4–11.)

Exemple: **a** *Rowan Rowe (Ro-Ro)*

a What is the man's name (and his nickname)?
b What does he do?
c Where does he live?
d What languages does he speak?
e When is his birthday?
f How old is he?
g What's his favourite thing?

Je m'appelle Rowan Rowe (ou 'Ro-Ro') et je suis cycliste. J'habite en Écosse. Je parle anglais et français. Mon anniversaire, c'est le vingt-huit avril et j'ai vingt ans. Mon objet préféré, c'est une médaille d'or!

4 Imagine you are a celebrity or sports personality. Write a paragraph to introduce yourself. (See pages 4–11.)

Give details about:

- your name
- your age
- where you live
- what language(s) you speak
- your eyes and your hair
- your birthday
- your favourite object

Remember, the more you can develop your answers, the better your work will be.

Simple detail.

For example: *J'habite en France.*

More detail.

For example: *J'habite en France, en Europe.*

Even more detail.

For example: *J'habite en France, en Europe. En France, je parle français!*

Vocabulaire

About me

Bonjour!	*Hello!*
Salut!	*Hi! Bye!*
Au revoir!	*Goodbye!*
Comment t'appelles-tu?	*What's your name?*
Je m'appelle ...	*I'm called ...*
Où habites-tu?	*Where do you live?*
J'habite en/au ...	*I live in ...*
l'Allemagne	*Germany*
l'Angleterre	*England*
la Belgique	*Belgium*
l'Écosse	*Scotland*
l'Espagne	*Spain*
la France	*France*
l'Italie	*Italy*
l'Irlande	*Ireland*
le pays de Galles	*Wales*
le Portugal	*Portugal*
la Suisse	*Switzerland*

Quelle langue parles-tu?	***What language do you speak?***
je parle	*I speak*
on parle	*we/they speak*
anglais/allemand/français/ gallois	*English/German/French/ Welsh*
Je suis ...	*I am ...*
allemand(e)/anglais(e)/ écossais(e)/espagnol(e)/ français(e)/gallois(e)/ irlandais(e)/belge	*German/English/Scottish/ Spanish/French/Welsh/ Irish/Belgian*
d'origine (tunisienne/ sénégalaise)	*of (Tunisian/Senegalese) origin*

Dates and birthdays

janvier	*January*	juillet	*July*
février	*February*	août	*August*
mars	*March*	septembre	*September*
avril	*April*	octobre	*October*
mai	*May*	novembre	*November*
juin	*June*	décembre	*December*

1–31

un	*1*	deux	*2*
trois	*3*	quatre	*4*
cinq	*5*	six	*6*
sept	*7*	huit	*8*
neuf	*9*	dix	*10*
onze	*11*	douze	*12*
treize	*13*	quatorze	*14*
quinze	*15*	seize	*16*
dix-sept	*17*	dix-huit	*18*
dix-neuf	*19*	vingt	*20*
vingt et un	*21*	vingt-deux	22

vingt-trois	*23*	vingt-quatre	*24*
vingt-cinq	*25*	vingt-six	*26*
vingt-sept	*27*	vingt-huit	*28*
vingt-neuf	*29*	trente	*30*
trente et un	*31*		

C'est quel jour aujourd'hui?	*What is the date today?*
Quelle est la date de ton anniversaire?	*What is the date of your birthday?*
C'est le premier/deux janvier.	*It's the first/second of January.*
Quel âge as-tu?	*How old are you?*
J'ai (onze) ans.	*I am (11) years old.*

Physical appearance

J'ai les yeux ...	***I have ... eyes.***
bleu/gris/marron/noisette/ vert/bleu foncé/bleu clair	*blue/grey/brown/hazel/ green/dark blue/light blue*
J'ai les cheveux ...	***I have ... hair.***
blond/brun/noir/roux	*blond/brown/black/red*
court/long/mi-long/ bouclé/natté/raide	*short/long/medium-length/ curly/braided/straight*
Je n'ai pas de cheveux.	*I don't have any hair.*

My favourite object

Ton objet préféré, c'est quoi?	*What's your favourite object?*
Mon objet préféré, c'est ...	*My favourite object is ...*
une collection de BD	*a comic book collection*
une console de jeux vidéo	*a games console*
une peluche	*a cuddly toy*
un (téléphone) portable	*a mobile phone*
une tablette	*a tablet*
une voiture	*a car*
un carré	*a square*
un ovale	*an oval*
un rectangle	*a rectangle*
un rond	*a circle*
une sphère	*a sphere*
un triangle	*a triangle*
Il/Elle est en ... /C'est en...	***It's made of ...***
bois/céramique/coton/ métal/papier/plastique/ tissu/velours	*wood/ceramic/cotton/ metal/paper/plastic/ fabric/velvet*

◎ Grammar and skills: I can...

- ◉ introduce myself and say dates
- ◉ use the present tense of *avoir*
- ◉ use adjectives and indefinite articles
- ◉ use prepositions
- ◉ ask and answer questions
- ◉ use strategies to learn new words
- ◉ recognise and apply French sound patterns

- Vocabulary: describe your personality
- Grammar: use adjectives and *être* (present tense)
- Skills: use memorisation strategies; use high-frequency structures to express thanks

1 Relie les mots et les images.
Match the words and the pictures.
Exemple: **a** 6

a	amusant	**d**	actif	**g**	travailleur
b	bavard	**e**	généreux	**h**	gentil
c	courageux	**f**	timide		

2 Écoute. Relie les personnes et les qualités.
Listen. Match the speakers and the qualities.

a Pauline   c, ...   **c** Faïza
b Julien   **d** Mohammed

✚ What is Pauline's motto at the end?

3 Fais un compliment à ton/ta partenaire. A ↔ B.
Pay your partner a compliment. Have a conversation.
Exemple: **A** *Tu es quelqu'un de ... travailleur.*
          B *Merci.*
          A *De rien.*
          B *Tu es quelqu'un d'amusant.*

◎ **Extend your sentences by using et (and) or et ... aussi
(and ... too):** *Tu es quelqu'un de travailleur* et *de gentil. Tu es
quelqu'un de gentil* et *d'amusant* aussi.

⚙ Grammaire   p. 168–169 / WB p.8

Present tense of *être* (to be)

je suis	I **am**
tu es	you **are**

Je suis quelqu'un de literally means 'I am someone of ...'. In English, we say 'I am someone who is ...'. This phrase is only ever followed by a masculine adjective, even if you are female.

🔧 Thank you

Use some of the phrases below to say 'thank you' and 'you're welcome'. These are high-frequency structures (they are used a lot) and they are highly transferable (you can use them in all sorts of situations).

Thank you.	You're welcome.
Merci.	Je t'en prie.
Merci bien.	Pas de quoi.
Merci beaucoup.	De rien.

Tu es comment? Écris six phrases positives.
What are you like? Write six positive sentences.
Exemple: *Je suis quelqu'un d'assez généreux et de très gentil.*

| je suis quelqu'un de/d' ... | très assez | amusant, sociable, courageux, actif, généreux, timide, travailleur, gentil |

 Look at the vocabulary in the grammar box for some more ideas.

Recopie et complète le diagramme de Venn.
Copy and complete the Venn diagram. Use adjectives from the grammar box.

actif   sociable   active

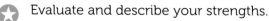 **Can you add some of your own?**

C'est qui, Pauline ou Julien?
Who is it? Pauline ou Julien?
Exemple: **a** *C'est Julien.*

a Je suis créatif.
b Je suis active.
c Je suis actif et timide.
d Je suis sportive et sociable.
e Je suis très généreuse et assez bavarde.
f Je suis un peu amusant et très travailleur.

Décris-toi. Écris cinq phrases.
Describe yourself. Write five sentences.
Exemple: *Je suis assez bavarde.*

très	*very*
un peu	*a bit*
assez	*quite*

 Use *Je ne suis pas* to say what you are not: *Je ne suis pas bavard(e).*

Plenary

★ Evaluate and describe your strengths.

◎ Identify strengths in your partner, then thank them when they do the same to you.

✚ Describe yourself using qualifiers alongside adjectives. Remember adjectival agreement.

Discuss in pairs for one minute the importance and relevance of what you have learnt so far in this unit.

Grammaire
p. 166
WB p.11–12, p.14

Adjectives

Adjectives are words that describe nouns (people, places, things). They change their spellings when describing *feminine* nouns. Can you identify the different types of spelling changes in the box below? Some don't change. Why, do you think?

	masculine	feminine
je suis ...	amusant	amusante
	intelligent	intelligente
	bavard	bavarde
	actif	active
	créatif	créative
	sportif	sportive
	courageux	courageuse
	paresseux	paresseuse
	travailleur	travailleuse
	sociable	sociable
	timide	timide
	adorable	adorable

Qualifiers (*très, un peu, assez*) slightly change the meaning of adjectives.

Memorisation strategies

You used some memorisation strategies in Unit 1. Try these too.

- Use what you know already, e.g. *intelligent* is a cognate.

- Use your senses. Visualise *paresseux* and *bavard* as Mr. Men. Say the words aloud and use mime/tone of voice to show what they mean.

- Spot the silent letters to remind you not to pronounce them, e.g. *bavard*.

- Spot which letter strings you rarely see together in English (*courageux*, *travailleur*) and use what you know already, e.g. *deux*, *acteur* to help you pronounce and spell them correctly.

2.2 C'est quoi, une famille?

- Vocabulary: describe and discuss your family
- Grammar: use possessive adjectives *mon/ma/mes* and *ton/ta/tes*
- Skills: show empathy in conversations and demonstrate good listening

ÉCOUTER 1 **Écoute et lis.**

> Je m'appelle Faïza. J'habite avec ma mère, mon père, mes deux frères, Habib et Iman, et ma sœur qui s'appelle Alia. Chez nous, il y a aussi mes grands-parents. Mon grand-père s'appelle Mustafa et ma grand-mère s'appelle Rachida.

mon grand-père   ma grand-mère   ma mère   mon père

mon frère   mon frère   ma sœur   moi

le beau-père   *stepfather*
la belle-mère   *stepmother*
le demi-frère   *stepbrother*
la demi-sœur   *stepsister*
papa   *dad*
maman   *mum*

ÉCOUTER 2 **Écoute et lis (1–3). Qui parle?**
Listen and read. Who's speaking? Work out the missing names.
Exemple: **1** *Aurélie*

Vincent

Aurélie

Loïc

1 Je m'appelle ***. Chez moi, il y a ma maman, mon papa et ma sœur. Je n'ai pas de frère … alors avec moi, chez nous, on est quatre!

2 Je m'appelle ***. Ma mère s'appelle Laurence et mon père s'appelle Philippe. Mes parents sont divorcés. J'habite avec ma mère et mon beau-père, Simon. J'ai deux sœurs qui s'appellent Rachel et Lauren. Simon, il a un fils. C'est mon demi-frère, David.

3 Je m'appelle ***. Mes parents sont séparés. J'habite avec ma mère. Je n'ai pas de frères ou de sœurs. Je suis fils unique. Maman, elle s'appelle Anne. Je passe un week-end tous les mois chez papa. Papa, il s'appelle Paul.

fils/fille unique   *only child*

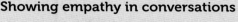

PARLER 3 **Décris ta famille. A ↔ B.**
Describe your family (real or imagined).
Exemple: **A** *J'habite avec ma mère.*
B *Moi aussi.*
A *Mes parents sont divorcés.*
B *D'accord.*

ÉCRIRE 4 **Écris un paragraphe sur 'Ma famille'.**
Write a paragraph about 'My family'
(real or imagined).
Exemple: J'ai une sœur. Je n'ai pas de frère.

ÉCOUTER 5 **Soraya décrit sa famille. Écoute et réponds aux questions en anglais.**
Soraya is describing her family. Listen and answer the questions in English.
Exemple: **a** *16 years old*

a How old is Soraya?
b Who are Hakim and Adèle?
c How many brothers and sisters does she have?

d How many stepbrothers or sisters does she have?
e What is her father like?
f What is her stepmother like?

Vrai ou faux?
La mère de Soraya s'appelle Adèle.

ÉCRIRE 6 **Complète le paragraphe de l'activité 4.**
Complete the paragraph you started in activity 4.

Use this checklist. Have you talked about ...

⭐ **family members? (their names)**

◎ **who you live with? (how many people live in your house)**

➕ **what members of your family (real or imaginary) are like?**

Showing empathy in conversations
Use some of these phrases to demonstrate good listening skills and empathy (understanding another person's feelings).
d'accord – OK
moi aussi – me too
c'est difficile, ça – that's difficult
c'est intéressant – that's interesting
ah bon? – really?

	mon père/ma mère	s'appelle ...
j'ai	un frère/une sœur	qui s'appelle ...
je n'ai pas de	frères/sœurs	
je n'ai plus de	père/mère	

Grammaire p. 167 WB p.25

Possessive adjectives ↖
These adjectives describe who something (or someone) belongs to. They follow a pattern, depending on whether the noun is masculine, feminine or plural: *mon père, ma mère, mes amis*.

masculine	feminine	plural	
mon	*ma*	*mes*	my
ton	*ta*	*tes*	your

Plenary

⭐ Describe a family member (real or imagined).

◎ Add the family member's name.

➕ In your description, use a mixture of positive and negative phrases.

Reflect on strategies for improving listening skills. Analyse the importance of body language when listening to other people. Is empathy important?

- Vocabulary: discuss the school subjects you do/don't like and why
- Grammar: use connectives to extend sentences; use *plus/moins* + adjective to compare subjects
- Skills: recognise and use transferable language

Écoute et lis (1–10). C'est quelle matière?
Listen and read. Which subject is it?
Exemple: **1** *l'anglais*

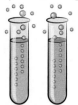    

les SVT (les sciences de la vie et de la terre) | les arts plastiques | l'anglais | la géographie | la technologie

les maths | la musique | le français | l'EPS (l'éducation physique et sportive) | l'histoire

Écoute (1–4). Note la matière en anglais et l'opinion.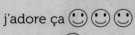
Listen. Note the subject in English and draw faces to show the opinions.
Exemple: **1** *maths* ☺

j'adore ça ☺ ☺ ☺
j'aime ça ☺
ça va 😐
je n'aime pas ça ☹
je déteste ça ☹ ☹ ☹

Lis et fais des paires.
Read and make pairs.
Exemple: **a** *1*

a J'adore le français.
b J'aime la musique.
c Je n'aime pas les maths.
d L'EPS, ça va.
e Je déteste la géographie.

1 C'est passionnant. C'est ma matière préférée!
2 C'est inutile et ennuyeux. C'est nul!
3 C'est créatif et relaxant.
4 C'est ennuyeux mais c'est utile.
5 C'est actif et c'est utile.

Transferable language: opinions

Learn these phrases off by heart, and you have a quick and easy way of saying how you feel about things. Note that *ça* is not always used in spoken language.

La pizza? J'adore (ça)!

Le football? Je déteste (ça)!

L'histoire? J'adore (ça)!

Remember qualifiers (see page 23)?
Rewrite some of the sentences or say them to a partner:
*J'aime le français. C'est **assez** intéressant et **très** utile!*

Invente des questions. Pose tes questions à ton/ta partenaire. A↔B.
Invent questions. Ask your partner the questions.
Exemple: **A** *Le français, tu aimes ça, toi?*
B *Oui, j'aime ça. C'est intéressant.*
B *L'anglais, tu aimes ça, toi?*
A *Non, je n'aime pas ça. C'est ennuyeux.*

Justify your opinion to improve your work:
Je n'aime pas ça parce que (because) *c'est ennuyeux.*

Complète les phrases. A↔B.
Complete the sentences.
Exemple: **A** *J'aime le français …*
B *… parce que c'est intéressant!*

Écris un mail à un(e) correspondant(e) français(e).
Write an email to a French penfriend. Say what subjects you like/don't like and why. Include your favourite subject.

> Sujet: Mes matières préférées
>
> Salut!
>
> Donc, ta matière préférée, c'est les maths. C'est intéressant, ça!
>
> Moi, j'aime ▆▆ parce que c'est ▆▆ mais je n'aime pas ▆▆ parce que c'est ▆▆
>
> J'adore ▆▆ car c'est ▆▆ mais je déteste ▆▆ parce que c'est ▆▆
>
> Et ma matière préférée? C'est ▆▆ car ▆▆ !

Grammaire WB p.15

Connectives
Connectives are used to link one sentence to another or to extend a sentence. Use *parce que* and *car* (because) to give reasons for your opinions.
*J'aime le français **parce que** c'est intéressant.*
*Je déteste les maths **car** c'est difficile.*
Use *mais* (but) to contrast.
*J'aime les maths, **mais** je n'aime pas les SVT.*

Écoute (a–f). Recopie et complète la grille. Note la matière, l'opinion et la raison en anglais.
Listen. Copy and complete the table. Note the subject, the opinion and the reason in English.

	subject	opinion	reason
a	French	like	more interesting than English
b			

Grammaire p. 167 WB p.12

Making comparisons
Use *plus* (more) or *moins* (less) in front of adjectives to make comparisons between subjects.

Le français, j'aime ça.	C'est	**plus**	intéressant	**que**	l'anglais.
L'anglais, je n'aime pas ça.	C'est	**moins**	intéressant	**que**	le français.

Plenary

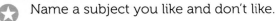

Name a subject you like and don't like.

Give reasons.

Compare subjects you like with subjects you don't like. Say what your favourite subject is and why.

Listen to your partner's opinions on subjects, then use the transferable language you have learnt to say whether you agree or disagree with them.

2.4 Les copains d'abord

- Vocabulary: talk about your friends and how long you have known them
- Grammar: use pronouns (*le*, *la* and *les*)
- Skills: use connectives *et* and *mais* to develop conversation

ÉCOUTER 1

Écoute et lis. Trouve la bonne image.
Listen and read. Find the correct picture.
Exemple: Martin c

a

c

b

d

Grammaire p. 166 WB p.16, p.29

le, la, les

Le, la, les mean 'the' but they can also mean 'him', 'her' and 'them'.

Mon meilleur ami s'appelle Baptiste.	Je **le** connais <u>depuis trois ans.</u>	I have known **him** <u>for three years.</u>
Ma meilleure amie s'appelle Emmeline.	Je **la** connais <u>depuis six ans.</u>	I have known **her** <u>for six years.</u>
Mes meilleurs amis s'appellent Jeanne et Luc.	Je **les** connais <u>depuis dix ans.</u>	I have known **them** <u>for ten years.</u>

Add *depuis*, and you can say how long you have known your friends for.

> Mes meilleurs amis s'appellent Mathieu et Raphaël.
>
> **Martin**

> Mon meilleur ami s'appelle Antoine.
>
> **Samuel**

e

> Mes meilleures amies s'appellent Anne et Mélanie.
>
> **Lauren**

> Un meilleur ami? Non, je n'en ai pas. Mais j'ai une grande bande de copains.
>
> **Guillaume**

> Ma meilleure amie s'appelle Sarah.
>
> **Rachel**

◎ **How long have they known them for?**

PARLER 2

'Tu as ... un meilleur ami/une meilleure amie?' A ↔ B.
Ask the question 'Have you a got a best friend?'.
Exemple: **A** *Tu as ... un(e) meilleur(e) ami(e)?*
  B *Oui. Elle s'appelle Rachel et je la connais depuis cinq ans.*
  B *Tu as un(e) meilleur(e) ami(e)?*
  A *Non, mais j'ai une bande de copains.*

Developing conversation

If you answer *oui*, continue with *et* ... and give details. If you answer *non*, continue with *mais* ... and develop your answer.

3 **Décris une photo de toi et de tes amis. Écris la légende.**
Describe a photo of yourself and your friends. Write a caption.
Exemple:
C'est moi sur la photo avec mon/ ma/mes meilleur(e)(s) ami(e)(s).
Il/Elle/Ils/Elles s'appelle(nt) ...
Je le/la/les connais ...

Je le/la/les connais depuis ...	I have known him/ her/them since ...
que je suis bébé	*I was a baby*
que je suis petit(e)	*I was small*
toujours	*always*
l'école primaire	*primary school*

4 **Recopie et complète les phrases.**
Copy and complete the sentences.
Exemple: **a** *Un bon ami, c'est quelqu'un de sympathique.*

a Un bon ami, c'est quelqu'un de méchant/ sympathique.
b Un vrai ami, c'est quelqu'un de sincère/ méchant.
c Un bon ami n'est pas moqueur/gentil.
d Un bon ami est fidèle/changeant.
e Une bonne amie est généreux/généreuse.
f Une vraie amie est gentil/gentille.

5 **Lis le mail. Remplis les blancs.**
Read the email. Fill in the gaps.

6 **Écoute (a–f). Recopie et remplis la grille.**
Listen. Copy and fill in the table.

	Friends?	How long?
a	*yes, a girl*	
b		
c		

➕ **What detail is given in d?**

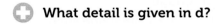
Plenary

⭐ Say what (best) friend(s) you have.

◎ Say what your friends' names are.

➕ Say how long you have known your friends.

Focus on speaking with accurate pronunciation.

Sujet: Mes meilleurs amis

Salut, Pierre!

Merci pour ton mail. J'ai une question pour toi. Tu as un meilleur ami? Moi, j'en ai deux!

1 Ma meilleure amie, Marie, je **2** ▄▄ connais depuis toujours. Elle est comme une sœur pour moi.

3 ▄▄ meilleur ami, Jack, je **4** ▄▄ connais depuis l'âge de dix ans. À part **5** ▄▄ deux meilleurs amis, Marie et Jack, j'ai une petite bande de copains.

À plus! James

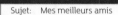
mon ma mes le la

2.5 Avant et maintenant

- Vocabulary: talk in detail about your family and home; analyse differences in your personality (past/present)
- Grammar: use a wider range of adjectives; recognise past tenses
- Skills: use connectives; use formal and informal language to express agreement/disagreement

Lis les deux lettres. Recopie et remplis la grille en anglais.

Read both letters. Copy and fill in the table in English. See page 33 for reading strategies.

	letter a	letter b
age		
personality		
lives ...		
opinion		
family		

a

Salut! Je m'appelle Sadie Starr. J'ai onze ans et mon anniversaire, c'est le huit mai — comme Tracy Beaker! Je m'identifie beaucoup à Tracy Beaker. Comme elle, je suis intelligente et adorable ☺. Je suis courageuse aussi — je n'ai peur de rien ni personne. Et comme elle, je ne connais pas mes parents. J'habite dans une maison d'enfance, mais je n'aime pas ça. Tracy, elle appelle la maison d'enfance "le (bon) débarras".

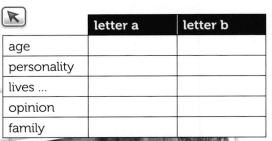

rien ni personne — *anything or anybody*
maison d'enfance — *children's home*
le débarras — *a cupboard or spare room where you put away things that are not needed or used*
Bon débarras! — *Good riddance!*

b

Bonjour! Je m'appelle Sadie Starr. J'ai seize ans. À onze ans, j'étais triste. Maintenant, je suis heureuse et j'ai plus confiance en moi. J'habite avec mes parents adoptifs dans une petite maison. J'adore ça. Ma mère adoptive s'appelle Michelle et mon père adoptif s'appelle Paul.

➕ **Can you give the meaning of the text in red as extra detail?**

Fais des phrases vraies ou fausses. Ton/Ta partenaire décide si elles sont vraies. A ↔ B.

Make up true or false sentences using the phrases below. Your partner decides if they are true.

a Je m'appelle ...
b J'ai ... ans.
c Je suis ... et ...
d J'habite avec ...

➕ **To add a past tense, make up a sentence using:**
Avant, j'étais ... et ...

Formal and informal language

Use formal language such as *c'est vrai* (it's true) or *c'est faux* (it's false) or informal language such as *Tu rigoles?* (Are you joking/having a laugh?) or *C'est ça, oui!* (Yeah, right!) — fine to reply to your friend's statements but not to your teacher.

3 **Relie les adjectifs et les images.**
Match the adjectives and the pictures.
Exemple: **a** *2*

a rêveur **c** paresseux **e** calme **g** agité
b motivé **d** sympathique **f** positif

4 **Recopie et remplis la grille.**
Copy and fill in the table.

masculine	feminine	meaning
positif		
motivé		
agité		
rêveur		
paresseux		
calme		
sympathique		

5 **Écoute (1–6). Recopie et remplis la grille.**
Listen to the six speakers. Copy and fill in the table.

> quand j'étais petit(e) *when I was little*

◎ **Can you spot any qualifiers (*très, un peu, assez*)?**

✚ **Can you spot any comparatives (*plus/moins que ...*)?**

		avant (before/ in the past)	*maintenant* (now)
1	Thomas	*(quite) lazy*	*(very) sporty*
2	Valentin		
3	Marine		
4	Dylan		
5	Éva		
6	Noémie		

6 **Compare-toi. Écris une lettre.**
Compare yourself. Write a letter as your 16-year-old self (use Sadie's on page 30 as a guide).

Plenary

Prepare a text message to a radio show about the changes you have noticed in your personality through childhood.

★ Make a sentence containing three adjectives to describe yourself.

◎ Add three adjectives to describe yourself as you were in the past.

✚ Link these two sentences with an appropriate connective.

Work with a partner. Do they agree with your opinion?

Varying connectives

To add more interest to your spoken and written French, use a variety of connectives, such as *et* (and) or *parce que/car* (because). To compare and contrast, you can use *mais* (but), or *par contre* (on the other hand).

2.6 Labo-langue

Present tense, avoir and être

1 Choose one of the verbs on the right to complete the sentences.

être	avoir
je suis	j'ai
tu es	tu as

a *J'ai* onze ans. *I am eleven years old.*
b _____ travailleuse et créative. *You are hard-working and creative.*
c _____ quelqu'un de bien. *I am a good person.*
d _____ une grande bande de copains? *Do you have a big group of friends?*
e _____ une meilleure amie qui s'appelle Solène. *I have a best friend who is called Solène.*
f _____ comment? *What are you like?*

Pronouns le, la, les

2 Fill in the gaps with the correct pronoun from the box.

a Ma meilleure amie, je *la* connais depuis quatre ans.
b Max, je _____ connais depuis un an.
c La prof de géographie? Je _____ déteste.
d Les cours de maths? Je _____ déteste.
e Mes camarades de classe? Je _____ connais depuis un an.
f Mon petit frère? Je _____ adore.

> Pronouns are short words that replace a noun.
> Maths? ('maths' = noun) I love **it**! ('it' = pronoun)
> We use **le** and **la** to refer to people ('him' and 'her') but they can also be used to refer to specific things.
> **le** – him/it   **la** – her/it   **les** – them
> *Mon collège? Je l'adore!* My school? I love it!
> *Mon meilleur ami, je le connais depuis trois ans.*
> I've known my best friend for three years.

Possessive adjectives

3 Read the interview with the 16-year-old Sadie and fill in the gaps with words from the box.

Journalist Alors, parle-moi de **1** *ta* famille, Sadie.
Sadie Je ne connais pas **2** _____ parents biologiques, mais **3** _____ mère adoptive s'appelle Michelle et **4** _____ père adoptif s'appelle Paul.
Journalist Parle-moi de **5** _____ parents adoptifs. Elle est comment **6** _____ mère et il est comment **7** _____ père?
Sadie **8** _____ père adoptif, il est très amusant et gentil. **9** _____ mère, elle est généreuse et charmante.

> Possessive adjectives are the words that describe who or what something (or someone) belongs to.

masculine	feminine	plural	
mon	ma	mes	my
ton	ta	tes	your

Adjectival agreement

4 Read the sentences below carefully. They are describing twins, a boy and a girl. Fill in the gaps.

a Daniel est élégant et Danielle est *élégante* aussi.
b Danielle est courageuse et Daniel est _____ aussi.
c Daniel est actif et Danielle est _____ aussi.
d Danielle est bavarde et Daniel est _____ aussi.
e Daniel est calme et Danielle est _____ aussi.

> Adjectives change their sound and spelling to be masculine or feminine like the noun they are describing.

Comparative structures

5 **Now compare school subjects. Follow the pattern in the box.**

a L'EPS est plus *amusante* que la musique. (*fun*)
b La musique est plus ▭▭▭ que les arts plastiques. (*creative*)
c L'anglais est plus ▭▭▭ que l'histoire. (*boring*)
d La géographie est moins ▭▭▭ que la technologie. (*useful*)
e Les maths sont moins ▭▭▭ que les SVT. (*interesting*)

> **Le** français est plus intéressant que la géographie.
>
> **La** géographie est moins intéressant**e** que le français.
>
> **Les** maths sont plus intéressant**es** que l'EPS.

Reading strategies

Use these strategies with activity 1, page 30.

1 Read the texts in activity 1, page 30, and write down three things you do when you see a word you don't know. These are your reading strategies.

2 Compare them to those your partner wrote. Have you got different strategies?

3 What about the whole class? How many strategies can the class come up with?

4 Try these new strategies. Using them together works best!

- **Look at the pictures:** they can give you clues as to what you will find in the text.
- **Skip** what you don't know and **use what you do know**. Some words are easy, as they are cognates (they look like English words, e.g. *adorable*). It can help you <u>before</u> you work on the hard bits of the text to underline all the cognates and chunks of language you know.
- <u>Before</u> you read, you can also **make predictions**. **Look at the task and predict** what information you will find in the text, e.g. Sadie will give her opinion of where she used to live and where she lives now. The opinions may well be different.
- Make inferences. Circle the word you don't know, e.g. *À onze ans, j'étais (triste)*. Say in English what you have worked out so far, using 'something' to help you guess the bit you don't know (*triste*), e.g. 'At 11 years old I was <u>something</u>'. You know she didn't like the children's home, so how might she have felt?

5 Now practise these new strategies with your partner. Read this text and work out two more things about Sadie.

Quand j'étais petite, je ne me séparais jamais de mon doudou. Il était doux et violet et un peu sale. Maintenant, je passe mon temps à fabriquer des bracelets pour donner à mes copines.

Pronunciation: silent letters

6 **Look at the list. Which words <u>will</u> sound their final consonant? Which words won't? Listen and check your answers.**

français, actif, bavard, Daniel, meilleur, sœur, généreux, amusant, travailleur

> Consonants at the end of words in French are usually silent. But there is a small group of consonants, C, R, F and L, that are sounded at the end of a word. These are sometimes called '**CaReFuL**' consonants to help you remember which ones to say.

2.7 Extra Star

- Vocabulary: practise using language from the unit
- Grammar: revise high-frequency verb structures (*j'ai*, *je suis*)
- Skills: numeracy (chronological order), literacy (developing reading skills)

Match the questions to the answers.
Exemple: **1** *c*

1 Comment t'appelles-tu?
2 Quel âge as-tu?
3 C'est quand ton anniversaire?
4 Tu es comment?
5 Tu habites avec ton père et ta mère?

a J'ai seize ans ... mais je suis très mature pour mon âge!
b Je suis angélique, charmante, intelligente et courageuse.
c Je m'appelle Sadie Starr.
d Avec mes parents adoptifs, en fait.
e C'est le huit mai.

Find the correct ending for each sentence.
Exemple: **1** *b*

1 J'ai ...
2 Mon père adoptif ...
3 Je n'ai pas de ...
4 Je suis quelqu'un ...
5 Ma meilleure amie s'appelle Estelle. Elle est ...
6 Je déteste le sport ...

a frères ou de sœurs.
b une famille adoptive.
c parce que c'est ennuyeux.
d de bien et de travailleur.
e sympathique et compréhensive.
f s'appelle Simon.

Imagine you are being interviewed for the school magazine or newspaper. Write your answers to the questions below to produce a short paragraph.

questions	phrases
Comment t'appelles-tu?	*Je m'appelle ...*
Tu es comment?	*Je suis quelqu'un de ...*
	Je suis un peu/assez/très + adjective
Parle-moi de ta famille.	*J'habite avec mon père/ma mère. J'ai deux sœurs ...*
Parle-moi de ton/ta meilleur(e) ami(e).	*Il(s)/Elle(s) s'appelle(nt) ...*
	Je le/la/les connais depuis ... ans.

Match the titles of these Jacqueline Wilson novels with their French translations.
Exemple: **1** *a*

1 La fabuleuse histoire de Jenny B.
2 Maman, ma sœur et moi
3 Mon amie pour la vie
4 Le site des soucis
5 Soirée pyjama
6 Ma meilleure amie
7 La double vie de Charlotte

a The Story of Tracy Beaker (1991)
b The Worry Website (2002)
c The Lottie Project (1997)
d Illustrated Mum (1999)
e Best Friends (2004)
f Sleepovers (2001)
g Vicky Angel (2000)

Tip: Do the easy ones first. Look for links between words.
Can you put the titles of the novels in chronological order?

2.7 Extra Plus

- Vocabulary: practise using language from the unit
- Grammar: recognise and use present and imperfect structures
- Skills: develop reading skills

Lis le texte. Recopie et remplis les blancs.
Read the text on Sadie Starr. Copy and fill in the gaps with a high-frequency structure from the box.

a *Je m'appelle* Sadie Starr. **b** ▨▨▨ dans une maison d'enfance.
c ▨▨▨ onze ans. **d** ▨▨▨ courageuse et intelligente mais **e** ▨▨▨ fille-fille. Je déteste la maison d'enfance. **f** ▨▨▨ "le bon débarras" ... comme Tracy Beaker!

> je suis   je ne suis pas   je m'appelle   je l'appelle
> j'habite   j'ai

Écris des phrases.
Write sentences to compare what you were like <u>before</u> to what you are like <u>now</u>.

*Exemple: Avant, **j'étais** paresseux mais maintenant, **je suis** actif.*

Lis le texte et réponds aux questions.
Read the text and answer the questions a–f in English.

*Exemple: **a** sincere, ...*

a What are the qualities of a good friend according to the text?
b What is this person's best friend called?
c What is he like?
d What does he say about their relationship?
e What was his best friend at primary school called?
f What was she like?

> Pour moi, un bon ami, c'est quelqu'un de sincère, de gentil et de fidèle ... comme mon meilleur ami. Il s'appelle Adrien. Il est sportif et travailleur. Il est un peu timide mais il est assez sociable. Je le connais depuis deux ans.
>
> À l'école primaire, ma meilleure amie, c'était Inès. Elle était très bavarde. Elle était rêveuse mais travailleuse aussi.

Le camion-école

Lilou a 13 ans. La famille de Lilou, ce sont des "gens du voyage". Ils n'ont pas de maison, et ils voyagent en camping-car. Ils sont souvent à Lyon, par exemple pour des réunions familiales.

Hussein a 12 ans. Il est malien. Les parents de Hussein n'ont pas de passeport français. Ils sont réfugiés et ils demandent l'asile. Ils n'ont pas de maison, ils habitent dans un squat à Lyon.

Lilou explique: "L'année dernière, on était toujours sur la route, toujours en voyage, alors impossible d'aller à l'école. Cette année, je suis contente, parce qu'il y a le camion-école. La prof s'appelle Mylène. Elle est amusante et super gentille. Mylène, je l'adore."

Et Hussein? "Je vais dans le camion-école tous les jours. L'année dernière, je n'étais pas très sociable. Maintenant, je parle français, alors je suis moins timide. Je n'aime pas les maths, c'est ennuyeux. Par contre, j'adore la géographie. C'est ma matière préférée.

Cédric, mon prof, est sympa, mais je voudrais un passeport français, pour aller dans un vrai collège."

Lilou ajoute: "Moi, je ne suis pas très travailleuse, mais j'aime bien les maths, parce que c'est utile. L'année prochaine, je voudrais aller dans un vrai collège."

le camion-école	*school van*
les gens du voyage	*travellers*
en camping-car	*in a camper van*
Lyon	*a very large city in Eastern France*
malien	*Mali*
réfugiés	*refugees*
ils demandent l'asile	*they are seeking asylum*

LIRE 1 **Read the text and answer the questions.**

a Why doesn't Lilou attend an ordinary school?
b Where do Lilou's family live?
c Why doesn't Hussein attend an ordinary school?
d Where do Hussein's family live?
e Which document would Hussein and his family like to have?
f What would both Lilou and Hussein like to do in the future?

LIRE 2 **What do Lilou and Hussein like and not like in their schooling? Copy out and fill in the table.**

	Cédric	Mylène	maths	geography
Lilou				
Hussein				

LIRE 3 **Find the French for these time phrases.**
Exemple: **a** *souvent*

a often
b last year
c always
d this year
e every day
f now
g next year

2.8 Vidéo

Notre bande

Regarde l'épisode 2. Choisis la bonne réponse.
Choose the correct answer.

a Diakouba has *two/three/four* best friends.
b Diakouba has known Asma for *two/five/ten* years.
c The group has *always/sometimes/not always* been very close.
d The girls are very *similar/different/positive*.
e Asma *plays a musical instrument/cooks/reads* a lot.
f Noura helps *Diakouba/Oumaïma/Asma* with her homework.

Recopie et remplis la grille.
Copy out and fill in the table.

	Diakouba	Noura	Oumaïma	Asma
active				
adorable				
amusante				
bavarde				
courageuse	✔			
créative				
intelligente				
motivée				
sociable				
sportive				
sympa				
timide				
travailleuse				

Comment dit-on en français … ?
How do you say this in French?

a What luck! *On a de la chance!*
b It's fun.
c Are you kidding?
d I'm kidding.
e Don't mention it.
f We get on well.

Choisis des adjectifs pour te décrire, ou pour décrire tes amis.
What adjectives would you use to describe yourself or your friends in French, and why?

Exemple: Moi, je suis timide …
Toi, XXX, tu es amusant et …

2.9 Test

Listen (1–10). Who speaks about topics a–d? (See pages 22–29.)

Exemple: **1** c

a what kind of a person they are
b their family
c their friends
d school subjects

Answer the questions. (See pages 22–29.)

1 Tu es comment?
2 Parle-moi de ta famille.
3 Parle-moi de ton meilleur ami/ta meilleure amie.
4 Quelle est ta matière préférée?

Read the text. Copy out the table. Supply information under each heading. (See pages 22–29.)

> J'habite avec mon père et ma belle-mère. Papa, il s'appelle François. Ma belle-mère, elle s'appelle Justine. Je ne connais pas ma mère. J'ai deux demi-sœurs qui s'appellent Charlotte et Clara.
> Je n'ai pas de meilleur ami mais j'ai trois bon amis. Ils s'appellent Mustafa, Julien et Enzo. On est camarades de classe. À l'école, ma matière préférée, c'est les maths. J'adore ça parce que c'est intéressant et utile. J'ai un bon prof aussi. Je suis sociable et amusant. Je suis quelqu'un de bien. C'est important ça.

family	friends	school	personality	
				1 detail
				2 details
				3 details

Imagine you are creating a main character for a novel. Write in the first person, using *je*, as if you are the character. Give yourself a new name, age and birthday. Then use the questions in activity 2 as a prompt for writing. (See pages 22–29.)

Je m'appelle …
Je suis …
J'ai …
Il(s)/Elle(s) s'appelle(nt) …
Mon/Ma meilleur(e) ami(e) …
Je le/la/les connais …
Ma matière préférée, c'est …

✚ *Avant, j'étais …*

Remember, the more you can develop your answers, the better your work will be.

A few simple structures. Lot of repetition. → Less repetition. Wider range of simple structures. Simple opinions. → Wide range of structures. Using connectives. Opinion and justification.

Vocabulaire

Describing personality

Tu es comment?	What are you like?
Je suis quelqu'un de (d') ...	I am a(n) ... person.
je suis/je ne suis pas	I am/I am not
tu es/tu n'es pas	you are/you are not
il/elle est	he/she is
un peu/assez/très	a bit/quite/very
actif	active
adorable	adorable
amusant	funny
bavard	chatty/talkative
courageux	brave
créatif	creative
fidèle	faithful
généreux	generous
gentil	kind
heureux	happy
intelligent	intelligent
méchant	horrible
sociable	sociable
sportif	sporty
timide	timid/shy
travailleur	hard-working

Family

J'habite avec ...	I live with ...
J'ai ... qui s'appelle/ s'appellent ...	I have ... who is/are called ...
il/elle s'appelle	he/she is called
ils/elles s'appellent	they are called
je l'appelle	I call him/her/it
Je n'ai pas de ...	I don't have a ...
Je n'ai plus de ...	I don't have a ... any longer.
séparés/divorcés	separated/divorced
adoptif	adoptive
Je suis fils/fille unique.	I am an only child.
une mère/belle-mère	mother/step-mother
un père/beau-père	father/step-father
des parents	parents
maman/papa	mum/dad
une sœur/demi-sœur	sister/half-/step-sister
un frère/demi-frère	brother/half-/step-brother
des grands-parents	grandparents

School

l'anglais	English
les arts plastiques	Art
l'EPS	Sport
le français	French
la géographie	Geography
l'histoire	History
les maths	Mathematics
la musique	Music
les SVT (sciences de la vie et de la terre)	Science
la technologie	Technology
Ma matière préférée, (c')est ...	My favourite subject is ...
j'adore (ça)	I love (it/that)
j'aime (ça)	I like (it/that)
ça va	it's OK
je n'aime pas (ça)	I don't like (it/that)
je déteste (ça)	I hate (it/that)
C'est ...	It's ...
créatif/ennuyeux/inutile/ passionnant/nul/ relaxant/utile	creative/boring/pointless/ exciting/rubbish/ relaxing/useful
C'est plus/moins intéressant que ...	It's more/less interesting than ...

Friends

J'ai un/une meilleur(e) ami(e).	I've got a best friend.
Je n'en ai pas.	I don't have one/any.
J'ai une grande bande de copains.	I have a big group of friends.
Je le/la/les connais depuis ...	I have known him/her/ them ...
... un an/deux ans.	... for one/two years.
... que je suis petit/bébé.	... since I was small/a baby
... toujours.	... always
... l'école primaire.	... since primary school

Opinions and connectives

À mon avis, ...	In my opinion, ...
Je pense que ...	I think that ...
On dit que ...	People say that ...
parce que / car	because
et	and
mais / par contre	but / on the other hand

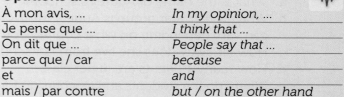

⦿ Grammar and skills: I can...

- ⦿ use adjectives
- ⦿ use *être* (present tense)
- ⦿ use connectives and make comparisons
- ⦿ use the pronouns *le/la/les*
- ⦿ recognise past tenses
- ⦿ use memorisation strategies
- ⦿ recognise and use transferable language
- ⦿ use formal and informal language for agreement and disagreement

3.1 Chez moi

- Vocabulary: describe school and where you live; talk about different places to live
- Grammar: use *j'* with verbs beginning with vowels
- Skills: identify and avoid false friends; convert miles to kilometres

 Écoute et lis.

What new words do you see here? How can you work them out?

> Salut! Je m'appelle Audrey et j'ai douze ans. Je vais au collège Victor-Hugo et je suis en sixième. J'habite à deux kilomètres de mon collège. Il y a vingt-huit élèves dans ma classe et j'ai beaucoup de copains. Dans mon collège les élèves restent dans la salle de classe et ce sont les profs qui changent de salle. C'est cool! J'aime bien mon collège parce que j'ai beaucoup de copains, les profs sont sympa et les matières sont intéressantes. Ma matière préférée, c'est les arts plastiques — j'adore dessiner!

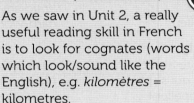

11–12 (Year 7)	sixième or 6ᵉ (6ᵗʰ year)
12–13 (Year 8)	cinquième or 5ᵉ (5ᵗʰ year)
13–14 (Year 9)	quatrième or 4ᵉ (4ᵗʰ year)
14–15 (Year 10)	troisième or 3ᵉ (3ʳᵈ year)

Faux amis (false friends)

As we saw in Unit 2, a really useful reading skill in French is to look for cognates (words which look/sound like the English), e.g. *kilomètres* = kilometres.

However, some words are *faux amis* (false friends). They look like a cognate, but they have a different meaning, and often they don't make sense in the rest of the text. *Collège*, for example, doesn't mean college, but secondary school.

Pick out all the cognates in the text in activity 1, then figure out which ones are *faux amis*, and what they really mean.

 Réponds aux questions en anglais.

Exemple: **a** *Victor-Hugo*

a What is the name of Audrey's school?
b What British year group is Audrey in? (Note: year groups can vary depending on what country you live in.)
c How far away does she live from her school?
d How many students are in her class?
e Where do the students and teachers go for different lessons?
f What **three** reasons does Audrey give for liking her school?
g What is her favourite subject?

 Sondage. Pose la question. Recopie et remplis la grille.

Class survey. Ask the question. Copy out and fill in the table.

Exemple: – Où habites-tu?
Tom – J'habite à **deux kilomètres** de mon collège.

<1km	1km	2km	3km	4km	5km	>5km
		Tom				

Converting miles to kilometres

1 mile = 1.6 kilometre

To work out the distance in kilometres you need to divide the miles by 0.6:

3 miles = 3 ÷ 0.6 = 5 kilometres

ÉCRIRE 4 Écris. Où habites-tu?

Exemple: J'habite à ... kilomètres de mon collège.

LIRE 5 Relie les mots et les images.

Exemple: **a** 3

a une maison individuelle
b une maison jumelée
c un appartement

d un pavillon
e à la campagne
f à la montagne

g en ville
h dans un village
i en banlieue

①
②
③

④
⑤
⑥

⑦
⑧
⑨

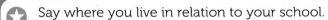

ÉCOUTER 6 Écoute et note (1–7). Relie les personnes et les endroits.
Listen and take notes. Match the speakers and the places.
Exemple: **1** *c, g*

◎ **Can you note down any additional information that is provided?**

Plenary

⭐ Say where you live in relation to your school.

◎ Talk about your school and where you live. Give your opinion.

➕ Describe your school and subjects and where you live. Include opinions and connectives to link your ideas together.

How does this lesson relate to your learning in other areas of the curriculum?

3.2 À la maison des jeunes

- Vocabulary: recognise personal items; identify activities at the youth club
- Grammar: use the present tense
- Skills: use connectives to extend sentences; interpret longer texts

ÉCOUTER 1

Écoute. Relie les mots et les images.

Exemple: **a** 3

a mon ordi(nateur)	**e** mes BD
b mon lecteur MP4	**f** ma télé
c ma console de jeux vidéo	**g** mes DVD
d mes romans	**h** mon portable

ÉCRIRE 2

Qu'est-ce que tu aimes faire? Écris des phrases.
Choose three activities you enjoy from the list below and complete the sentences with a matching item from activity 1.

Exemple: J'aime lire donc j'adore mes romans.

Extending sentences

In Unit 2 you met *et* and *mais* which you can use to add detail and contrast sentences.

You can use another connective, *donc*, 'therefore', to give extra information after an opinion and make your sentences even more detailed:

J'aime lire **donc** *j'adore mes romans*.

See page 51 for writing strategies.

J'aime						
lire	écouter de la musique	regarder un match de foot	jouer aux jeux vidéo	surfer sur internet	regarder un film	envoyer des textos

◎ **Can you add any activities that you enjoy to this list?**

PARLER 3

En groupe.

Exemple: **A** Qu'est-ce que tu aimes faire?
B J'aime regarder des films donc j'adore ma télé.

 Lis le blog de Paul et traduis les extraits soulignés.
Read Paul's blog and translate the underlined extracts.

Exemple: je retrouve mes copains – I meet up with my friends

La maison des jeunes		Accueil Profil Compte

Là où j'habite, il y a une super maison des jeunes où je vais tous les mercredis et tous les samedis. Là-bas, <u>je retrouve mes copains</u> et <u>je joue au baby-foot</u> – j'adore ça! Aussi, <u>je bavarde avec mes copains</u> ou <u>je joue au billard</u> parce que c'est marrant. D'habitude, <u>je vais au bar</u> et je bois un coca. De temps en temps, <u>je joue au foot</u> avec l'équipe – c'est génial! Je joue de la guitare donc quelquefois <u>je fais des concerts</u> avec mon groupe. Quand je veux me détendre, <u>je regarde un film</u> avec mes copains – c'est très sympa!

 Vrai ou faux?

Exemple: **a** *faux*

  a Paul goes to the youth club on Thursdays.
  b At the youth club Paul meets his friends and plays table football.
  c Paul likes to drink lemonade at the bar.
  d Paul plays football for the youth club team.
  e Paul likes to watch concerts at the youth club.
  f Paul likes to watch films with his friends.

 Find the words in the text that prove a sentence is false.

  En groupe. Que fais-tu le week-end?

je retrouve mes copains	je vais au bar
je joue au baby-foot	je joue au foot
je bavarde avec mes copains	je fais des concerts
je joue au billard	je regarde un film

Grammaire   p. 168–169
WB p.30, p.36

The present tense

The present tense is used to describe things **you do** or **are doing**.

For verbs that end in *-er* you remove the *-er* and add the following endings:

I	je	**-e**	je jou**e**
you	tu	**-es**	tu jou**es**
he/she/we	il/elle/on	**-e**	il/elle/on jou**e**

regard**er** *to watch*	je regard**e**
	I watch, I am watching
jou**er** *to play*	je jou**e**
	I play, I am playing
bavard**er** *to chat*	je bavard**e**
	I chat, I am chatting

Some verbs are irregular:

aller *to go*	je **vais** *I go, I am going*
faire *to do*	je **fais** *I do, I am doing*

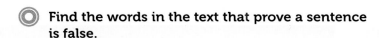 **Écoute Jules et note. Recopie et remplis la grille.**

When?	Activities (3)	Favourite activity	Who with?	Snack?
Wednesdays, ...				

Plenary

⭐ Write a sentence to say what activities you do.

◎ Add a sentence using the *tu* form.

➕ Add a sentence to say what activities other people do, using connectives to link your sentences.

Explain to your partner how the present tense of regular *-er* verbs works.

3.3 Les animaux chez moi

- Vocabulary: describe animals and colours
- Grammar: practise colour agreement; use *avoir*, *je voudrais* and *j'avais*
- Skills: use statistics; apply tenses

1 Écoute. Relie les animaux, les images et les couleurs.
Match the animals, the pictures and the colours.

Exemple: **a** *orange 4*

a	un chat	**noir(e)**
b	un chien	**blanc(he)**
c	un lapin	**marron**
d	un cochon d'Inde	jaune
e	un cheval	orange
f	une tortue	**gris(e)**
g	un oiseau	**bleu(e)**
h	un lézard	**vert(e)**
i	un phasme	**rouge**
j	un poisson	rose
k	un hamster	**violet(te)**

    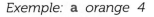

2 Lis les informations. Vrai, faux ou pas mentionné?
Read the information. Are the statements true, false or not in the text?

Exemple: **a** *vrai*

a The most popular animal in France is fish.
b The least popular type of animal is birds.
c There are two million more horses than small mammals.
d There are over 30 million fish in France.
e The difference between the number of cats and dogs in France is 2.41 million.
f Dogs and cats combined are more popular than fish.

Les animaux en France	
animal	millions
chiens	7,59
chats	10,96
petits mammifères (lapins, hamsters, etc.)	3,0
poissons	31,58
oiseaux	6,04

3 Sondage: 'Tu as un animal?'
Class survey. Find out who's got a pet.

Exemple: **A** *Tom, as-tu un animal?*
B *Oui, j'ai un chien.*

 Describe your results using statistics:
La moitié de la classe a un chat.

%	pour cent
$\frac{1}{3}$, 33%	un tiers
$\frac{2}{3}$, 66%	deux tiers
$\frac{1}{4}$, 25%	un quart
$\frac{3}{4}$, 75%	les trois quarts
$\frac{1}{2}$, 50%	la moitié

Grammaire p. 168–169 WB p.7

Avoir (to have)

Avoir is an irregular verb.

j'ai	*I have*
tu as	*you have* (sing)
il/elle a on a	*he/she has we have*
nous avons	*we have*
vous avez	*you have* (pl)
ils ont	*they have*

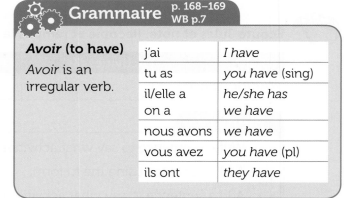

Traduis.
Translate the sentences.

Exemple: **a** *J'ai un chat blanc.*

a I have a white cat.
b He has two green lizards.
c We have three black dogs.
d You have (pl) a grey tortoise.
e They have a red stick insect.
f I have four blue hamsters.

Est-ce qu'ils ont un animal? Écoute. Recopie et remplis la grille en anglais (1–5).

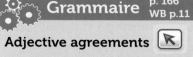
Grammaire p. 166 WB p.11

Adjective agreements ▶

- The colour always goes **after** the noun:
  un chien noir – a black dog

- The colour usually has to agree with the noun it is describing:
  un chien noir   *deux chien**s** noir**s***
  une tortue noire   *deux tortue**s** noire**s***

If the colour already ends in -e, you don't add an extra 'e' when describing a feminine noun:
un chien jaune   *une tortue jaune*
Some colours don't ever change to agree with the noun they are describing:
deux tortues marron

animal ⭐	animal + couleur ◉
1	two dogs	two black dogs
2		

Lis le texte. Mets les images dans le bon ordre.
Put the pictures into the correct sequence from the earliest pet to an ideal future pet.

Exemple: **c** ...

J'ai une tortue marron qui s'appelle Chloé et elle est timide mais sympa. J'ai aussi trois lapins noirs qui s'appellent Athos, Portos et Aramis. J'adore mes lapins mais je voudrais avoir un grand chien blanc – ça serait super. Quand j'étais petit, j'avais un chat marron qui s'appelait Bruno. Il était amusant et très mignon mais malheureusement, il est mort.

je voudrais   *I would like*
j'avais   *I used to have*
mort   *dead*

Décris tes animaux.
Write a description of your pets. Use activity 6 as a model.

Plenary

⭐ Describe your pets, saying their names and colour.

◉ Add a pet you would like to have.

➕ Add something about pets you used to have.

Are you moving from being able to recognise the past tense to using it confidently? How can you keep improving your knowledge of tenses?

3.4 Au parc safari

- Vocabulary: describe wild animals
- Grammar: recognise and use the past tense; use adjectives to describe wild animals
- Skills: use a dictionary; use writing strategies to structure a paragraph

Sépare les mots. Relie les mots et les images.
Unjumble the words then match them to the pictures.

Exemple: le lion f

lelionlesingelagirafeléléphantletigrelezèbrelhippopotamelerhinocéros

Lis le texte et réponds aux questions.
Exemple: **a** On Saturday.

- **a** When did Sophie visit the safari park?
- **b** Who did she go with?
- **c** What is her favourite animal?
- **d** Which animals does she prefer monkeys to?
- **e** What animal didn't she see?
- **f** What was her overall impression of the day?

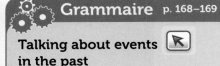

Grammaire p. 168–169

Talking about events in the past

The **perfect** tense in French is formed by using *j'ai* (from the verb *avoir*) and the past participle form of the verb (*visited*, *seen*, etc. in English):

j'ai visité – I have visited/ I visited
j'ai vu – I have seen/I saw

The **imperfect** tense is used to describe what something <u>was</u> like:

c'était – it was

La visite de Sophie

Bonjour! Samedi, j'ai visité le parc safari avec ma famille. Tout d'abord, j'ai vu un éléphant – c'est mon animal préféré! C'était super – l'éléphant est magnifique. Ensuite, j'ai vu un lion et aussi un tigre mais je préfère le singe. Après ça, j'ai vu un hippopotame mais je n'ai pas vu le rhinocéros, c'était nul. C'était une journée fantastique!

⭐ **Can you list all the different animals that Sophie saw?**

➕ **Can you translate the text into English? Use a dictionary if there are any new words that you can't work out.**

 Écoute. Recopie la grille et note les animaux en anglais (1–5).

	j'ai vu	je n'ai pas vu
1	*lion*	*monkey*
2		

 Cherche les adjectifs dans le dictionnaire. Traduis les phrases.
Look up the adjectives in the dictionary. Translate the sentences.

Exemple: **a** *The tiger is ferocious.*

a Le tigre est féroce.
b Le lion est fort.
c Le rhinocéros est effrayant.
d L'éléphant est sage.
e L'hippopotame est grincheux.
f Le singe est méchant.

Now look up five new animals and find five new adjectives to describe them using the model sentences above.

Dictionary skills

- When you look for a noun the *m* or *f* beside it tells you whether the noun is masculine or feminine:

monkey singe *m*

- When you look for an adjective, you will see the letters *adj*:

big *adj* grand

The dictionary only gives the masculine form. To describe a feminine noun, you normally add an ending to the adjective, usually just an *-e*. (See page 23.)

le grand chien
la grand**e** tortue

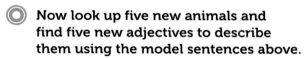

ce week-end	j'ai visité	tout d'abord	et	c'est/c'était … super, fantastique, génial, nul
samedi	j'ai vu	ensuite	mais	j'adore
dimanche		puis	avec	mon animal préféré
		après ça	aussi	je préfère

Décris une visite au parc safari.
Describe a visit to a safari park.
See page 51 for writing strategies.

Exemple: Samedi, j'ai visité …

Plenary

⭐ Describe an animal that you like.

◎ Add some new adjectives to describe the animal.

➕ Compare this animal to your favourite animal, adding as much extra detail as you can.

Careful listening and reading for key details in class leads to productive use of language. Set your partner a target to include a specific amount of new vocabulary in his/her description and check if he/she has done this. What do you need to do to keep acquiring new words?

Structuring a paragraph

To improve your work you need to write in paragraphs which include:

time expressions
different verbs
sequencing words
connectives
opinion phrases

Look at Sophie's description in activity 2 to see the different structures in use.

3.5 Mon animal préféré

- Vocabulary: recognise farm animals and sounds; describe favourite animals
- Grammar: practise using plurals and adjectives; recognise present tense of *être*
- Skills: practise pronunciation; justify opinions; talk about others

LIRE 1 **Relie les animaux et les images.**

Exemple: **a** *le cochon*

le mouton	le canard
le chien	le cochon
la vache	l'âne
le chat	le cheval

LIRE 2 **Relie les sons et les animaux.**

Exemple: **a** *le chien*

Predict how the words will sound in French.
How are they different from the English animal sounds?

a	Ouah! Ouah!	**d**	Coin coin	**g**	Bêêh
b	Miaou	**e**	Hi-han	**h**	Hiiiiiii
c	Meuh	**f**	Groin-groin		

LIRE 3 **Lis la conversation. C'est qui?**

Pierre J'adore les tigres parce qu'ils sont féroces et magnifiques!
Jules Mon animal préféré, c'est le lézard. C'est super cool, les lézards!
Marie Moi, je préfère les chevaux parce qu'ils sont beaux et gentils.
Céline J'aime les chats et les hamsters parce qu'ils sont mignons.

a Céline/<u>Marie</u>/Jules aime bien un animal qu'on utilise pour faire un sport.
b Jules/Pierre/Marie adore un type de reptile.
c Pierre/Céline/Marie adore les petits animaux domestiques.
d Piere/Jules/Marie aime les animaux dangereux.
e Jules/Marie/Céline aime bien deux animaux différents.
f Marie/Jules/Céline adore un animal qui est à sang froid.

j'aime 🖤		
j'adore 🖤🖤	je n'aime pas ✖	parce qu'ils/
je préfère	je déteste ✖ ✖	elles sont
mon animal préféré, c'est		

Pronunciation

Look at the different sounds in French. Practise saying them. Then listen to the words, check and repeat. ⎍⎍

a	qu**a**tre
i	d**i**x
an	t**an**te, enf**an**t
eu	n**eu**f
oi	au rev**oi**r
ou	d**ou**ze
ê	s**ê**pt
h (silent)	**h**uit

⚙️ Grammaire p. 166

Plurals

Plural nouns usually have an -s at the end, just like in English. You don't pronounce it though; it is a silent -s.

Cheval is an exception:

*un chev**al** – des chev**aux***

Adjectives describing a plural noun have to be plural as well:

*Les tigre**s** sont féroce**s**.*

*Les tortu**es** sont lente**s**.*

ÉCOUTER 4

Écoute (1–5). Recopie et remplis la grille en anglais.

	J'adore ♥♥	parce qu'ils/ elles sont	Je n'aime pas ✗
1	cats	cute	tortoises
2			
3			
4			
5			

mignon	beau *masc.*
féroce	belle *fem.*
gentil	beaux *masc. pl.*
amusant	belles *fem. pl.*
sympa	
magnifique	mais
super cool	par contre
intéressant	

PARLER 5

👥 **À deux ou en groupe: 'Quel est ton animal préféré?'**
A ↔ B.

Speak in pairs or in a group. Which is your favourite animal?

Exemple: Mon animal préféré, c'est le lion.

◎ **Can you include a reason for your opinion? Can you say what animal you don't like and why?**

ÉCRIRE 6

Écris des phrases.
Write down sentences for the answers in activity 5.

Exemple: John adore les lions.

✚ **Extend your sentences to give reasons and contrasting opinions:**
John adore les lions parce qu'ils sont magnifiques. Par contre, il n'aime pas les tigres parce qu'ils sont féroces.

⚙ **Grammaire** p. 168–169 WB p.9

Être

The present tense of the verb 'to be', *être*, has its own pattern. It is an **irregular verb**.

je suis	*I am*
tu es	*you are*
il/elle est on est	*he/she is we are*
nous sommes	*we are*
vous êtes	*you are*
ils/elles sont	*they are*

Plenary

Before you aim for your medal, reflect on your progress in this unit. What grammar rules have you learnt? Can you apply them in the medal task?

⭐ Say what your favourite animal is and mention an animal you don't like.

◎ Add a reason why you like and don't like them.

✚ Include descriptions of other people's opinions.

Adjectives

An adjective describes a noun. In French, the adjective agrees with the noun.

Most **feminine** adjectives end in **-e**.
Most **masculine plural** adjectives end in **-s**.
Most **feminine plural** adjectives end in **-es**.

masculine singular un chien	feminine singular une tortue	masculine plural deux chiens	feminine plural deux tortues
noir	noire	noirs	noires

Some adjectives follow a slightly different pattern.

blanc	blanche	blancs	blanches
jaune	jaune	jaunes	jaunes
gris	grise	gris	grises
violet	violette	violets	violettes

Some adjectives, called **invariable**, never change:

des tortues orange   *des lapins marron*

1 Create sentences using the following words. Don't forget to make the colours agree.

Exemple: **a** *J'ai un lapin marron mais ma sœur a une tortue grise.*

a lapin / marron / tortue / gris
b chien / noir / chat / blanc
c tortue / vert / oiseau / orange
d deux / lapin / blanc / noir
e phasme / marron / trois / serpent / rose
f lion / jaune / tigre / noir / orange

Present tense

2 Choose the correct present tense verb to complete the sentences.

a Je *joue* au basket avec mon frère.
b Je ▦▦▦ à la maison des jeunes tous les lundis.
c Je ▦▦▦ la télé le soir.
d Je ▦▦▦ mes copains quand je ▦▦▦ au collège.
e J' ▦▦▦ de la musique sur mon lecteur MP4.
f Je ▦▦▦ les courses avec mes copains le week-end.

> vais   retrouve   écoute   regarde   ~~joue~~   vais   fais

Most verbs that end in *-er* follow the pattern shown with *aimer*. These are called **regular -er verbs**.

Aller doesn't follow that pattern. It is called an **irregular verb**.

aim**er**	aller
j'aime	je vais
tu aime**s**	tu vas
il/elle/on aime	il/elle/on va

Faire is another common irregular verb: *je fais*.

To add detail to your work, talk about other people using the *il/elle* ('he/she') form of the verb.

Present tense, *être* (to be) and *avoir* (to have)

3 ***Être*** **or** ***avoir*?** **Fill in the gaps with the correct form of the verb.**

a Nous *sommes* super cool.
b Je m'appelle Claire. Je ▭ sympa.
c ▭-tu gentil?
d J'ai un lapin. Il ▭ deux ans.
e J'adore les tigres. Ils ▭ magnifiques.
f Vous ▭ une maison jumelée?
g Tu ▭ un chien?

être (to be)		avoir (to have)	
je suis	*I am*	j'ai	*I have*
tu es	*you are*	tu as	*you have*
il/elle est on est	*he/she is we are*	il/elle a on a	*he/she has we have*
nous sommes	*we are*	nous avons	*we have*
vous êtes	*you are*	vous avez	*you have*
ils/elles sont	*they are*	ils ont	*they have*

Writing strategies

Use these strategies with activity 5, page 47.

When you're writing a text of your own, it can be hard to know where to start.
Here are some suggestions **before** you start writing:

- **Brainstorm ideas** for what you could include and record them on a spidergram or mind map.
- **Collect and recycle language** from somewhere else: not just individual words, but chunks of language too, even if you don't know the grammar, e.g. *il faisait beau, il y avait* ... Use your coursebook, exercise book, posters, displays, etc.
- Put your ideas in a **sensible order**. Think about what you've learnt in English lessons about how to sequence ideas.

While you are writing, try out these strategies:

- If you don't know the French for something you want to say, either **use a dictionary**, or think of an easy way of saying it. For example, rather than *climbing up* the branch, simply say the monkey was *on* the branch.
- Put your ideas in a **logical order** using time expressions and sequencing words, e.g. *samedi matin, d'abord, ensuite, l'après-midi* ...
- Make your written work more interesting by using **connectives**, **different verbs** and **opinion phrases**.
- **Re-read what you've written** so far to get a sense of the 'flow'.

With your partner, talk about which of these strategies you already use, and which new ones you'll try out to describe a visit to a safari park.

Pronunciation: accents

4 **Listen and repeat the words that you hear.**

5 **Use the pronunciation rules to practise saying these words.**

collège   éléphant   zèbre   rhinocéros   lézard   nationalité   visité   c'était

6 **Do you know any other words in French that have these two accents? Write a list of them and practise saying them with a partner.**

The signs on some letters in French words are called **accents** and they can help us pronounce a word:

j'écoute
le kilomètre

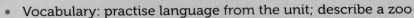

- Vocabulary: practise language from the unit; describe a zoo
- Grammar: use adjectives of colour
- Skills: read for detail; describe a scenario

1 **Read and find the odd one out. Justify your choice.**

a le lion	le tigre	l'éléphant	le singe
b le chat	le chien	le lapin	le serpent
c la tortue	le mouton	le cochon d'Inde	le phasme
d le zèbre	le lion	la girafe	le cheval

2 **Read and complete the sentences.**

Exemple: **1** *d*

1 Je vais au		**a**	jouer sur ma console.
2 J'habite dans une maison		**b**	le singe.
3 Dans ma chambre, j'adore		**c**	je n'aime pas les serpents.
4 Chez moi, j'ai un lapin		**d**	collège Albert-Camus.
5 J'adore les lions mais		**e**	jumelée en banlieue.
6 Mon animal préféré, c'est		**f**	et un chat.

3 **Read Juliette's message. Are the sentences a–f true or false? Correct the false sentences.**

Exemple: **a** *false – She lives two kilometres away.*

- **a** Juliette lives 3km from her school.
- **b** Juliette doesn't like her maths teacher.
- **c** She likes listening to music but doesn't like watching TV.
- **d** She goes to the youth club on Fridays and Saturdays.
- **e** Juliette loves animals.
- **f** Her favourite animal is a dog.

| Ma vie | | Accueil | Profil | Mon compte |

Salut! Je m'appelle Juliette. Je vais au collège Albert-Camus et j'habite à deux kilomètres de mon collège. J'aime bien mon collège mais je n'aime pas mon prof de maths. Il n'est pas sympa! Chez moi, j'aime écouter mon lecteur MP4 et j'aime aussi regarder la télévision.

Je vais à la maison des jeunes le vendredi, c'est cool. Je joue au billard et je bavarde avec mes copains. J'adore les animaux. Mon animal préféré, c'est le cheval!

4 **Describe a crazy zoo with unusually coloured animals. Include pictures to illustrate your work.**

Exemple:
Dans mon zoo fou,
il y a un lion vert,
un zèbre rouge …

un lion
un tigre
un zèbre
un singe
un éléphant
une tortue
une girafe
un rhinocéros
un hippopotame

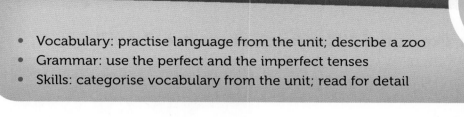

3.7 Extra Plus

- Vocabulary: practise language from the unit; describe a zoo
- Grammar: use the perfect and the imperfect tenses
- Skills: categorise vocabulary from the unit; read for detail

1 **Recopie la grille et classe les mots. Ajoute *un/une/des*.**
Copy the table and categorise the words. Add the article *un/une/des*.

> ordi   lion   chien   cochon d'Inde   vache
> console de jeux vidéo   BD   télé   tigre   cochon
> mouton   tortue   singe

animaux domestiques	un chien, ...
animaux sauvages	
animaux de la ferme	
objets dans la chambre	

2 **Lis les phrases a–e. Corrige les erreurs.**
Correct the mistakes. There is at least one mistake in every sentence.
Exemple: **a** ~~Au~~ À la maison des jeunes, je joue au foot avec ~~ma~~ mes copains.

a Au maison des jeunes, je joue au foot avec ma copains.
b Dans mon chambre, j'aime je regarde la télé.
c Ma mère adores les éléphants et le tigres.
d Chez moi, j'ai une chien et deux chat marron.
e J'adore les singe parce qu'ils sont mignon.

3 **Lis le texte et réponds aux questions.**

Exemple: **a** *She lives five kilometres away.*

a How far away from school does Maeva live?
b Why does Maeva like school?
c What is her favourite subject?
d Why doesn't she like History?
e What two activities does she like to do at home?
f What activities does she do at the youth club?
g Who is Max and what happened?
h What is her favourite animal?

> Salut! Je m'appelle Maeva. Je vais au collège Lafontaine et j'habite à cinq kilomètres de mon collège. J'aime bien mon collège parce que je retrouve mes copains. J'adore les SVT, c'est ma matière préférée, mais je n'aime pas l'histoire parce que c'est difficile. Chez moi, j'aime écouter mon lecteur MP4 et j'aime aussi jouer sur l'ordi. Je vais à la maison des jeunes le vendredi avec ma sœur Karine et c'est vraiment cool. Je joue au billard et je bavarde avec mes copains. Chez moi, j'ai un lapin noir qui s'appelle Belle. J'avais un chien marron qui s'appelait Max; il était très gentil mais malheureusement, il est mort. J'adore les animaux. Mon animal préféré, c'est le poisson!

4 **Décris une visite au zoo.**
Describe a visit to a zoo. Include a labelled map of the zoo to illustrate your work.
Exemple: J'ai visité le zoo avec mon amie Sarah. J'ai vu les lions ...

Conte du Burkina-Faso: Pourquoi l'Homme est maître du village

1   Au début des temps, l'Homme, l'éléphant, le lion, le léopard et le singe habitent dans le même village. L'Homme n'est pas maître du village.

2   Tous les jours, l'éléphant, le lion, le léopard et le singe vont à la chasse dans la brousse. Ils rapportent des gazelles au village et ils mangent avec l'Homme.

3   Un jour, les animaux disent à l'Homme: "On va à la chasse et on rapporte des gazelles. Mais toi, tu ne rapportes rien. Maintenant, c'est fini: tu ne manges plus avec nous."

4   L'Homme a un lance-pierre, caché dans sa maison. Le lendemain, il prend son lance-pierre et il va à la chasse dans la brousse. Il rapporte une gazelle.

5   Les animaux disent à l'Homme: "Bravo! Quel est ton secret?" Mais l'Homme ne montre pas son lance-pierre aux animaux.

6   Le lendemain, l'Homme retourne à la chasse. Mais le singe est caché dans un arbre et il observe l'Homme. Ensuite, le singe explique à l'éléphant, au lion et au léopard: "L'Homme est dangereux! Il lève le bras, et la gazelle tombe morte." Les animaux ont peur! Ils quittent vite le village.

7   Voilà pourquoi maintenant, les animaux sont dans la brousse et l'Homme est maître du village.

maître	*master*	le lance-pierre	*catapult*
à la chasse	*hunting*	caché	*hidden*
dans la brousse	*in the bush*	montre	*shows*
ils rapportent	*they bring back*	il lève le bras	*he raises his arm*
ils partagent	*they share*	tombe morte	*falls dead*

This is a traditional story from Burkina-Faso, a French-speaking country in West Africa.

Match the summaries with the paragraphs in the story.

Exemple: **a** 5

a The animals are surprised, but they don't know the man has got a catapult.

b This is why the man is now the only master in the village.

c The animals do the hunting and share their prey with the man.

d Man and animals live together in the same village.

e The monkey, having watched the man hunting, tells the animals he can kill just by raising his arm. They are scared and run away.

f The man goes hunting with his catapult and brings a gazelle back.

g The animals tell the man that as he never brings any food, they won't share their meal with him any more.

Read the text and find:
- five animals
- two natural features of the landscape
- a part of the body
- a weapon

Exemple: l'éléphant, ...

In story-telling, sequencers and time markers are important. Match the French and the English words and phrases.

Exemple: **a** 4

a	au début des temps	**1**	but
b	tous les jours	**2**	this is why
c	un jour	**3**	now
d	mais	**4**	at the beginning of time
e	maintenant	**5**	the day after
f	le lendemain	**6**	one day
g	ensuite	**7**	then
h	voilà pourquoi	**8**	every day

3.8 Vidéo

Au zoo

 Regarde l'épisode 3. Réponds aux questions en anglais.

Exemple: **a** *monkey, …*

a What animals are there at the zoo? Make a list.
b Which animal does Zaied want to pose with?
c What does Zaied want to put in the time capsule?
d Which part of the world does Clarisse's favourite animal come from?

Parc Zoologique
«Montpellier préserve et cultive la biodiversité»

 Clarisse et Zaied <u>ne</u> parlent <u>pas</u> de quels animaux? (1–5)

Exemple: *un cheval, …*

> un chien   un chat   ~~un cheval~~   un insecte   un singe
> un rhinocéros   un lapin   une tortue   un zèbre
> un lion   un poisson   une grenouille   un hamster

 Vrai ou faux? Corrige les phrases fausses.

a Zaied n'a pas de chien. *Vrai*
b Zaied est allergique aux chats.
c Zaied a un phasme.
d L'animal préféré de Zaied, c'est la girafe.
e L'animal préféré de Clarisse est blanc.
f L'animal préféré de Clarisse n'est pas féroce.
g L'animal préféré de Clarisse habite en Afrique.
h L'animal préféré de Clarisse est très long.

 Quel est l'animal préféré de Zaied? Et de Clarisse?
Which are Zaied and Clarisse's favourite animals?

Quel est ton animal préféré au zoo de Montpellier? Pourquoi?
Which is your favourite animal at the Montpellier zoo? Why?
Exemple: *Mon animal préféré au zoo de Montpellier, c'est …*

3.9 Test

ECOUTER 1

Listen to the four interviews and fill in the table in English (1–4).
(See pages 40–41, 44–49.)

		where they live	pets (number and colour)	favourite animal	pet they would like to have
1	Jules	*a flat in the suburbs*			
2	Amélie				
3	Arthur				
4	Céline				

PARLER 2

Give a presentation about yourself. (See pages 40–49.)
You could include:
- where you live and your school
- your hobbies; what you like to do with your friends
- a description of your pets at home
- a pet you would like to have
- your favourite animal

LIRE 3

Read the text and answer the questions.
(See pages 40–49.)

a How far away does Sarah live from her school?
b What is her favourite subject at school?
c What **two** things does she like doing in her room?
d When does she go to the youth club?
e What **two** pets does she have?
f What pet would she like?
g What is her favourite animal?

ECRIRE 4

Write a paragraph about you and your world. (See pages 40–49.)
You could include:
- a description of where you live
- a description of your pets at home and a pet you would like to have
- your favourite an imal and why
- your friends' or family members' favourite animals
- animals you don't like and why
- what happened the last time you went to a zoo/farm/park

Remember, the more you can develop your answers, the better your work will be.

Ma vie à Rouen   Accueil   Profil   Compte

Salut! Je m'appelle Sarah et j'ai douze ans. J'habite à Rouen et je vais au collège Jeanne d'Arc. J'habite à deux kilomètres de mon collège – c'est bien! J'aime mon collège parce que les profs sont sympa et j'adore les maths. C'est ma matière préférée. Chez moi, dans ma chambre, j'ai une télé et un lecteur MP4. J'adore regarder des DVD et écouter de la musique pop. Tous les mercredis, je vais à la maison des jeunes avec ma sœur Émilie. Là-bas, je joue au billard ou je bavarde avec mes amis. J'ai un chat marron qui s'appelle Claude et un chien blanc qui s'appelle Oscar, mais je voudrais avoir un lapin. J'adore les lapins mais mon animal préféré, c'est le tigre.

Vocabulaire

School and home

la sixième	Year 7
la cinquième	Year 8
la quatrième	Year 9
la troisième	Year 10
une classe	class
un collège	secondary school
le copain	friend, mate
un(e) élève	pupil, student
un kilomètre	kilometre
une matière	subject
un(e) prof(esseur)	teacher
une salle (de classe)	(class)room
j'habite	I live
dans	in
un appartement	flat
une chambre	bedroom
une maison individuelle	detached house
une maison jumelée	semi-detached house
un pavillon	bungalow
en banlieue	in the suburbs
à la campagne	in the countryside
à la montagne	in the mountains
dans un village	in a village
en ville	in town

Possessions and activities

des BD	comics
une console de jeux vidéo	console
des DVD	DVDs
un lecteur MP4	MP4 player
un ordi(nateur)	computer
un roman	novel
une télé	TV
un (téléphone) portable	mobile (phone)
je bavarde avec mes copains	I chat with my friends
je fais des concerts	I do concerts
je joue au baby-foot	I play table football
je joue au billard	I play pool
je joue au foot	I play football
je regarde un film	I watch a film
je retrouve mes copains	I meet up with my friends
je vais au bar	I go to the bar

Pets

un animal	animal
un chat	cat
un cheval	horse
un chien	dog
un cochon d'Inde	guinea pig
un lapin	rabbit
un lézard	lizard
un oiseau	bird
un phasme	stick insect
une tortue	tortoise

Wild animals

un éléphant	elephant
une girafe	giraffe
un hippopotame	hippo
un lion	lion
un rhinocéros	rhino
un singe	monkey
un tigre	tiger
un zèbre	zebra

Useful verbs

je vais	I go
j'ai visité	I visited
j'ai vu	I saw
je n'ai pas vu	I didn't see
c'était	it was
j'avais	I had / I used to have
je voudrais	I would like

Connectives

et	and
aussi	also
donc	therefore
mais	but
par contre	on the other hand
tout d'abord	first of all
puis	then
ensuite	next
après ça	after that

⊙ Grammar and skills: I can...

- ⊙ use the present tense
- ⊙ practise agreement for adjectives of colour
- ⊙ use *je voudrais* and *j'avais*
- ⊙ use the perfect tense of common verbs
- ⊙ use adjectives to describe animals
- ⊙ avoid false friends
- ⊙ interpret longer texts
- ⊙ apply tenses
- ⊙ use a dictionary
- ⊙ use writing strategies to structure a paragraph

4.1 Boire et manger

- Vocabulary: talk about food
- Grammar: use *du/de la/de l'/des*; use the present tense
- Skills: use memorisation strategies; improve writing

 Écoute et lis. Qu'est-ce que c'est?

Exemple: 1 **b**

1	de la pizza	**8**	du jambon
2	du pain	**9**	des œufs
3	de la salade	**10**	du coca
4	des saucisses	**11**	du fromage
5	des fruits	**12**	de l'eau
6	des gâteaux	**13**	du chocolat
7	du pâté	**14**	des chips

🍴 *See page 69 for strategies to remember new words.*

 Écoute. Qu'est-ce qu'il y a dans le chariot de Marie?
What's in Marie's trolley?
Exemple: 8, 4 ...

 Écris. Envoie une liste de courses à tes copains par mail.
Email a shopping list to your friends. Say what you or they are going to buy for a party.
Exemple:

Sujet: La fête de samedi

Salut! Pour la fête de samedi, je vais acheter des chips ...
Lucie va acheter ...

Grammaire
p. 166
WB p.26

Partitive articles

Use **du**, **de la**, **de l'** or **des** in front of food items to say 'some'.

	singular	plural
masculine	**du** pain	**des** œufs
feminine	**de la** salade	**des** chips

Use *de l'* for a singular word starting with a vowel: *de l'eau.*

je vais acheter   *I am going to buy*
Lucie va acheter   *Lucie is going to buy*

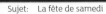

4 Écoute et lis. Trouve les expressions françaises qui correspondent.

Exemple: **a** *Le matin*

a in the morning **b** for breakfast **c** I drink **d** at midday
e for lunch **f** I eat **g** after school **h** in the evening **i** for dinner

08:00 Le matin, au petit déjeuner, je mange une ou deux tartines et je bois du jus d'orange. Le week-end, je mange des céréales avec du lait. Puis à midi, **12:00** pour le déjeuner, je mange de la viande ou du poisson avec des frites ou des pâtes. Je mange aussi du fromage et je bois de l'eau. Au goûter, **16:30** après le collège, je prends une banane ou une pomme et je bois un coca. Le soir, au dîner, on mange de la soupe, des œufs ou de la salade et un yaourt ou un fruit.

5 En groupe. Qu'est-ce que tu manges/tu bois …
- au petit déjeuner? • au déjeuner? • au dîner?
Exemple: Au petit déjeuner, je mange … et je bois …

◎ Can you add opinions and/or time descriptors to your answers?

6 Lis le mail. Recopie et remplis les blancs avec *du, de la, de l'* ou *des*.

Sujet: Qu'est-ce qu'on mange en France?

En France, on mange **1** _du_ pain frais tous les jours, en général **2** _____ baguette. Aussi, on mange **3** _____ escargots et **4** _____ cuisses de grenouilles … mais pas tous les jours!
Les Anglais n'aiment pas ça. Ils pensent que c'est dégoûtant. On mange aussi **5** _____ viande:
6 _____ poulet, **7** _____ bœuf avec **8** _____ frites, **9** _____ riz ou **10** _____ légumes et on boit **11** _____ eau du robinet ou **12** _____ eau minérale.
Chez toi, qu'est-ce qu'on mange? Rebecca

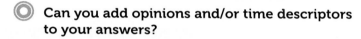

escargots *snails*
cuisses de grenouilles *frogs' legs*

➕ Translate Rebecca's email into English.

7 Écris un petit article sur la nourriture chez toi. Utilise le texte de Rebecca.

Exemple: Chez moi, au petit déjeuner, je mange …

Grammaire p. 168–169

Manger* and *boire

Manger is a regular *-er* verb.
je mang**e**
tu mang**es**
il/elle/on mang**e**

Boire is an irregular verb.
je boi**s**
tu boi**s**
il/elle/on boi**t**

Writing strategies
Improve your written work by:
- using connectives: *mais, aussi, et*
- adapting Rebecca's expressions, e.g. *Les Français n'aiment pas ça*
- expanding your work with as much detail as possible, e.g. using adjectives
- paying attention to accuracy, e.g. *du, de la, de l', des*.

Plenary
You have 60 seconds to write down as much as you can about food and meals.
★ Use single words.
◎ Add verbs and write a few sentences.
➕ Make more complex sentences and use a near future (going to) tense.
Show your list to your partner and ask him/her to assess your work, then do the same for them.

4.2 Tu aimes ça?

- Vocabulary: give your opinion on food and drinks
- Grammar: use negative forms; use *pouvoir*
- Skills: identify language patterns; recycle language you already know

1 Lis. Qui dit ... ?

Exemple: **a** *Sophie*

a I eat anything.
b I love vegetables.
c I hate green vegetables.
d I love fruit.
e I love eating.

Language patterns

Look at what the three youngsters in activity 1 say. What article do they use after opinion verbs? Which one do they use after negative forms such as *ne ... pas* and *ne ... jamais*?

Can you make a sentence to say what you like/dislike and never eat?

J'adore les fruits et les légumes mais je ne mange jamais de poisson.

Margaux

J'adore la viande mais je déteste les légumes verts et je ne mange pas de fruits.

Hugo

Moi, j'aime tout, je ne suis pas difficile et j'adore manger!

Sophie

2 Écoute. Hugo parle à quatre copains. Vrai ou faux?

Hugo speaks to four friends. True or false?

Exemple: **a** *vrai*

a Vanessa does not like cereals but she loves bread for breakfast.
b Théo is fussy with his food.
c Zarah likes eating vegetables.
d Thomas does not like meat.
e Hugo likes fish and green vegetables.

◎ Choose two food items that are mentioned. What is the friends' opinion?

Grammaire
p. 167
WB p.13

Negative forms

Remember **ne ... pas** goes around the verb to make it negative:

J'aime les chips. → *Je n'aime pas les chips.*
I like crisps. → I do not like crisps.

The same goes for *ne ... jamais*:

Je ne mange jamais de poisson.
– I never eat fish.

3 Sondage. 'Tu aimes ça?'

Pose les questions à cinq personnes.

Do a class survey to find out about favourite foods and drinks. Choose three items and ask five people.

Exemple: – *Tu aimes la viande?*
– *Oui, j'adore ça, c'est top/c'est super bon.*
– *Non, je n'aime pas ça, c'est dégoûtant/j'ai horreur de ça.*

	♥♥	♥	✗✗✗
a *la viande*	✓		
b			
c			

j'adore	l'eau,	c'est super bon
j'aime bien	le coca,	c'est top
	le fromage,	
	le jambon,	c'est dégoûtant
je déteste	la viande,	j'ai horreur de ça
je n'aime pas du tout	les chips,	ça me fait vomir

➕ **Can you talk about your findings?**
Quatre personnes aiment ... , mais ...

60 *soixante*

Lis les messages et trouve les paires.

Exemple: **a** *je ne peux pas manger*

a I cannot eat
b because of my religion
c I am a Muslim
d it makes me sick
e I am a vegetarian
f I don't eat meat
g it is disgusting
h it is full of vitamins

À table   Accueil   Profil   Compte

Moi, j'adore la viande mais je ne peux pas manger de porc à cause de ma religion, je suis musulmane! J'aime aussi les fruits, ça donne de l'énergie et des vitamines. C'est super parce que je suis sportive. Par contre, le poisson, c'est horrible, ça me fait vomir!

Zarah

Moi, j'adore les animaux donc je suis végétarien et je ne mange pas de viande du tout. C'est dégoûtant! J'aime beaucoup les légumes et le fromage, c'est plein de vitamines et de calcium!

Léo

 Écoute. Recopie et remplis la grille. C'est qui?

Qui ...	Zaïd	Sarah	Kévin	Sophie
est végétarien?	✓			
n'aime pas manger de poisson?				
mange beaucoup de pâtes?				
mange beaucoup de fruits?				

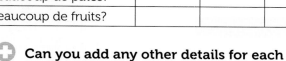 **Grammaire** p. 168–169 WB p.20

Pouvoir

Pouvoir (can) is a modal verb and is always followed by an infinitive:

je peux manger – I can eat
tu peux jouer – you can play
il/elle/on peut aller – he/she/we can go

To say 'cannot', you wrap *ne ... pas* around *peux/peut*:

*Je **ne** peux **pas** manger de viande.* – I cannot eat meat.

➕ **Can you add any other details for each of them in English?**

 Lis et trouve les paires.
Find the pairs.
Exemple: **a 3**

a Je ne peux pas manger de viande
b Je ne peux pas boire de lait
c Je mange beaucoup de fruits
d Je ne peux pas manger de porc
e Je ne mange pas de bœuf

1 parce que je suis musulman.
2 parce que je suis allergique.
3 parce que je suis végétarien.
4 parce que ma famille est hindoue.
5 parce que ça apporte des vitamines.

 Qu'est-ce que tu manges et bois? Tu aimes ça? Écris des phrases.
What do you eat and drink? Write sentences giving your opinions and saying what you can and cannot eat and drink (and why).
Exemple: J'adore le jambon, c'est top ...

Plenary

Recycling known language is vital to success when learning French. Practise the skills of substitution when you tackle the task below. How have you improved your learning skills? Can you write about food? Use the expressions from activity 4. Your partner will assess your work.

⭐ Build a complete sentence.

◎ Build a complete sentence and add an opinion.

➕ Build a complete sentence, add an opinion and a reason. Can you also add a near future tense?

4.3 Glace ou crêpe?

- Vocabulary: talk about your favourite restaurant and order food
- Grammar: use *je voudrais* to order ice cream
- Skills: express opinions; use knowledge of verb forms in a new context

Lis. C'est quel restaurant? Relie les menus et les images.
Exemple: 1 ...

 1

Lasagnes maison

Pâtes:
carbonara/au fromage

Pizza:
tomates/fromage/
champignons

Boissons:
limonade/orangina

2

Crêpes salées:
au fromage/au jambon/à l'œuf

Crêpes sucrées:
au beurre/au sucre/
à la confiture/au Nutella

Gaufres chantilly

Boissons: cidre/chocolat chaud

3

Hamburger:
fromage
bacon
poulet

Nuggets

Frites

Salades

Boissons:
coca light
eau minérale

a

b

Écoute. Recopie et remplis la grille.

	Ahmed	Enzo	Sarah	Marie
le fast-food				
la pizzeria				
la crêperie				

c

Lis le texte de Léo. Vrai, faux ou pas mentionné?
Exemple: **a** *vrai*

Moi, j'aime aller à la pizzeria. C'est mon resto préféré parce que j'adore les pizzas jambon/fromage et les spaghettis bolognaise. Mais je n'aime pas manger dans les fast-food. Les hamburgers, ce n'est pas mon truc. Berk, j'ai horreur de ça! Par contre, j'aime manger des crêpes. J'habite en Bretagne donc il y a beaucoup de crêperies, c'est une spécialité bretonne.

Léo

a Léo aime les pizzerias.
b Il aime les lasagnes.
c Il aime les fast-food.

d Il déteste les hamburgers.
e Il n'aime pas les crêpes.
f Il aime les gaufres.

Which connectives can you find in the text?

Quel restaurant tu préfères? Écris un petit texte.
What is your favourite restaurant? Write a short review.
Exemple: J'aime manger à la pizzeria ...

Verb forms

If a verb follows *j'aime/j'aime bien/je déteste/je n'aime pas/je préfère*, what form will the verb take? Can you find examples in Léo's text?

Can you complete these sentences?

I like to drink – *J'aime/J'adore ...*
I don't like drinking – *Je n'aime pas/Je déteste ...*
I prefer eating – *Je préfère ...*

(See Workbook, page 18)

J'aime manger/aller à la/au ...
J'aime manger/aller dans les ...
C'est mon restaurant préféré parce que j'aime manger ...
J'aime aller ... mais je déteste aller ...

5 Écoute et lis.

Glace italienne

Glace 1, 2 ou 3 boules

Coupe de glace avec ou sans chantilly

Parfums

Glaces: vanille/chocolat/noisette/café/pistache/caramel

Sorbets:

fraise

framboise

citron

cassis

Prix
Glace italienne: 2€50
1 boule: 1€50
2 boules: 2€
3 boules: 2€50
Supplément
chantilly: 0€50

Si, mais   *Yes, but*
C'est combien?   *How much is it?*
C'est tout?   *Is that all?*

Vendeuse	Bonjour!
Coralie	Je voudrais une glace *trois boules* s'il vous plaît.
Vendeuse	Oui, dans un cornet ou un pot?
Coralie	Dans *un cornet* s'il vous plaît.
Vendeuse	Quel parfum?
Coralie	*Vanille, fraise* et *chocolat*.
Vendeuse	Avec de la chantilly?
Coralie	*Non* merci.
Vendeuse	Tu n'aimes pas *la chantilly*?
Coralie	Si, mais je préfère sans! C'est combien?
Vendeuse	*2€50*. C'est tout?
Coralie	Oui, c'est tout, merci. Au revoir!
Vendeuse	Au revoir!

 6 Lis le dialogue et réponds aux questions.
Exemple: **a** 3

a How many scoops does Coralie want?
b Does she have a tub or a cone?
c Which flavours does she choose?
d Does she want any chantilly?
e How much does she pay?

 7 À deux. Adaptez le dialogue.
Make up a similar dialogue changing the words in italics in activity 5.

Grammaire WB p.17

Je voudrais + noun/verb

je voudrais une glace – I would like an ice cream
je voudrais manger – I would like to eat

Plenary

How many full sentences can you remember? Say them aloud to your partner and assess each other.

⭐ Two or three correct sentences.
◎ Four or five correct sentences.
➕ Six or more correct sentences.

4.4 On cuisine

- Vocabulary: understand quantities and recipes
- Grammar: use quantities accurately; use *il faut*
- Skills: explain number patterns and use them with familiar vocabulary

Écoute. Relie les images et les mots.
Exemple: 1 g

a
b
c
d
e
f
g
h

1 un paquet de chips
2 un morceau de fromage
3 une bouteille de coca
4 une bouteille d'eau
5 une tranche de jambon
6 un pot de yaourt
7 une tablette de chocolat
8 cent grammes de pâté

Quantities

Can you see a pattern when you use a quantity? Which word do you use in front of the item of food?

Recopie la liste d'Affreux Jojo. Corrige les erreurs.
Copy out Jojo's list. Correct the mistakes.
Exemple: une tablette de chocolat, ...

une tablette de chips
un pot de jambon
un morceau de yaourt
un paquet d'eau minérale
4 tranches de chocolat
une bouteille de fromage

JOJO

Lis, écoute et répète les nombres. Attention à la prononciation!
See page 69 for strategies to help you learn these numbers.

Au marché on utilise les grammes et les kilos. Trouve les paires.
In markets, we use grammes and kilos. Find the pairs.
Exemple: a 3

a 150 g
b 260 g
c 500 g
d 180 g
e 460 g
f 1 kg

1 cinq cents grammes
2 quatre cent soixante grammes
3 cent cinquante grammes
4 un kilo
5 deux cent soixante grammes
6 cent quatre-vingts grammes

40	quarante
41	quarante et un
50	cinquante
60	soixante
70	soixante-dix
71	soixante et onze
80	quatre-vingts
81	quatre-vingt-un
90	quatre-vingt-dix
91	quatre-vingt-onze
100	cent
200	deux cents
250	deux cent cinquante
300	trois cents

LIRE 5 — Lis et trouve les quatre phrases correctes.

Read the recipe and find the four correct sentences below.
Correct the wrong ones.
Exemple: **1** *correcte*

Recette du croque-monsieur
Ingrédients

Il faut:

2 tranches de pain

1 tranche de fromage

1 tranche de jambon

50 g de fromage râpé

2 cuillères à soupe de
crème fraîche

Méthode

Il faut:

a étaler la crème
sur le pain

b poser le
jambon sur la
crème

c poser le
fromage sur
le jambon

d poser le pain
sur le fromage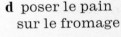

e mettre le
fromage râpé
sur le pain

f mettre au four

Bon appétit!

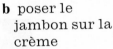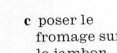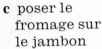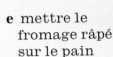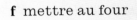

1 spread the cream on the bread
2 place the ham on the cream
3 spread the cream on the ham
4 place the bread on the ham
5 put the grated cheese on the bread
6 put in the oven

Grammaire WB p.19

il faut

Use *il faut* to say what you need or must have:

Il faut deux œufs. – You need two eggs.

Use *il faut* + infinitive to say what you have to do:

Il faut mettre le beurre … – You must put the butter …

ÉCOUTER 6 — Écoute. Qui gagne *Superchef Junior*? Avec quelle note?

Whose sandwich wins the contest? What mark does it get?

Le challenge: créer un sandwich "fou"

Le sandwich de Théo   Le sandwich de Zarah   Le sandwich de Salomé

◎ **Name two ingredients in the winning sandwich.**

✚ **Translate the judge's description of the winning sandwich.**

ÉCRIRE 7 — Écris. Crée un sandwich fou.
Invent a crazy sandwich.
Exemple: Mon sandwich: il faut du pain, …

du beurre   des smarties
de la moutarde   du poisson   du Nutella
du ketchup   du chocolat   des oignons

Plenary

Work with a partner. Check on each other's recipes from exercise 7. Read them aloud and comment on each other's pronunciation. Pay particular attention to the use of *il faut*.

⭐ Pronunciation OK.
◎ Good pronunciation.
✚ Very good pronunciation.

4.5 La cuisine et l'art

- Vocabulary: talk about food and about art; give opinions
- Grammar: identify and use different tenses
- Skills: use a wider range of language to express opinions; recycle food vocabulary in a different context

 Lis le blog de Marion et réponds aux questions en anglais.
Read Marion's blog and answer the questions in English.
Exemple: **a** *in Marseille*

La soupe de poissons | Accueil Profil Compte

Aujourd'hui: *10 juillet*

Salut à tous!

Je suis *en France*, à *Marseille: la région du soleil, de la mer!*

Ici, la spécialité, c'est *la soupe de poissons*. J'ai goûté: c'est vraiment délicieux! J'ai demandé la recette.

Il faut *500g de poissons, une boîte de tomates, 4 cuillères d'huile, 2 oignons hachés, du sel et du poivre. Il faut mélanger tous les ingrédients ensemble et faire cuire trente minutes!* C'est tout et c'est super bon!

Demain, je vais visiter *le musée*. Il y a *des grands artistes comme Cézanne et Picasso et des peintures très célèbres!* Je vais mettre des photos sur mon blog.

À plus!

FRANCE

Provence

hachés   *chopped*
faire cuire   *to cook*
des peintures   *paintings*

---

a Where is Marion today?	**f** Name two other ingredients.
b Why is this region famous?	**g** How long do you cook it for?
c What is the traditional dish?	**h** Where is Marion going tomorrow?
d What does Marion think of it?	**i** Name two famous artists.
e How much oil do you need?	

➕ **Marion uses verbs in a past tense in parts of her blog. Can you spot them? She also talks about the future. Can you spot these verbs too?**

 Adapte le texte et change les mots en *italique*.
Adapt the text and change the words in *italics*.
Exemple: Je suis en Angleterre, à ... La spécialité, c'est ...
         Demain, je vais visiter ...

la spécialité	je vais visiter
le musée	c'est super/c'est top
j'ai visité	c'est délicieux
j'ai goûté	j'adore ça
j'ai adoré	je n'aime pas beaucoup

  Fais une présentation à ton groupe.
Present your work from activity 2 to your group.

4

Lis et écoute Hanan et Yussef. Trouve les phrases.

Exemple: **a** ça me fait peur

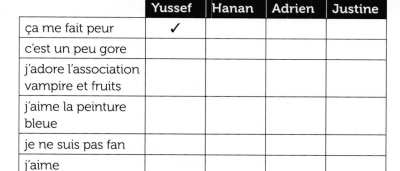

Tu aimes la peinture numéro 1?

Oui, j'adore l'association vampire et fruits, c'est original. C'est un peu gore, mais j'adore! Quel talent!

Non, je déteste les vampires. Ça me fait peur! Et toi?

La peinture numéro 3 est très intéressante. Elle représente un chien mais c'est très bizarre, il y a juste des fruits et des légumes. Mais ça marche! C'est trop cool, j'adore.

Moi je préfère la peinture numéro 2. Je suis fan du bleu alors j'aime.

a it scares me	**c** I am a fan of	**e** it represents
b I love the association	**d** I like it	**f** it works

 5

Écoute. Recopie et remplis la grille. Qui dit quoi?

Listen. Copy and complete the table. Who says what?

	Yussef	Hanan	Adrien	Justine
ça me fait peur	✓			
c'est un peu gore				
j'adore l'association vampire et fruits				
j'aime la peinture bleue				
je ne suis pas fan				
j'aime				

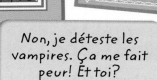 **6**

Écris la critique d'une peinture.

Write a review of a painting (one from activity 4, or a different one). Use the phrases below and from activity 4.

je pense que	c'est super
Quel talent!	j'aime
ça marche	
je trouve ça horrible/super	

⭐ Use at least five phrases to describe it.

◎ Can you add connectives?

Plenary

In pairs, you have 30 seconds to describe one of the three paintings in activity 4 to your partner. Listen and assess each other's description.

⭐ Use single words.

◎ Use simple sentences with opinions.

✚ Make longer sentences and give opinions.

Partitive articles

1 **Fill in the missing word for 'some'.**

a   *du*   jambon
b   ▭▭   fruits
c   ▭▭   eau minérale
d   ▭▭   frites
e   ▭▭   fromage
f   ▭▭   viande
g   ▭▭   coca
h   ▭▭   œufs
i   ▭▭   café
j   ▭▭   pain

You have to use **du**, **de la**, **de l'** or **des** in front of food items. In English, you would say 'some'.

	singular		plural	
masculine	*un/le*	**du chocolat**	*des/les*	**des gâteaux**
feminine	*une/la*	**de la soupe**		**des chips**
vowel	*l'*	**de l'eau**		

Regular -er verbs

2 **Choose the correct form of the verb.**

a   Nous aime/<u>aimons</u>/aimez la pizza.
b   Charlotte aimes/aime/aiment le chocolat.
c   Les jeunes adores/adorent/adorez le fast-food.
d   Nous aiment/aimes/aimons la cuisine française.
e   Loïc et Bastien détestes/détestent/détestez les légumes.
f   Vous aimes/aimez/aiment les escargots?
g   Tu habite/habites/habitez où?

Verbs that end in *-er* are regular; they all follow the same pattern. They include **aimer** (to like, to love), **adorer** (to love), **détester** (to hate), **jouer** (to play), **habiter** (to live)… The only exception is **aller**, which is irregular – see page 43.

To form the present tense, remove the *-er* and add the following endings:

j'aim**e**   nous aim**ons**
tu aim**es**   vous aim**ez**
il/elle/on aim**e**   ils/elles aim**ent**

Negative forms

3 **Make the sentences negative.**

Exemple: **a** *Je ne mange pas de viande.*

a   Je mange de la viande.
b   Je bois de la limonade.
c   Il mange des légumes verts.
d   J'ai du chocolat.
e   J'aime les frites.
f   Tu aimes les glaces?

To make a sentence negative you put *ne … pas* (or *n' … pas*) around the verb:

*je mange – je **ne** mange **pas***
*j'aime – je **n'**aime **pas***

A verb in the negative form is normally followed by *de*:

*Je mange du fromage, mais je ne mange pas **de** yaourt.* – I eat cheese but I do not eat yoghurt.

Ne … jamais means 'never':

*Je **ne** mange **jamais** de frites.* – I never eat chips.

The exception to the *de* rule is *aimer*. When talking about likes and dislikes, you use *le/la/l'/les* in front of the noun:

*J'aime le fromage, mais je n'aime pas **le** yaourt.* – I like cheese but I don't like yoghurt.

Aimer + infinitive, *je voudrais* + infinitive

4 **Translate these sentences.**

Exemple: **a** *J'aime manger de la pizza.*

a I like eating pizza.
b I don't like eating meat.
c I like to drink water.
d I hate going to fast-food restaurants.
e I would like to buy an ice cream.
f I would like to eat some bread.

> When you talk about what you like or dislike doing, or what you would like to do, you use the infinitive form for the second verb:
> *J'aime **manger** au restaurant.* – I like eating out.
> *J'adore **visiter** les musées.* – I love visiting museums.
> *Je n'aime pas **aller** dans les fast-food.* – I don't like going to fast-food restaurants.
> *Tu aimes **jouer** au foot?* – Do you like playing football?
> *Je **voudrais** manger de la pizza.* – I would like to eat some pizza.

Memorisation strategies

You have already seen some memorisation strategies in Units 1 and 2.

Use these new strategies with activity 1, page 58 and activity 3, page 64.

- To remember the gender of new words, e.g. food, group them together using colour-coding, e.g. **blue** for masculine, pink for feminine.

- Put 10–15 new words to a memorable tune, e.g. a rap, TV theme, nursery rhyme, etc.

- Memorise new words using a dice. Roll the dice and complete the following activities. If you roll:

  1 = write your word out three times
  2 = draw a picture of the word
  3 = write your word in a sentence
  4 = write your word backwards
  5 = write the word in a word snake
  6 = write what the word means in English

- Memorise spellings by writing words four ways: **1 in pencil, 2 in pen, 3 in colour, 4 in crayon.**

- Test yourself using **Look** – **Cover** – **Test** – **Check.**

- If you make a mistake, copy the word five times and re-test yourself the next day.

- Memorise how to say the word correctly, paying attention to the sound strategies covered in other units.

Silent letters at the end of words

5 **Listen to the list of words. Can you hear any exceptions to this rule? There are two.**

> In French, the letters **s, t, d, x** are normally silent when they are at the end of a word.

- Vocabulary: practise talking about food
- Grammar: revise the use of *du/de la/de l'/des*
- Skills: develop reading skills

 1 **Can you crack the code and read the names of drinks and items of food? Write out the words.**

Exemple: **a** = *du chocolat*

a d❷ ch❸c❸l❶t

b d❷ p❸❷l❹t

c d❹s fr❷❺ts

d d❷ p❶❺n

e d❹ l'❹❶❷

 2 **Match the answers to the questions.**

Exemple: **a 2**

a Vous désirez?

b Quel parfum?

c Combien de boules?

d Un cornet ou un pot?

e C'est combien?

f C'est tout?

1 2€50.

2 Je voudrais une glace.

3 Un cornet, s'il vous plaît.

4 Vanille/fraise.

5 Oui, merci.

6 Deux boules, s'il vous plaît.

 3 **Unjumble these sentences.**

Exemple: **a** *J'aime manger des pizzas avec de la salade.*

a des j'aime avec de pizzas manger salade la.

b je pas dans n'aime les manger fast-food.

c au je du au petit bois déjeuner lait café.

d déteste de manger je viande suis je la parce que végétarienne.

e manger il des chantilly avec aime la de crêpes.

 4 **Read Théo's email about his summer camp and answer the questions.**

Exemple: **a** *toasted bread with butter and jam*

Sujet: La colo

Salut! Je suis en colonie depuis une semaine. C'est super! Le matin, au petit déjeuner, je mange du pain grillé avec du beurre et de la confiture et je bois du chocolat chaud. À midi, on mange du poulet avec des légumes (carottes, haricots verts …) et comme dessert, on mange une tarte au citron ou un yaourt. Le soir, on mange de la soupe, une pizza avec une salade verte ou une omelette et je bois un coca … J'adore ça!
À plus!

a What does Theo eat for breakfast?

b What does he drink?

c What do they eat at lunchtime?

d Which vegetables do they eat?

e What dessert do they eat? (two answers)

f What is served for dinner? (two answers)

4.7 Extra Plus

- Vocabulary: practise higher numbers; talk about different food and meals
- Grammar: develop the use of *j'aime/je n'aime pas* + infinitive
- Skills: become confident in dealing with unfamiliar words in longer texts

Écris les nombres.
Write these numbers out.
Exemple: **a** *cent cinquante*

a 150	**c** 520	**e** 340	**g** 390
b 200	**d** 180	**f** 250	

Qu'est-ce que tu aimes/n'aimes pas manger et boire?

Exemple: **a** *J'aime manger du jambon, mais je n'aime pas manger …*

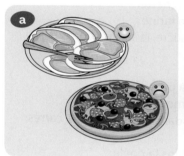   

Lis le texte.
Trouve les trois phrases justes et corrige les autres.
Find the three correct sentences and correct the others.
Exemple: **a** *true*

- **a** In Belgium they eat mussels.
- **b** Belgians eat chips with ketchup.
- **c** Beer is the traditional Canadian drink.
- **d** 'Créole' cooking is from Belgium.
- **e** 'Cari' is made with meat or fish.
- **f** Caroline likes chicken cari.
- **g** In Quebec they eat chicken with maple syrup.
- **h** Caroline loves the Canadian dish.

> l'île de La Réunion   *Reunion Island*
> épicé   *spicy*
> le sirop d'érable   *maple syrup*

Plats traditionnels   Accueil   Profil   Compte

Bonjour! Aujourd'hui on va parler des plats traditionnels dans des pays francophones. En Belgique, on mange des moules-frites avec de la mayonnaise et on boit de la bière. À l'île de La Réunion, c'est la cuisine créole. On mange du cari de viande ou de poisson avec du riz. C'est un plat très épicé! À La Réunion, on mange un cari de poulet. C'est super bon, j'adore ça. Au Québec, il y a un plat très bizarre, le jambon au sirop d'érable. C'est un peu sucré et salé. Je ne suis pas fan!

À plus

Caroline, de Paris

La recette des merveilles

Ingrédients

- 500 g de farine
- 3 œufs
- 125 g de beurre
- 3 cuillères de sucre
- le jus de 2 ou 3 citrons
- un peu de sel
- un peu d'huile

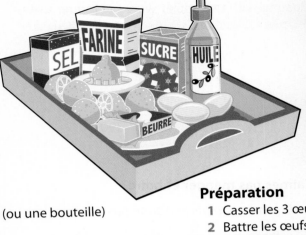

Ustensiles

- un grand bol
- une fourchette
- une cuillère
- un rouleau à pâtisserie (ou une bouteille)
- un couteau
- une poêle

le rouleau à pâtisserie

le papier absorbant

la bouteille

le bol

la poêle

la cuillère

la fourchette

le couteau

Préparation

1. Casser les 3 œufs dans un grand bol.
2. Battre les œufs à la fourchette.
3. Mélanger les œufs et la farine.
4. Ajouter 3 cuillères de sucre, le sel, le beurre, le jus de citron.
5. Mélanger.
6. Faire une boule avec la pâte.
7. Étaler la pâte très finement.
8. Découper des formes dans la pâte: étoiles, carrés, ronds, ovales…
9. Faire chauffer l'huile dans la poêle.
10. Mettre les formes dans l'huile très chaude pendant 30 secondes.
11. Mettre les merveilles sur du papier absorbant.
12. Ajouter du sucre.

LIRE 1 Read the *Préparation* section. Match the verbs.

Exemple: **a** *1*

a	to add	**1**	ajouter
b	to break	**2**	battre
c	to cut out	**3**	casser
d	to heat up	**4**	découper
e	to mix	**5**	étaler
f	to place	**6**	faire chauffer
g	to roll into a ball	**7**	faire une boule
h	to roll out	**8**	mélanger
i	to whisk	**9**	mettre

LIRE 2 Answer the questions in English.

Exemple: **a** *flour*

- **a** Which do you think is the main ingredient?
- **b** Which is probably the least important ingredient?
- **c** What shapes does the recipe suggest for making *merveilles*?
- **d** Which step requires a rolling pin?
- **e** Which step requires a knife?
- **f** Which words in the recipe suggest the dough should be rolled out thinly?
- **g** Why do you have to place the *merveilles* on kitchen paper?
- **h** What do you do with the dough straight after mixing all the ingredients?

Le sandwich fou

 Regarde l'épisode 4. Combien de temps ont les jeunes pour faire le sandwich?
How long do they have to make their sandwich?

2 **Qu'est-ce qu'il y a dans le sandwich des filles? Et dans le sandwich des garçons?**
Le sandwich des filles: *du pain, …*
Le sandwich des garçons: *du pain, …*

du pain

du fromage

du chocolat

de la pizza

des carottes

des chips

du jambon

des œufs

des sardines

des tomates

du ketchup

de la salade

 Réponds aux questions en anglais.
Exemple: **a** *ham, because …*

- **a** What is it that Noura never eats, and why?
- **b** What is it that Clarisse never eats, and why?
- **c** What is it that Basile eats with everything? (2 answers)
- **d** What kind of bread do they use for their sandwiches?
- **e** Which ingredient can't the boys get?
- **f** Why does Diakouba take a photo?

 Quel sandwich préfères-tu, le sandwich des filles ou le sandwich des garçons? Pourquoi?
Which sandwich do you prefer, the boys' or the girls'? Why?

Exemple: Je préfère le sandwich des garçons, parce que je n'aime pas … et j'ai horreur de … mais j'adore …

4.9 *Test*

 1 Listen to four young people. Which meal do they talk about?
What do they eat and drink? What do they think?
(See pages 58–59.)

		meal	food/drink	opinion
1	Samuel		*yoghurt, ...*	
2	Jade			
3	Martin			
4	Louna			*favourite drink, it's great*

 2 Discuss food and drink with a partner.
Speak for a minute each. (See pages 60–61 and 64–65.)

● Ask for the following quantities of food.

Exemple: Je voudrais un paquet de chips ...

● Say what you like and don't like eating and drinking
and say why.

Exemple: J'adore manger des ... parce que ... Et toi?

3 Read Océane's email and answer the questions
below in English. (See pages 60–61.)

Exemple: a the food,...

a What does Océane like about England?
b Which English dish does she like?
c How does Océane drink her tea?
d What does she eat for breakfast?
e Why is Rebecca a vegetarian?
f Does Océane like custard?
g When is Océane going back to England?
h Where is she going to stay?

 4 Write an article on what you like to eat
and drink for a French school magazine.
(See pages 58–65.)
You could include:

● what you eat for breakfast/lunch/dinner
● what you can/cannot eat and why
● information about your favourite
restaurant
● information about a recipe –
the ingredients and how to make it.

Exemple: Au petit déjeuner, je mange ...

**Remember, the more you can develop your
answers, the better your work will be.**

Sujet: Vive l'Angleterre

Salut à tous!

J'adore l'Angleterre! J'adore la cuisine anglaise,
la musique anglaise (Adele, elle est trop cool!) et
Primark pour le shopping. J'adore une spécialité
anglaise, les scones avec de la crème et de la
confiture, c'est très "british" et c'est vraiment
délicieux! Ici, je bois beaucoup de thé au lait. Le
matin, au petit déjeuner, je mange des céréales avec
du lait. Rebecca ne peut pas manger de viande parce
qu'elle adore les animaux, donc elle est végétarienne.

Avec les desserts, les Anglais mangent toujours
une crème qui s'appelle la "custard". C'est comme
la crème anglaise, mais c'est chaud. C'est bizarre
mais j'adore ça! Je vais retourner chez Rebecca en
Angleterre en août.

Regardez mes photos sur Facebook, elles sont super!

À plus!

Bisous

Océane

Vocabulaire

Meals

au petit déjeuner	*for breakfast*
au déjeuner	*for lunch*
au goûter	*for a snack*
au dîner	*for dinner*
du lait	*milk*
du chocolat chaud	*hot chocolate*
du pain grillé	*toasted bread*
du jus d'orange	*orange juice*
du beurre	*butter*
de la confiture	*jam*
une tartine	*a slice of bread*
des céréales	*cereals*
des produits laitiers	*milk products*
le dessert	*pudding*

Food and drink

Qu'est-ce que tu manges/bois?	*what do you eat/drink?*
Je mange	*I eat…*
Je bois	*I drink…*
du pain	*bread*
du poulet	*chicken*
du bœuf	*beef*
du jambon	*ham*
du yaourt	*yoghurt*
du gâteau	*cake*
du poisson	*fish*
du riz	*rice*
du fromage	*cheese*
de l'eau	*water*
de la viande	*meat*
de la salade	*green salad*
de la baguette	*French stick*
de la pizza	*pizza*
des saucisses	*sausages*
des œufs	*eggs*
des chips	*crisps*
des légumes	*vegetables*
des frites	*chips*
des pâtes	*pasta*
une glace	*ice cream*
une crêpe	*pancake*

Ordering food

Vous désirez?	*What would you like?*
C'est tout?	*Is that all?*
Quel parfum?	*What flavour?*
Combien de boules?	*How many scoops?*
C'est combien?	*How much is it?*
Comme boisson?	*For drinks?*
un cornet	*a cone*

un pot	*a tub*
un plat régional	*a regional dish*
une spécialité	*a speciality*

Quantities

un paquet de	*a packet of*
un morceau de	*a piece of*
un pot de	*a pot of*
une tablette de	*a bar of*
une boîte de	*a box of*
une bouteille de	*a bottle of*
une tranche de	*a slice of*
une cuillère de	*a spoonful of*

Useful structures and verbs

Je peux	*I can*
Je ne peux pas	*I cannot*
Je vais	*I am going to*
Je voudrais	*I would like*
J'aime	*I like to*
Je n'aime pas	*I don't like to*
Il faut …	*You have/it is necessary …*
étaler	*to spread*
poser	*to place/to put*
allumer	*to switch on*
mettre	*to put*
mélanger	*to mix*
faire cuire	*to cook*

Opinions

je suis fan (de)	*I am a fan (of)*
c'est mieux que	*it is better than*
ce n'est pas mon truc	*it is not my thing*
trop bon/super bon	*really nice/really good*
c'est top	*it's great*
délicieux	*delicious*
dégoûtant	*disgusting*
ça me fait vomir	*it makes me sick*
j'ai horreur de ça	*I can't stand it*

◎ Grammar and skills: I can…

- ◎ use *du, de la, de l', des*
- ◎ use negative forms
- ◎ use the present tense and *je voudrais*
- ◎ apply *il faut*
- ◎ identify and explain language patterns, including numbers
- ◎ recycle language I already know
- ◎ express opinions
- ◎ use memorisation strategies to learn new words

5.1 Deux îles

- Vocabulary: understand places in town; describe a town
- Grammar: use *il y a* and *il n'y a pas*; use correct word order
- Skills: create contrasting sentences; reflect on writing

 Écoute (1–7). C'est quelle île?
Listen to the descriptions. Which island is it, A or B?

Exemple: **1** Island A

un cinéma

un centre sportif

une patinoire

un collège

A

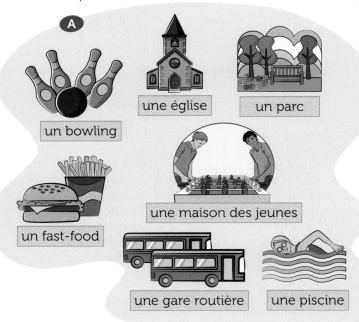

une église

un parc

un bowling

une maison des jeunes

un fast-food

une gare routière

une piscine

un centre commercial

un skatepark

un supermarché

Grammaire   p. 167   WB p.22

Saying *there is* and *there isn't*

Il y a means 'there is':

Il y a un cinéma. – There is a cinema.

Il n'y a pas means 'there isn't'. After *il n'y a pas*, you use *de* instead of *un/une/des* (*d'* if the word begins with a vowel):

Il n'y a pas de parc. – There isn't a park.
Il n'y a pas d'église. – There isn't a church.

 En groupe. Qu'est-ce qu'il y a en ville?

Exemple: **A** *Il y a une piscine.*
B *Il y a une piscine et un bowling.*
◎ **C** *Il y a une piscine et un bowling mais il n'y a pas de maison des jeunes ...*

Contrasting sentences

Combine positive and negative statements to create variety in your language. Use *mais* (but) and *par contre*.

Il y a un cinéma **mais** *il n'y a pas de parc.*
Il y a une église. **Par contre**, *il n'y a pas de collège.*

 Écris des phrases.

Exemple: **a** *Il y a une piscine mais il n'y a pas de bowling. / Il y a une piscine. Par contre, il n'y a pas de bowling.*

a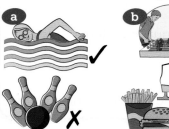

b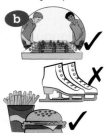

c

d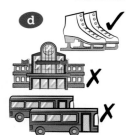

e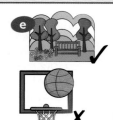

f

**Lis les textes.
C'est quelle photo?**

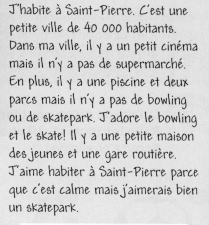

J'habite à Saint-Pierre. C'est une petite ville de 40 000 habitants. Dans ma ville, il y a un petit cinéma mais il n'y a pas de supermarché. En plus, il y a une piscine et deux parcs mais il n'y a pas de bowling ou de skatepark. J'adore le bowling et le skate! Il y a une petite maison des jeunes et une gare routière. J'aime habiter à Saint-Pierre parce que c'est calme mais j'aimerais bien un skatepark.

J'habite à Neuville. C'est une grande ville de 95 000 habitants. Dans ma ville, il y a un supermarché et un petit centre commercial. Il y a aussi deux piscines et un petit skatepark, mais il n'y a pas de patinoire. J'adore faire de la natation – c'est très amusant! En plus, il y a trois parcs et une gare routière. Par contre, il n'y a pas de maison des jeunes. J'aime habiter à Neuville parce que c'est grand et parce qu'il y a beaucoup d'activités.

Lis les textes. Vrai ou faux?
Correct the false statements.

Exemple: **a** *faux – Saint-Pierre is a smaller town than Neuville.*

a Neuville is a smaller town than Saint-Pierre.
b Saint-Pierre is the only town with a youth club.
c Both towns have a bus station.
d Saint-Pierre has more parks than Neuville.
e Neuville has an ice rink and two swimming pools.
f Saint-Pierre has neither a bowling alley nor a skate park.
g Both teenagers love their towns and are totally happy with them.

aussi   *also*
en plus   *furthermore*
j'aimerais (bien)   *I would like*

Décris ta ville.
Write a description of your town. Include descriptions of what there is and isn't in the town.

Exemple: J'habite à Lewes. C'est calme. Il y a une grande piscine. Par contre, il n'y a pas de skatepark.

➕ **Include contrasting sentences and justified opinions about your town.**

⚙ **Grammaire** p. 166

Position of adjectives
Short, common adjectives sometimes come <u>before</u> the noun:
une grande ville
un petit skatepark

Plenary

⭐ Write a description of a famous town or city.

◎ Give your opinion on a famous city and give reasons.

➕ Your town is being shortlisted for 'The UK's Best Town'. Summarise what is great about your town. Give reasons.

Reflect as you are writing on what helps the most when something gets tricky. A friend, the teacher, the glossary of the book? Swap your work with a partner for them to check and together set targets for improvement.

5.2 Qu'est-ce qu'on peut faire?

- Vocabulary: combine activities with places using *on peut*
- Grammar: use *au/à la/à l'/aux* with places; combine verbs
- Skills: create more complex sentences

Qu'est-ce qu'on peut faire sur les deux îles?
Relie les mots (1–10 et a–j) et les images (A–J).
Écoute et vérifie.

Exemple: **A** *7 h*

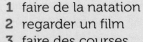

On peut ...

1 faire de la natation	6 chercher un trésor
2 regarder un film	caché
3 faire des courses	7 jouer au foot
4 retrouver des	8 acheter des
copains	vêtements
5 faire du patin à	9 faire du bowling
glace	10 faire du skate

a au cinéma	g à la maison des
b à la patinoire	jeunes
c au bowling	h au parc
d au skatepark	i dans la forêt
e au supermarché	j au centre
f à la piscine	commercial

Écoute (1–7). Où est Jérémie?

Exemple: **1** *Jérémie est à la piscine.*

J'aime	aller au parc faire du skate ...	parce que c'est	amusant. intéressant. cool. génial. extra. facile. super. magnifique.
Il y a	un parc une piscine ...	où on peut	faire du skate. jouer au foot. faire de la natation. regarder un film.

Grammaire   p. 167 / WB p.24

Saying 'to the' and 'at the'

In French there are four different ways of saying 'at the' or 'to the' + name of a place.

masculine noun	feminine noun
à + le = **au**	à + la = **à la**
le cinéma = **au** cinéma	la piscine = **à la** piscine
words starting with a vowel or a h	**plural noun**
à + l' = **à l'**	à + les = **aux**
l'hôpital = **à l'**hôpital	les États-Unis = **aux** États-Unis

3 **Lis les textes et réponds aux questions.**

Exemple: **a** *Éloi*

> Moi, c'est Éloi. J'aime retrouver mes copains pour jouer au foot ou au basket mais je n'aime pas le shopping. Je n'aime pas aller au skatepark mais j'adore aller à la maison des jeunes et au cinéma.

> Moi, je suis Anna. Je n'aime pas la natation ou le patin à glace mais j'adore les magasins. J'aime aller au centre commercial mais je n'aime pas aller à la patinoire.

a Who prefers the youth club to the skate park?
b Who doesn't like swimming or ice skating?
c Who dislikes skateboarding?
d Who would be most likely to organise a shopping trip?
e Who would accept an invitation to watch a film?
f Who enjoys meeting up with friends to play sport?

 4 **En groupe. Où aimes-tu aller? A↔B.**

Exemple: **J'aime aller au parc. Et toi?**

 Include what you like to do there:
J'aime retrouver mes copains au parc.

 5 **Écoute. Vrai ou faux?**
See page 87 for listening strategies.

Exemple: **a** *vrai*

a Lucie likes going ice skating because it's fun.
b Paul likes to play sports in the park with his friends.
c Christelle likes to go shopping with her sister.
d Pierre likes skateboarding with his brother because it's great.
e Sarah likes watching films at her friend's house.
f Arthur likes swimming at the pool with his cousin.

 Correct the false sentences.

Grammaire p. 168 / WB p.20

Using *on peut* + infinitive

On peut regarder un film. – We can watch a film.

Add the word *où* (where) to make your sentences more detailed:
où on peut – where we can

Il y a un centre sportif **où on peut** *faire du basket.* – There is a sports centre **where we can** play basketball.

Plenary

Write an advert for an island.

 Write five sentences describing the activities you can do in different places.

 Include some opinions.

 Produce longer sentences including *où on peut*.

Read your own advert critically then give yourself a target. Think about the use of connectives, opinions and reasons. Now take five minutes to spot where you could make your sentences even better. Highlight the spot and add an extra opinion, connective and reason. What connection can you make between today's learning and what you have learnt in French before?

 6 **Écris des phrases. Qu'est-ce que tu aimes faire en ville?**
Write some sentences describing what you like to do in town.

Exemple:
Personnellement, j'aime aller au skatepark avec mon frère ...

 Include some reasons for your opinions using *parce que*:
... parce que c'est génial.

 7 **Décris ta ville.**
Exemple:
Il y a un cinéma où on peut regarder des films. J'adore aller au cinéma parce que c'est amusant ...

5.3 Trouve le chemin!

- Vocabulary: ask for and give directions
- Grammar: use *au/à la/à l'/aux*; use the imperative
- Skills: use connectives

ÉCOUTER 1

Écoute (1–10). C'est quelle direction?

Exemple: d, ...

a Tournez à droite.

b Tournez à gauche.

c Allez tout droit.

d Traversez le pont.

e Traversez la place.

f Traversez la rue.

g Prenez la première rue à droite.

h Prenez la deuxième rue à droite.

i Prenez la première rue à gauche.

j Prenez la deuxième rue à gauche.

LIRE 2

Lis. Pour aller au ...?

Where do they want to go? Follow the map to find out the destination then write the question. Always start at X.

Exemple: **a** *Pour aller au collège?*

a Prenez la première rue à gauche puis traversez la rue et c'est à droite.

b Allez tout droit puis traversez le pont et prenez la première rue à droite. C'est à gauche après le parc.

c Prenez la première rue à gauche et ensuite allez tout droit. Après la patinoire, traversez la rue et puis traversez la place. C'est à gauche.

d Allez tout droit après la piscine et le fast-food et c'est à droite.

e Allez tout droit puis traversez le pont et prenez la première rue à gauche. Allez tout droit et puis c'est à droite après la gare routière.

f Prenez la première rue à droite et puis allez tout droit. C'est à gauche après le fast-food.

g Allez tout droit et ensuite prenez la première rue à droite. C'est à droite.

le centre sportif — le supermarché — le parc — le skatepark

la gare routière

l'église — le bowling — le collège — le centre commercial

place de l'Église — le fast-food — la maison des jeunes

la patinoire — la piscine — place de la Liberté — le cinéma

Commence ici — X

3 **Écoute et regarde le plan de l'activité 2 (1–7). Où vont-ils?**
Listen and look at the map in activity 2. Where are they going?
Always start at X.

Exemple: **1** *à la patinoire*

4 **Regarde le plan de l'activité 2. Explique le chemin.**
Give the directions. Always start at X.

Exemple: **a** *Pour aller au fast-food, allez tout droit.*
Ensuite, tournez à droite ...

a Pour aller au fast-food?   **d** Pour aller au cinéma?
b Pour aller à la patinoire?   **e** Pour aller au bowling?
c Pour aller au parc?   **f** Pour aller à la gare routière?

5 **Parle avec un(e) partenaire.**
Take turns to ask and give directions to places on the map
in activity 2. Use connectives to link the directions:

Exemple: **A** *Pour aller au collège?*
B *D'abord, allez tout droit puis prenez
la première rue à gauche. C'est à droite.*

Grammaire p. 167

Asking for directions
*Pour aller **au** cinéma?* – How do
I get to the cinema?
*Pour aller **à la** gare routière?* –
How do I get to the bus station?
*Pour aller **à l'**église?* – How do I
get to the church?

Using connectives
Use these connectives to link together
several instructions.

d'abord – first   *ensuite* – then, next
puis – then   *pour finir* – finally
après – after

Grammaire p. 170 WB p.23

Using imperatives
Imperatives are used to give instructions: *Tournez à
gauche!* (Turn left!), *Écoutez!* (Listen!), *Regardez!* (Watch!)

In French they end in *-ez* when you are talking to more
than one person:

tourner	to turn	**tournez** à droite	turn right
traverser	to cross	**traversez** la rue	cross the road

Plenary

In groups, devise a mark
scheme for the task on the
right, giving marks out of
5 for spelling and grammar.
You must be able to
explain the marking criteria
yourselves. Analyse at the
end of the task how you
worked as a group and the
purpose of your learning.

★ Design a map and create directions to five places. Exchange with a
partner and follow their directions. Where are they taking you?

◎ Design a map and number the landmarks. Write directions to five places
giving the name of each place and swap with a partner. Match the
numbers to the places.

✚ Design a map and include 10 different landmarks. Number five of them
and label the remaining five. Write directions, including sequencing
connectives, to the five numbered places giving the name of each place
and then swap with a partner.

Don't forget to give your partner a mark out of 5 plus a comment on
how to improve.

5.4 Tu veux sortir?

- Vocabulary: arrange to go out; discuss meeting places
- Grammar: use *vouloir* and *pouvoir*
- Skills: use reading and listening strategies

La sortie de classe: recopie la grille, écoute et note.
Tally the choices the students are making in the second column.

Écoute et note.
The teacher is counting all the votes. Write the total number of votes for each outing in the third column in the table.

Sondage: 'Tu veux ...?'
Agree on six activities and create a table like the one in activity 1.
Listen to each person's choice and tally the options to find out the class choice of activity.

je veux ...		choix	total
regarder un film			2
faire du skate			
faire de la natation		✓	
aller à la maison des jeunes			
faire du shopping			
aller au bowling			
aller au parc d'attractions			
voir un match de foot au stade			
faire un pique-nique			

je veux   I want to

Grammaire   p. 168   WB p.20–21

Using *vouloir* and *pouvoir*

vouloir	to want to	pouvoir	to be able to
je veux	I want	je peux	I can
tu veux	you want	tu peux	you can
il/elle veut on veut	he/she wants we want	il/elle peut on peut	he/she we can

Vouloir and *pouvoir* are two very useful verbs. You can combine them with other verbs to talk about what you want to do or what you can do:

*Je **veux** faire du skate.* – I want to go skateboarding.

*On **peut** aller au cinéma.* – We can go to the cinema.

*Tu **veux** aller à la maison des jeunes?* – Do you want to go to the youth club?

*On **peut** aller au cinéma. Tu **veux** bien?* – We can go to the cinema. Would you like that?

Écoute et lis la conversation.

Céline Coucou Marie! Ça va? Tu veux sortir samedi soir?
Marie Salut Céline! Oui, ça va bien! Oui, je veux bien sortir. Qu'est-ce que tu veux faire?
Céline On peut aller au cinéma? J'adore aller au cinéma!
Marie Bof! Non, je n'aime pas ça. Je préfère faire du patin à glace. Alors, on peut aller à la patinoire. Tu veux bien?
Céline Oui, j'aime bien! On peut manger au fast-food et on peut aller à la patinoire après.
Marie D'accord. On se retrouve où?
Céline À la gare routière, ça va?
Marie Non, je ne veux pas. On se retrouve chez moi?
Céline D'accord! À bientôt!
Marie À bientôt!

 Vrai ou faux? Relis la conversation.

Exemple: **a** *vrai*

a Céline is inviting Marie out on Saturday night.
b Céline likes going to the cinema.
c Marie prefers the skate park to the cinema.
d Marie suggests eating at the fast-food restaurant after they go ice skating.
e Céline suggests meeting at the bus station.
f They agree to meet at Céline's house.

 Écris des phrases. Tu veux …?

Exemple: **a** *Tu veux faire du patin à glace?*

 Jeu de rôles. Écris avec un(e) partenaire.
Write a role-play arranging to go out, similar to the conversation in activity 4.

○ **Add in extra details including opinions and reasons.**

(samedi) matin	au parc
(dimanche) après-midi	au café
(vendredi) soir	sur la place
on se retrouve	chez moi
devant le cinéma	chez toi
à la gare routière	d'accord

 Faites le jeu de rôles.
Perform your role-play to another pair. Give feedback to the other pair on their pronunciation and accuracy. Give a mark out of 5 for pronunciation and another mark out of 5 for accuracy (how many mistakes they made).

Reading and listening strategies
You have already looked at some of the differences between spoken and written French. As you read and listen to the conversation in activity 4, what do you notice?

- *Salut* and *peut* have a silent letter, *t*. How might you say *tout, c'est, tournez, d'accord, droit*?
- Look at the punctuation (*!* and *?*) How and where does it influence intonation (tone of voice)?
- Listen out for strings of sounds which are actually separate words but which sound like one long word, e.g. *On peut aller* and *patin à glace*. Listen again **without reading the text**, and **visualise** how the words are broken up.

Plenary
Create an advert for a new leisure centre opening in your area.
★ Include five activities.
◎ Add opinions and reasons.
✚ Add connectives and include other people's opinions.
As you complete the task, reflect on the type of language you are choosing to use.

5.5 La chasse au trésor

- Vocabulary: identify more places on a map; use place prepositions
- Grammar: give directions using the imperative; use *du/de la/de l'/des* with prepositions
- Skills: develop map skills

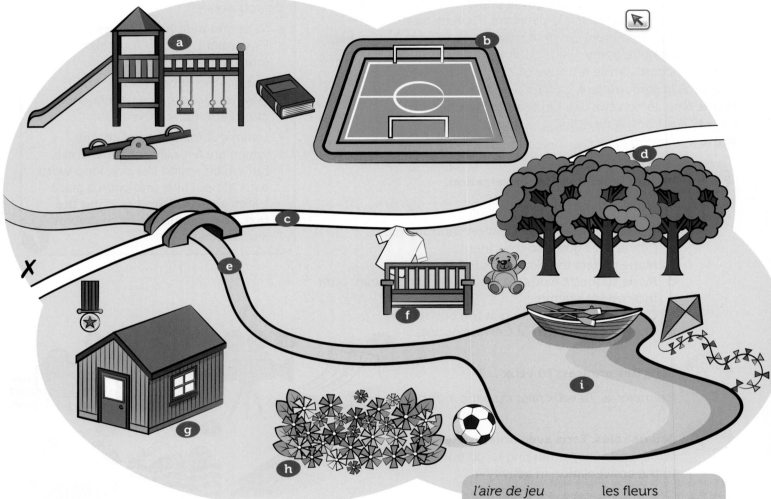

Complète la carte.
Find the correct labels for the map in the vocabulary box.

Exemple: **a** *l'aire de jeu*

l'aire de jeu	les fleurs
les arbres	le lac
le banc	le ruisseau
la cabane	le terrain de sport
le chemin	

Écoute et note (1–7). Pour trouver le trésor …?
Listen to the clues to find each item of treasure on the map.
Always start at X.

Exemple: **1** *a teddy bear* (un nounours, une peluche)

○ **Use a dictionary to find out the French word for each item of treasure.**

suivez	*follow*
devant	*in front of*
derrière	*behind*
à côté de	*next to*
en face de	*opposite*
à droite de	*to the right of*
à gauche de	*to the left of*
entre	*between*

Grammaire
p. 167
WB p.24

Using de + le/la/l'/les

On page 78 you learnt how to use à + le/la/les (au/à la/aux).

De follows a similar rule:

masculine noun	de + le = du	de + le chemin: le lac est à côté **du** chemin
feminine noun	de + la = **de la**	de + la cabane: le banc est à droite **de la** cabane
words starting with a vowel or a *h*	de + l' = **de l'**	de + l'aire de jeu: le terrain de sport est à droite **de l'**aire de jeu
plural noun	de + les = **des**	de + les arbres: la cabane est à gauche **des** arbres

3 Écris des phrases avec un(e) partenaire. C'est quoi?
Write some clues based on your own town for other groups to work out.

Exemple: C'est entre le supermarché et le cinéma. – C'est le café.

4 Lis tes phrases.
Read your clues to another pair. Can they work out the answer? Don't forget to give feedback on accent and accuracy to the pair reading their clues to you.

5 Regarde les deux images. A décrit une image. B devine. A↔B.

Exemple: **A** *C'est devant le café.*
B *Un arbre?*
A *Tu as raison!*

le cinéma
la patinoire
le bowling
le skatepark
le supermarché
la piscine
la maison des jeunes
le parc
la gare routière
le centre commercial
le fast-food
l'église
le collège
le centre sportif

la boulangerie *baker's*
la boucherie *butcher's*

Plenary

⭐ Use the map on the opposite page to create your own treasure hunt and clues.

◎ Create a new map with new clues.

➕ Plan a treasure hunt around your school.

Working in groups, read your clues to another pair. Can they work out your words? Give feedback on the pronunciation, accent and accuracy to the pair reading their clues to you.
Analyse how your written preparation of this task can help you to improve your spoken French.

Saying 'there is' and 'there isn't'

1 **Translate the sentences into French.**

Exemple: **a** *Il y a un bowling.*

a There is a bowling alley.

b There is a shopping centre.

c There isn't a cinema.

d There is a bus station.

e There isn't a youth club.

f There isn't a park.

> *Il y a* means 'there is':
> *Il y a un cinéma.* – There is a cinema.
> *Il n'y a pas* means 'there isn't'. After *il n'y a pas*, you use *de* instead of *un/une/des* (*d'* if the word begins with a vowel):
> *Il n'y a pas de piscine.* – There isn't a swimming pool.
> *Il n'y a pas d'église.* – There isn't a church.

Saying 'to the' and 'at the'

2 **Copy the sentences and choose the correct article.**

Exemple: **a** *On peut faire de la natation **à la** piscine.*

a On peut faire de la natation **au/à la** piscine.
b On peut faire les courses **au/à la** supermarché.
c On peut faire du skate **au/à la** skatepark.
d On peut faire du patin à glace **au/à la** patinoire.
e On peut regarder un film **au/à la** cinéma.
f On peut retrouver des amis **au/à la** maison des jeunes.

masculine noun	à + le = **au**	le cinéma = **au** cinéma
feminine noun	à + la = **à la**	la piscine = **à la** piscine
words starting with a vowel or a *h*	à + l' = **à l'**	l'aire de jeu = **à l'**aire de jeu
plural noun	à + les = **aux**	les États-Unis = **aux** États-Unis

Using imperatives

3 **Copy and complete the sentences by choosing the right verb from the box.**

Exemple: **a** *tournez*

a Au supermarché, *tournez* à gauche.
b Après la piscine, _____ la première rue à droite.
c _____ la rue de la Liberté.
d Après la patinoire, _____ tout droit.
e Max et Karima, _____ le tableau!
f _____ les stylos, tout le monde!

> posez   tournez   traversez   prenez
> allez   regardez

> Imperatives are used to give instructions: *Tournez à gauche!* (Turn left!), *Tournez à droite!* (Turn right!), *Écoutez!* (Listen!), *Regardez!* (Watch!)
>
> In French they end in *-ez* when you are talking to more than one person:
>
> | tourner | to turn | **tournez** à droite | turn right |
> | --- | --- | --- | --- |
> | traverser | to cross | **traversez** la rue | cross the road |
>
> If you are talking to one person, informally, you say *tourne à droite* or *traverse la rue.*

Using *vouloir* and *pouvoir*

4 **Match the sentence halves and translate the sentences into English.**

Exemple: **1 c** – *Do you want to go to the cinema?*

1	Tu veux aller	**a**	un hamburger?
2	On peut faire	**b**	de la musique?
3	Tu veux manger	**c**	au cinéma?
4	On peut regarder	**d**	des courses en ville.
5	Tu veux écouter	**e**	la télévision.
6	On peut jouer	**f**	au foot au parc.

vouloir	to want to	**pouvoir**	to be able to
je veux	I want	je peux	I can
tu veux	you want	tu peux	you can
il/elle veut on veut	he/she wants we want	il/elle peut on peut	he/she can we can

You can combine *vouloir* and *pouvoir* with other verbs to talk about what you want to do or what you can do:

*Je **veux** faire du skate.* – I want to go skateboarding.

*On **peut** aller au cinéma.* – We can go to the cinema.

*Tu **veux** aller au parc?* – Do you want to go to the park?

*On **peut** aller au cinéma. Tu **veux** bien?* – We can go to the cinema. Would you like to?

Listening strategies

Use these strategies with activity 5, page 79.

Before you listen:
- **Look at the task** and identify the **key words** to listen out for so you recognise them quickly: all you need to listen for is *amusant* to know that Lucie likes ice skating.
- Try saying some of the words in the task out loud so you recognise them when you hear them. Remember the sound might be different from the spelling. Try these with your partner: *Arthur*, *sport*, *cousin*. Pay special attention to the underlined letters.

While you're listening:
- **Work out the context.** Is it a conversation? An interview? An advert? How many voices are there? What can you tell from the tone of voice? Is there any background noise?

- **Make inferences (sensible guessing).** For example, you don't need to understand the whole text to guess that *génial* or *cool* mean something positive.
- **Don't panic** if you don't understand every word first time. Carry on listening, but try and hold the sound or word in your head until you hear the recording for the second time.
- **Listen for key words** such as names of people or places. This can help you break down the stream of sound.

After listening:
- **Check back** to see if your first answers make sense.

Pronunciation: the silent letter *h*

5 **Listen and repeat these words.**

heureux   horrible   hôpital   hôtel

The letter *h* at the start of a word is never pronounced in French.

6 **Write a list of five other French words starting with *h*. Practise saying them.**

- Vocabulary: use directions; describe an ideal town
- Grammar: use *il y a*/*il n'y a pas*
- Skills: apply map skills

1 **Write sentences with *il y a* or *il n'y a pas de*.**

Exemple: **a** *Il n'y a pas d'église.*

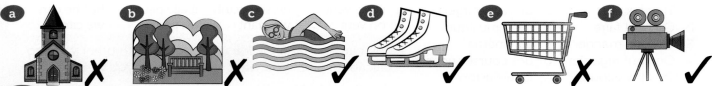

2 **Where is it? Follow the instructions to find the place marked on the map.**

a Allez tout droit et prenez la deuxième rue à droite, puis c'est à gauche.
le cinéma/la piscine/l'église

b Allez tout droit puis prenez la première rue à gauche et c'est à droite.
le parc/le cinéma/la gare routière

c Allez tout droit et prenez la première rue à droite. C'est à gauche après la maison des jeunes.
le skatepark/la piscine/l'église

d Allez tout droit et puis prenez la deuxième rue à gauche. C'est à droite.
la piscine/le cinéma/le parc

e Après le centre commercial, traversez la rue et allez tout droit. C'est à droite.
l'église/la maison des jeunes/la piscine

3 **Read the text and the statements. True or false?**

Exemple: **a** *false – there is a big swimming pool*

a In Charlotte's ideal town there is a small swimming pool.
b There is a cinema and an ice rink.
c There are three secondary schools.
d Charlotte doesn't like school.
e There is a big park.
f There is a shopping centre.

4 **Write a description of your dream town.**
Adapt the model text from activity 3. The most useful phrases are in italics.

Exemple: Dans ma ville de rêve, il y a …

Sujet: Ma ville de rêve

Salut! Je m'appelle Charlotte et *dans ma ville de rêve il y a* une grande piscine *parce que* j'adore faire de la natation. *Il y a aussi* un cinéma et une patinoire *mais il n'y a pas de* collège parce que c'est nul! *Pour finir*, il y a un grand parc pour faire du sport et il y a deux centres commerciaux – j'adore le shopping!

5.7 Extra Plus

- Vocabulary: use directions; describe an ideal town
- Grammar: use *il y a/il n'y a pas*
- Skills: apply map skills

Écris des phrases avec *il y a* ou *il n'y a pas de*.

Exemple: **a** *Il y a un hôpital mais il n'y a pas de supermarché.*

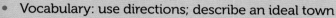

**Regarde la carte page 88. Explique le chemin.
Remets les mots dans le bon ordre. Ajoute *et* ou *puis*.**

Exemple: **a** *le skatepark – Prenez la première rue à droite **puis** allez tout droit. C'est à gauche après la maison des jeunes.*

a le skatepark – allez tout droit / après la maison des jeunes / prenez la première rue à droite / c'est à gauche

b le parc – après la gare routière / prenez la première rue à gauche / c'est à gauche / allez tout droit

c le cinéma – prenez la deuxième rue à gauche / allez tout droit / c'est à droite

d la piscine – allez tout droit / c'est à gauche / prenez la deuxième rue à droite

e l'église – c'est à droite / allez tout droit

Lis le mail de Félix et réponds: vrai, faux ou pas mentionné?

Exemple: **a** *vrai*

a In Félix's ideal town there is a swimming pool.
b There isn't a primary school.
c There is a big park and a bowling alley.
d There isn't a youth club.
e His brother likes skateboarding but Félix doesn't.
f At the weekend he is going to have a game of football.

Décris ta ville de rêve. Utilise les mots en *italique* dans l'activité 3.

Exemple: *Dans ma ville de rêve, il y a … Je vais …*

Sujet: Ma ville de rêve

Salut! Je m'appelle Félix et *dans ma ville de rêve, il y a* une grande piscine *parce que j'adore* faire de la natation avec mes copains. *Il y a aussi* un cinéma *où on peut* regarder un bon film et une patinoire mais *il n'y a pas de* collège parce que c'est nul! *En plus*, il y a un grand parc où on peut faire du sport et un bowling – j'adore le bowling! *Pour finir*, il y a une maison des jeunes et un grand supermarché mais il n'y a pas de skatepark. *Le week-end, je vais* retrouver mes copains au parc pour faire un match de foot et après on va faire un pique-nique – c'est cool!

La Fête des voisins: créer un vrai réseau social

La Fête des voisins existe en France depuis 1999. Les habitants d'un quartier, d'un immeuble, d'un village se retrouvent dans la rue. C'est d'habitude à la fin du mois de mai ou au début du mois de juin, parce qu'il fait beau.

Tout le monde apporte quelque chose à manger, quelque chose à boire. On installe des grandes tables et beaucoup de chaises, et on partage tout.

L'objectif, c'est de faire connaissance avec ses voisins, les personnes âgées, mais aussi les personnes plus jeunes.

Et quand la fête est finie, on n'oublie pas ses voisins. On peut faire des courses pour une dame âgée, inviter un monsieur seul à prendre le café. On peut aider quelqu'un qui ne parle pas bien français, échanger des plantes avec un voisin jardinier.

En 1999, il y avait 10 000 personnes à la première Fête des voisins, à Paris. Maintenant, plus de 10 millions de personnes participent en France. Et depuis 2003, on célèbre aussi la Fête des voisins en Belgique, au Québec et ailleurs.

un réseau social	*social network*
les habitants	*inhabitants*
un immeuble	*block of flats*
se retrouvent	*meet up*
tout le monde apporte	*everyone brings*
on partage	*they share*
faire connaissance	*to get to know*
les personnes âgées	*elderly people*
on n'oublie pas	*they don't forget*

True or false?
Correct the false sentences.

Exemple: **a** *false*

a French-speaking countries have been holding neighbourhood street parties since 1999.
b They take place on a fine autumn day.
c Everyone brings food and drink to share.
d The street parties are held in towns, usually around a block of flats.
e The street parties are not just for elderly people.
f Once they've got to know their neighbours, many people stay in touch.

Complete the sentences in French. Sometimes, there is more than one possible answer.

Exemple: **a** *1999*

a La première Fête des voisins en France, c'est en …
b La première Fête des voisins en Belgique, c'est en …
c Les habitants d'un quartier mangent ensemble dans …
d On installe des chaises et …
e On mange, on boit et on parle avec …
f Ensuite, on peut aider les personnes …

Find the French for …

Exemple: **a** *au début*

a at the beginning
b something to drink
c they set up
d go shopping
e a gentleman living on his own
f have a coffee
g to swap
h gardener

5.8 *Vidéo*

La visite à Odysseum

 Regarde l'épisode 5.
Where are they at the start of the episode, and why have they come?

 Dans quels endroits vont-ils?
What places do they visit?

Exemple: **b** *le bowling*

a le centre commercial	**d** le centre d'escalade	**g** la patinoire
b le bowling	**e** le planétarium	**h** le fast-food
c le karting	**f** l'aquarium	**i** le cinéma

 Basile préfère quels endroits? Clarisse préfère quels endroits?

Exemple: Basile – *les centres sportifs, ...*
        Clarisse – ...

 Trace le chemin.
Draw the directions as you hear them.

Exemple: **a** *Tout droit, et ...*

a Pour aller au bowling?   **c** Pour aller au centre d'escalade?
b Pour aller au karting?   **d** Pour aller au planétarium?

  Qu'est-ce que tu préfères dans le quartier Odysseum?

Exemple: J'aime le planétarium parce que ...

Listen to the teenagers. Copy and complete the table with the information that they give. (See pages 76–83.)

	suggested place	why not?	alternative place	meeting point
Paul	cinema	doesn't like the films	fast food restaurant	in the square
Marie				
Youssef				
Claire				
Pierre				

Talk about your hobbies and what you like to do in your town. (See pages 76–83.)

Give the following information:

● two places there are in town (and what you can do there): *En ville, il y a ... (où on peut ...)*
● one place there isn't in town: *Il n'y a pas de ...*
● two activities you like to do (and why, to add more information): *En ville, j'aime ... parce que ...*
● one activity you don't like to do (and why): *Je n'aime pas ... parce que ...*
● one activity you are going to do at the weekend: *Samedi/Dimanche, je vais ...*

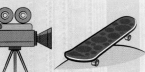

Read the text and answer the questions in English. (See pages 76–79.)

Exemple: **a** *historic monuments and museums*

a What can you visit to do cultural activities?
b What activity can you do at the *centre commerciaux*?
c What can you do in the parks?
d Where can you go for food if you don't want to eat in the restaurants and cafés?
e What two active hobbies can you do and where?
f Why is Villedieu a good place to live?

Villedieu est une très grande ville. Il y a beaucoup de monuments historiques et de musées où on peut faire des activités culturelles. À Villedieu, on peut faire des courses parce qu'il y a beaucoup de centres commerciaux. On peut aussi visiter les parcs et les jardins publics où on peut pique-niquer avec des copains. En plus, il y a beaucoup de cafés et de restaurants où on peut bien manger et il y a aussi des petits supermarchés où on peut acheter du pain, etc. Pour finir, on peut faire du sport au grand centre sportif ou faire du patin à glace à la patinoire. Habiter à Villedieu, c'est super parce qu'il y a toujours beaucoup de choses à faire!

Write a paragraph on your town for a visiting school. What is and isn't there? What activities can you do there? What do you like to do? What are you going to do at the weekend? (See pages 76–83.)

j'habite à ...
en ville
il y a ... où on peut ...

il n'y a pas de ...
j'aime/je n'aime pas ... parce que ...
samedi/dimanche, je vais ...

Remember, the more you can develop your answers, the better your work will be.

Places in a town

Qu'est-ce qu'il y a dans … ?	What is there in … ?
il y a	there is
il n'y a pas	there isn't
un bowling	bowling alley
un centre commercial	shopping centre
un centre sportif	sports centre
un cinéma	cinema
un collège	secondary school
une église	church
un fast-food	fast food restaurant
une gare routière	bus station
un magasin	shop
une maison des jeunes	youth club
un parc	park
un parc d'attractions	theme park
une patinoire	ice rink
une piscine	swimming pool
une place	town square
un quartier	neighbourhood
une rue	street
un supermarché	supermarket
un terrain de sport	playing field

Activities

Qu'est-ce qu'on peut faire?	What is there to do?
on peut	we can/you can
acheter des vêtements	to buy clothes
faire de la natation	to go swimming
chercher un trésor	to look for treasure
faire du bowling	to go bowling
faire du patin à glace	to go ice skating
faire du skate	to go skateboarding
faire des courses	to go shopping
jouer au foot	to play football
prendre le bus	to take the bus
regarder un film	to watch a film

Asking for and giving directions

Pour aller à … ?	How do I get to … ?
allez tout droit	go straight ahead
prenez la deuxième rue à droite	take the second road on the right
prenez la deuxième rue à gauche	take the second road on the left
prenez la première rue à droite	take the first road on the right
prenez la première rue à gauche	take the first road on the left
tournez	turn
traversez	cross

Arranging to go out

Tu veux sortir?	Would you like to go out?
où (?)	where (?)
le matin	morning
l'après-midi	afternoon
le soir	evening
on se retrouve	let's meet
devant (le cinéma)	in front of (the cinema)
au café	at the café
à la gare routière	at the bus station
au parc	at the park
sur la place	in the square
chez moi	at my house
chez toi	at your house

Sequencing connectives

d'abord	first of all
puis	then
après	after
ensuite	next
pour finir	finally

⊙ Grammar and skills: I can…

- ◉ use il y a / il n'y a pas de
- ◉ use au/à la/à l'/aux with places
- ◉ use the imperative
- ◉ use vouloir and pouvoir
- ◉ use du/de la/de l'/des with prepositions
- ◉ create more complex sentences
- ◉ use connectives
- ◉ use reading and listening strategies

6.1 Mon look

- Vocabulary: talk about clothes and say what style you like
- Grammar: use *porter* and *j'aime porter*
- Skills: recycle adjectives you already know and express opinions

 Écoute et fais deux listes.
What are Yasmine and Paul packing?

Exemple: Yasmine – b, ...
Paul – f, ...

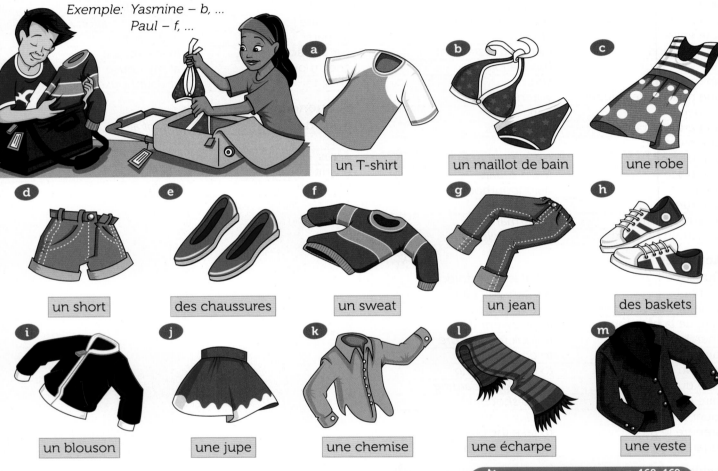

a un T-shirt

b un maillot de bain

c une robe

d un short

e des chaussures

f un sweat

g un jean

h des baskets

i un blouson

j une jupe

k une chemise

l une écharpe

m une veste

 Qu'est-ce que tu portes? A↔B.
Imagine your favourite outfit. Your partner guesses it.

Exemple: **A** Tu portes un sweat?
B Oui, je porte un sweat./Non, je ne porte pas de sweat.

 Give the French word, your partner gives the English.

Can you add a colour and/or size to your items?
Je porte un sweat bleu/une grande écharpe ...

Grammaire p. 168–169 WB p.31

Present tense of regular -er verbs

Porter (to wear) is a regular -er verb.

je port**e**   nous port**ons**
tu port**es**   vous port**ez**
il/elle/on port**e**   ils/elles port**ent**

*Je **ne** porte **pas** d'écharpe.* – I don't wear/I'm not wearing a scarf.

See page 105 for grammar memorisation strategies.

Ça, c'est mon truc 6.1

3 Lis et trouve les paires.

Exemple: **a** *J'aime porter*

Les looks d'aujourd'hui

J'aime porter des vêtements de marque comme Nike, Hollister ou Fred Perry, des jeans slim, des Converse. J'aime aussi les écharpes. C'est la classe et c'est très à la mode aujourd'hui!

Le look fashion

Ce look est très confortable. En général, je porte un survêtement très large, des baskets, un T-shirt. En plus, je porte une casquette.

Le look rappeur

J'adore le noir. J'aime porter une jupe noire, des bottes noires, des gants noirs, un pull noir et même du maquillage blanc et noir. Tout est noir! J'aime le look gothique parce que c'est différent.

Le look gothique

a I like to wear	**e** moreover
b designer clothes	**f** I wear a cap
c It's classy	**g** everything is black
d a tracksuit	**h** black and white make-up

Adjectives of colour

Why is *noir* spelt four different ways in the last speech bubble? Look back on page 50. Try some of the strategies on page 105 to help you remember the pattern.

4 **Décris ton look.**

Exemple:
*J'aime le look rappeur. Je porte ...
parce que c'est ...*

➕ **Add colours and connectives (*aussi, et, mais, par contre*).**

je porte j'aime porter	un jean/T-shirt	noir/blanc/rouge	parce que ...
	une veste/robe/jupe	noire/blanche/rouge	
	des gants	noirs/blancs/rouges	
	des bottes	noires/blanches/rouges	

j'aime le look	rappeur/gothique/fashion	parce que c'est	cool/confortable/différent/à la mode

5 **Écoute. Recopie et remplis la grille. Qui aime porter quoi (1–4)?**

	skirt	jeans	boots	jacket	trainers	scarf	shirt	sweatshirt	others
1		✓							
2									

➕ **Choose one person and transcribe what they say.**
Saskia: J'aime la mode ...

Plenary

Describe a style to your partner. Review and reflect on each other's descriptions.

 Use simple phrases.

 Use sentences with adjectives.

 Use longer sentences and opinions.

quatre-vingt-quinze 95

6.2 Qu'est-ce que tu portes?

- Vocabulary: talk about the weather and what you wear for different occasions
- Grammar: learn how to use *son/sa/ses*
- Skills: use *quand* to build longer sentences

p. 167
WB p.25

ÉCOUTER 1 **Quel temps fait-il? Lis, écoute et trouve les expressions.**

Exemple: **1** d

a Il fait du vent.	**c** Il fait chaud.	**e** Il gèle.	**g** Il y a du soleil.
b Il fait froid.	**d** Il pleut.	**f** Il y a de l'orage.	**h** Il neige.

LIRE 2 **Complète les phrases.**

Exemple: **a 2** – *Je porte un anorak, des gants et un bonnet quand il fait froid.*

a Je porte un anorak, des gants et un bonnet		**1** il y a du soleil.
b Je porte un imper et j'ai un parapluie		**2** il fait froid.
c Je porte des lunettes de soleil	quand	**3** il pleut.
d Je porte un maillot de bain		**4** il neige.
e J'ai des bottes de ski		**5** il fait chaud.

➕ **Translate the five sentences.**

PARLER 3 **Mime et complète la phrase. A↔B.**

Exemple: **A** *(mimes 'rain')*
B *Quand il pleut, je porte un imper.*

⭐ **Can you add a colour to your description?**

◎ **Can you say what your friend wears?**
Quand il pleut, ma copine Clara porte …

⚙ Grammaire

How to say 'his/her'

masculine word, or word starting with a vowel	**son** T-shirt	his/her T-shirt
	son écharpe	his/her scarf
feminine word	**sa** veste	his/her jacket
plural word	**ses** baskets	his/her trainers

🦿 *See page 105 for grammar memorisation strategies.*

Making sentences longer with *quand*

You can use *quand* at the beginning or in the middle of your sentence:
***Quand** il pleut, je porte un blouson.* – When it rains I wear a jacket.
*Je porte un blouson **quand** il pleut.* – I wear a jacket when it rains.
(See Workbook, page 28)

Écoute (1–4). Vrai ou faux? Corrige.

Exemple: **a** *faux – Elle aime sa chemise.*

a Virginie déteste sa chemise blanche.
b Elle porte souvent son écharpe blanche.
c Xavier adore son blouson en cuir.
d Il n'aime pas porter son jean noir.

e Caroline aime ses baskets Nike.
f Sarah n'aime pas sa robe bleue et rouge.
g Elle porte souvent son blouson.

Lis le texte et corrige les cinq erreurs.

Exemple: **a** *Charlotte wears a tracksuit …*

a Charlotte wears a pair of shorts for sports.
b When she goes to town she wears a pair of jeans and a sweatshirt.
c When it is cold she wears her black scarf.
d Luna wears a tracksuit for sports.
e When she goes to town she wears jeans.

Qu'est-ce que tu portes? Adapte le texte de Charlotte.

Exemple: *Quand je fais du sport, je porte mon survêtement Nike …*

Moi, *quand je fais du sport*, j'aime porter des vêtements confortables, comme mon survêtement avec mes baskets et mon T-shirt. *Quand je vais en ville* avec mes copains, je porte souvent mon jean slim avec ma chemise blanche et ma veste en cuir. Je porte aussi mon écharpe bleue et blanche quand il fait froid.

Par contre, ma copine Luna est différente. *Quand elle fait du sport*, elle préfère porter son short, son T-shirt et ses baskets Nike. *Quand elle va en ville*, elle aime porter des vêtements chics comme sa robe noire ou sa jupe Fred Perry avec ses bottes ou ses chaussures à talons. C'est très classe!

Charlotte

| comme | *like* |
| des chaussures à talons | *high-heel shoes* |

Can you add adjectives and opinions?
Je porte mon survêtement blanc, c'est ma couleur préférée.

Can you describe what your friend wears?
Ma copine porte son jean bleu.

Quand	je vais il/elle va	à une fête/en ville,	je porte il/elle porte	un jean/un sweat. une robe/une jupe. des baskets.
	je fais il/elle fait	du sport,		
	il fait	chaud/froid,		
	il pleut,			
	je reste il/elle reste	à la maison,		

Plenary

Discuss in groups <u>what</u> you have learnt about the importance of the word *quand* and <u>how</u> you have mastered this. Produce at least two 'grow me' sentences.
Pass them to the next group for feedback, which you must use to set yourself an individual target before aiming at your medal.

 Tell your group what you wear when it's raining.

 Tell your group what your friend wears when it's sunny and why.

 Tell your group what you and your friend wear when you go to a party and why.

6.3 Tu en fais souvent?

- Vocabulary: say how often you do an activity
- Grammar: use *faire* and *jouer* with activities
- Skills: use time expressions effectively and build longer sentences; use listening strategies

 Trouve les paires.

See page 33 for reading strategies.

Exemple: **a 5**

 Écoute et lis. Mets les images dans le bon ordre.

Exemple: **a, ...**

a	le week-end	1	always
b	deux fois par semaine	2	on Thursdays
c	tous les jours	3	often
d	le jeudi	4	sometimes
e	souvent	5	at the weekend
f	le samedi soir	6	on Saturday nights
g	toujours	7	twice a week
h	quelquefois	8	every day

a Tous les jours, je passe deux heures sur mon ordi.

b Le dimanche matin, je joue sur ma console de jeux vidéo.

c Je joue au handball une fois par semaine.

d Le week-end, je vais quelquefois en ville avec mes copains.

e J'écoute souvent de la musique.

f Le samedi soir, je vais au cinéma.

g Le dimanche soir, je regarde quelquefois la télé.

 Écris cinq phrases.

Write about your free time. Use a variety of time expressions.

Exemple: <u>Le vendredi soir</u>, je joue <u>souvent</u> sur ma console de jeux vidéo.

 Parle. Quelle activité? A↔B.

Choose an activity from pictures a–g. Your partner finishes the sentence with a time expression.

Exemple: **A** *Je regarde la télé ...*
B *... tous les soirs.*

> le week-end   tous les jours   une fois par semaine
> tous les soirs   le samedi après-midi

◎ **Add *souvent*, *quelquefois* or *toujours*. Watch out for the position:**
Je vais <u>souvent</u> en ville <u>le samedi</u>.

✚ **How would you say the following?**
When it rains I often stay at home.
When it is sunny I sometimes play tennis.

 **Grammaire** p. 168–169 WB p.30, p.36

Jouer and faire

Jouer is a regular verb (see page 43).
Faire is irregular.

je fais	tu fais	il/elle/on fait

Use them with sport and leisure activities.

Je joue sur l'ordi. *I play on the computer.*
Je fais du sport. *I do sports.*

Je joue Il/Elle/On joue		au foot/handball sur ma console de jeux vidéo aux jeux vidéo	
Je fais Il/Elle/On fait	quelquefois/ souvent/ toujours	du sport/shopping. des courses.	tous les jours/week-ends. une/deux fois par jour/semaine. le samedi après-midi/soir.
Je regarde Il/Elle/On regarde		la télé, des clips vidéo	
Je vais Il/Elle/On va		sur Internet en ville au cinéma	

Écoute l'interview de Benjamin et réponds aux questions.

Exemple: **a** *7am*

a What time does Benjamin get up?
b How many hours does he train in the morning?
c How many hours does he train every week?
d How many matches does he play at the weekend?
e Name a celebrity he admires.
f How many hours does he spend chatting to friends?
g How many games has he got on his mobile?

Lis le blog de Mathieu et corrige **les erreurs dans les phrases a–f.**

Exemple: **a** *Yannick has been swimming <u>since the age of eight</u>.*

a Yannick has been swimming for eight years.
b He trains every weekend.
c He has a lot of time for leisure activities.
d He does not like video games.
e He goes on the Internet in the afternoons.
f He writes messages.

Mon héros		Accueil Profil Compte

Mon héros, c'est Yannick Agnel. Il fait de la natation depuis l'âge de huit ans. C'est sa passion! Il s'entraîne tous les jours et passe plus de quatre heures dans la piscine. Il n'a pas beaucoup de temps pour ses loisirs mais il adore jouer sur sa play station parce que c'est cool! Il est champion de jeux vidéo. Le soir, il aime aussi aller sur Internet et lire les messages de ses fans.

Écris un article sur une personne célèbre ou sur un copain/une copine.
Adapt the text in activity 6.
Include the activities he/she does and how often he/she does them. You can invent if you don't know.

Plenary

Work in groups of four. Read aloud your description from activity 7 to the group. Discuss the descriptions and award a medal to each person. Peer assess and suggest one improvement for each description.

 Simple sentences.

Simple sentences with time expressions.

 Full description with opinions and time expressions.

 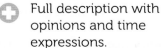

6.4 Mon week-end

- Vocabulary: talk about your weekend activities
- Grammar: use simple reflexive verbs
- Skills: become confident in understanding time and talking about activities

Écoute, lis et trouve les paires. Quelle heure est-il?

Exemple: **1** d

Il est …

1	dix heures	**5**	dix heures dix
2	minuit	**6**	dix heures moins dix
3	dix heures et demie	**7**	midi
4	onze heures moins le quart	**8**	dix heures et quart

Quelle heure est-il? Il est …

11 midi/minuit 1
une heure
10 deux heures moins dix — une heure dix 2
deux heures moins le quart 9 — une heure et quart 3
deux heures moins vingt — une heure vingt
8 — une heure et demie 4
7 6 5

Lis et réponds aux questions.

Exemple: **a** *midday in Paris, …*

Paris, France, Sophie

Nouméa, Nouvelle-Calédonie, Nathan

Basse-Terre, Martinique, Zarah

a When it is 7am in Martinique, what time is it in Paris/in Nouméa?
b What does Sophie do when Zarah gets up?
c When it is midday in Paris, what time is it in Nouméa?
d When Nathan goes to bed, what does Zarah do?

Ils habitent au bout du monde

Quand il est sept heures du matin à Basse-Terre en Martinique, Zarah se lève. À Paris, Sophie mange parce qu'il est midi. Nathan, qui habite en Nouvelle-Calédonie, est au lit parce qu'il est onze heures du soir à Nouméa. Quand Zarah se lève, Nathan se couche!

Quelle heure est-il? Change les mots soulignés.

Exemple: **A** *Il est <u>dix heures</u> à <u>Paris</u>. Quelle heure est-il à Basse-Terre?*

B *Il est <u>cinq heures du matin</u>.*

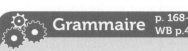 **Work out the time for other cities (New York, Delhi, Sydney …).**

Grammaire
p. 168–169
WB p.43

Reflexive verbs

*je **me** lève* – I get up
*tu **te** lèves* – you get up
*il/elle/on **se** lève* –
he/she gets up, we get up

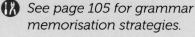 *See page 105 for grammar memorisation strategies.*

Trouve les paires. Écoute et vérifie.
Find the pairs. Listen and check your answers.

Exemple: **a** *4*

1 Je fais du shopping.
2 Je me lève à 7 heures.
3 J'écoute de la musique sur mon lecteur MP4.
4 Je joue aux jeux vidéo sur ma console de jeux.

5 Je tchate sur Internet.
6 Je vais à des fêtes.
7 Je me couche.
8 Je vais au cinéma.

 Trouve les expressions dans le texte.

Exemple: **a** *Jamel passe*

a Jamel spends
b in front of his computer screen
c when he gets up
d to chat on line
e to share photos
f to send SMS
g he downloads video clips

⭐ **Name two activities Jamel does:**
Jamel regarde ses messages et …

◎ **Name four more activities.**

écran *screen*

ADOS ET ÉCRAN

Aujourd'hui, l'ordinateur est indispensable. Jamel passe plus d'une heure et demie devant son écran d'ordinateur. Quand il se lève, il regarde immédiatement ses messages. Il aime aussi discuter en ligne, partager des photos et bloguer. Il adore envoyer des SMS ou des MMS. Il écoute souvent de la musique et de temps en temps, il télécharge des clips vidéo.

Écris un paragraphe sur ton week-end.

Exemple: Le week-end, je me lève à neuf heures …

◎ **Change your paragraph to say what your friend does and add opinions:**
Mon copain Louis se lève …

➕ **Add times, opinions, reasons, connectives:**
Mon copain Louis se lève à neuf heures …

Plenary

Explain to your teacher what a reflexive verb is, how to use one and, if you can, why you think they might exist. Then discuss leisure activities with your partner.

⭐ Say two activities that you do, and at what time.

◎ Add an opinion.

➕ Talk about a celebrity, what they do and at what time. Give opinions.

Discuss who was most successful and why.

6.5 La musique, j'adore!

- Vocabulary: talk about music and national events
- Grammar: express likes and preferences
- Skills: use leisure vocabulary in a different context

 Qui aime quoi?

Exemple: **a** Lisa

Who likes …?
- **a** rap music
- **b** electronic music
- **c** French rock music
- **d** pop music
- **e** African music
- **f** R&B

> Le rock français, c'est mon genre de musique préféré. J'adore le groupe BB Brunes. Ils sont incroyables et super beaux!
>
> Salomé

> Moi, mon chanteur préféré, c'est Christophe Maé. C'est de la musique pop un peu africaine. J'adore le rythme.
>
> Simon

> Moi, j'adore David Guetta, c'est de la musique électronique et c'est trop cool!
>
> Enzo

> Moi, j'adore le rap. Mon groupe préféré, c'est Sexion d'Assaut. Je les adore! J'aime aussi le R&B.
>
> Lisa

Tu aimes/Tu préfères quel genre de musique?	J'aime/Je préfère …	parce que c'est cool/fun.
Quel(le) est ton groupe/ ton chanteur/ta chanteuse préféré(e)?	Mon … préféré, c'est …	parce qu'il/elle est génial(e).

  Pose les deux questions à cinq personnes.

Exemple: **A** *Tu aimes quel genre de musique?*
B *J'aime …*
A *Quel(le) est ton groupe/ton chanteur/ta chanteuse préféré(e)?*
B *Mon groupe préféré, c'est …*

➕ **Can you add a reason for your choice? Which connectives could you use to give your opinion?**

 Lis le blog de Léa. Remplis les blancs. ⬚

> mon   j'aime   ~~écouter~~   joue
> porte   anglais   chante   blouson
> français   discuter   écoute

BB Brunes   Accueil   Profil   Compte

J'adore **1** *écouter* de la musique rock. **2** _____ groupe préféré, c'est BB Brunes. C'est un groupe **3** _____.
Ils sont quatre. Adrien Gallo **4** _____ de la guitare et il **5** _____. Karim Réveillé joue de la batterie. C'est le plus beau et j'adore son look! Il **6** _____ toujours un **7** _____ en cuir noir. La chanson que **8** _____ le plus s'appelle *Nico Teen Love*. Je pense que c'est le meilleur groupe de rock en ce moment!

◉ **Adapt Léa's blog and write a short paragraph about a group of your choice.**

> In the blog about BB Brunes, there are three interesting expressions to say what you like best and what is the best. Can you find them?

Écoute et réponds aux questions.

Exemple: **a** *21 June*

a When is the *Fête de la musique*?
b Name two activities you can do.
c What time does it start?
d When does it finish?
e Is it expensive?
f What time is the concert?

Lis le texte sur la Fête du cinéma. Trouve les six erreurs dans la traduction.

Find the six errors in the translation.

Exemple: **1** *the last weekend*

Tous les ans, le dernier week-end de juin, c'est la Fête du cinéma en France. Pendant quatre jours, on peut aller au cinéma pour seulement 3€50 la place! J'y vais avec mes copains tous les ans et on regarde plus de six films pendant les quatre jours.

Every year on the first weekend in July, there is the *Fête du cinéma* in Paris. For fourteen days you can go to the cinema for just 3€50 a ticket! I go there with my sister every year and we watch more than ten films during the four days.

Plenary

Work with a partner. Answer the following questions without saying either *oui* or *non*.
• Tu aimes la musique pop?
• Tu aimes faire du sport?
• Tu aimes tchater sur Internet?

 Use only a verb.
 Add a reason.
 Develop your answer.

Look back at activity 5. Discuss with your partner why you think translation might be an important skill for the modern world.

Regular and irregular verbs

1 **Choose the correct verb form.**

a Ils *jouent*/joues/jouez au foot.
b Nous portent/portons/portes un pull.
c Tu aimez/aimes/aime la musique?
d Vous portent/portez/portes un jean.
e Elle télécharge/téléchargent/télécharges de la musique.
f Je portes/porte/portez une robe rouge.

2 **Find the pairs.**

Exemple: **a** *6*

a	il fait	1	you go (informal)
b	je vais	2	we do
c	on fait	3	you do (informal)
d	elle va	4	I go
e	tu fais	5	she goes
f	tu vas	6	he does

> **Porter** (to wear), **jouer** (to play), **télécharger** (to download) are regular -er verbs just like *aimer*. See page 68.

> **Aller** (to go) is the only irregular -er verb and you have to learn its forms by heart. **Faire** (to do, to make) is another irregular verb.
>
> | aller | faire |
> |---|---|
> | je vais | je fais |
> | tu vas | tu fais |
> | il/elle/on va | il/elle/on fait |

Expressions of time

3 **Translate into French.**

Exemple: **a** *Je télécharge quelquefois de la musique*

a I sometimes download music.
b He often wears a leather jacket.
c She always listens to music.
d I sometimes play video games.
e I often play handball.
f I watch TV every Sunday.

> Most time expressions can be added either at the start or at the end of the sentence:
>
> *Je vais au cinéma <u>tous les samedis</u>.*
> *<u>Tous les samedis</u>, je vais au cinéma.*
>
> *Souvent* (often) and *toujours* (always) come immediately *after* the verb:
>
> *Je vais <u>souvent</u> au cinéma.* – I often go to the cinema.

Possessives adjectives: how to say 'his/her'

4 **Use the correct possessive adjective for each word.**

Example: **a** *son*

a jean (her)
b jupe (her)
c veste (his)
d baskets (her)
e chemise (his)
f écharpe (her)
g maillot de bain (his)
h short (her)
i T-shirt (his)
j survêtement (her)

> Possessive adjectives are words to say 'my', 'your', 'his', 'her'.
>
> | masculine | feminine | starts with a vowel | plural |
> |---|---|---|---|
> | son | sa | son | ses |
>
> a mobile – **un** portable
> his mobile – **son** portable
> her mobile – **son** portable
> his mobiles – **ses** portables
> her mobiles – **ses** portables
>
> a games console – **une** console de jeux
> his console – **sa** console
> her console – **sa** console
> his consoles – **ses** consoles
> her consoles – **ses** consoles

Quand

5 **Translate the sentences.**

Exemple: **a** *Quand je vais en ville, je porte mon jean avec mon sweat.*

a When I go to town, I wear my jeans with my sweatshirt.
b When I do sports, I wear a tracksuit and trainers.
c I wear a jacket when it is cold.
d When I stay at home, I wear comfortable clothes.
e I wear my leather jacket when I go to town
f I wear my trainers when I play tennis.

> *Quand* means 'when'. You can use it to build more complex sentences. The phrase with *quand* can be at the beginning or at the end of your sentence.
>
> **Quand il pleut,** *je porte une veste.*
> *Je porte une veste* **quand je vais en ville**.

Grammar memorisation strategies

Use these strategies on pages 94, 96 and 100.

There are lots of grammar rules to learn in this unit. If you try learning grammar in different ways, it makes it more interesting and more effective. Choose the ones that work best for you.

1 **Use your senses.**
- **Make up a song** to memorise a rule, e.g. *mon ma mes, ton ta tes* (to the tune of *Frère Jacques*).
- **Colour-code nouns** according to their gender.
- **Design a card/board game** to test your memory, e.g. cut up sentences with time expressions, reflexive verbs and opinions, then jumble up and re-order. For example, *Tous les samedis matin, je me lève tard car je ne vais pas à l'école. C'est chouette!*
- **Use colour strips** to list the six parts of a verb.
- Also **use colour strips** to list 'word families', e.g. *porter, porteur, portable, portefeuille* on one strip. This can help you understand the meaning of unfamiliar words.

- **Create a linking map** for a topic, e.g. *les vêtements* in the middle, and bubbles around with colour, sizes, style/look, etc.

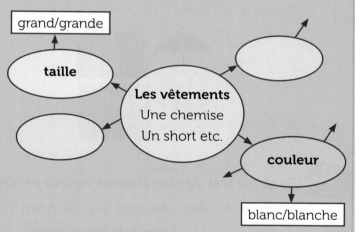

2 **Be on the look-out …**
- … for grammatical rules when you read or hear a text, or listen to your teacher talking, e.g. why is it **ma chemise blanche**?
- … when listening or reading for useful expressions which you can recycle in your own spoken or written work.

Pronunciation: speaking with a good accent

6 **Read these words aloud, then listen and check your pronunciation. What do they mean?**

> indispensable   incroyable   immangeable
> impensable   inoubliable

6.7 Extra Star

- Vocabulary: practise using clothes and leisure vocabulary
- Grammar: practise using familiar verbs
- Skills: extend basic sentences by adding details

 1 Find the clothes.

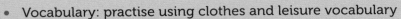

unjeandesbasketsunshortunsweatunerobeunblousonunevesteunechemise

 2 Match the pictures with the words in activity 1.

Exemple: **a** un jean

 3 Write captions for the pictures.

Exemple: **a** *Quand il pleut, je regarde la télé.*

a Quand ...

b Quand ...

c Quand ...

 **32°**
d Quand ...

 4 Read the text. Are the statements true or false?

Exemple: **a** *false – she goes with her mum*

a Salomé goes to town with her friends.
b She always buys CDs.
c She loves wearing jeans.
d She plays on her games console in the evening.
e She talks with her cousin on the Internet.
f She goes to bed at 9.30pm.

> Salut!
>
> Le samedi matin, je vais souvent en ville avec ma mère. J'achète toujours des vêtements! J'adore porter des jeans slim. L'après-midi, je joue sur ma console de jeux vidéo pendant une heure et après je discute quelquefois avec mes copines sur Internet. Le soir, je regarde des clips vidéo et je me couche à neuf heures et demie.
>
> À plus!
>
> Salomé

 5 Rewrite the text with connectives and time phrases. Use all the words in the box.

Exemple: *Le week-end, je fais du sport ...*

> Je fais du sport. Je vais en ville avec mes copains. J'aime envoyer des mails. Je joue aux jeux vidéo. J'écoute de la musique sur mon portable. Je télécharge de la musique.

> et   aussi
> le week-end   le soir
> le dimanche après-midi
> tous les soirs
> pendant deux heures

6.7 Extra Plus

- Vocabulary: practise using clothes and leisure vocabulary
- Grammar: apply correct word order with verbs
- Skills: build up more complex sentences

1 **Trouve le code et écris le nom des vêtements.**

Exemple: **a** *un ...*

❶= j ❷= ❸= ❹= ❺=
❻ = ❼= ❽= ❾= ❿=

a u❸ ❶ea❸
b u❸e ❶u❷e
c ❼e❹ ❽a❹❺e❾❹

d u❸ ❽❿ou❹o❸
e u❸e ❻o❽e
f u❸ ❹ho❻❾

2 **Mets les mots dans le bon ordre. Traduis les phrases.**

Exemple: **a** *Je porte un jean bleu et un sweat Hollister. – I am wearing blue jeans ...*

a un bleu porte et sweat je jean Hollister un.
b Bieber des porter Justin kaki baskets un aime blanches avec pantalon.
c Madonna chaussures robe avec porte noire des une rouges.

d porter quand ville mon slim j'aime jean je vais en.
e Internet mes quand lève discute je sur copains me je avec.

3 **Lis les blogs de Claire et de Julie. Recopie et remplis la grille.**

Claire   Accueil   Profil   Compte

Salut, *je m'appelle* Claire. *J'habite* à Paris et *le samedi matin*, je fais une heure et demie de basket. *L'après-midi*, je fais du shopping en ville. Le soir, je regarde une vidéo sur mon ordi. *Le dimanche matin*, je me lève à onze heures. *L'après-midi,* je joue à des jeux en ligne, j'adore ça! *Le soir*, je me couche à dix heures.

Julie   Accueil   Profil   Compte

Je m'appelle Julie et j'habite à la Martinique. Le samedi, je me lève à sept heures et je regarde mes mails. L'après-midi, on joue au volley-ball avec les copains et le soir, je regarde la télé pendant une heure. Le dimanche matin, je parle sur Internet avec mes copines et l'après-midi, je vais à la plage. Le soir, j'écoute souvent de la musique.

	Claire	Julie
Saturday morning afternoon evening	basketball, 1½ hour	
Sunday morning afternoon evening		
Other details		

4 **Utilise les mots en *italique* de Claire et écris ton blog. Parle de ton week-end.**

Exemple: *J'habite à Londres ...*

6.8 *Lire*

RENCONTRE AVEC ... SLIMANE AL-SALAM, JEUNE MANNEQUIN

- **Slimane, on voit souvent ta photo sur des catalogues, des panneaux publicitaires, quelquefois même à la télé ... C'est ton choix, d'être mannequin?**

Slimane: Absolument! Je fais des photos publicitaires depuis l'âge de onze ans. À neuf ans, j'étais passionné de mode et de photographie. J'ai demandé à mes parents et ils ont trouvé une agence.

- **Et l'école?**

Slimane: Je vais au collège, comme tout le monde. Le travail de mannequin, c'est seulement le samedi. Je travaille aussi pendant les vacances, mais seulement la moitié des vacances.

- **Raconte ta journée typique de jeune mannequin.**

Slimane: Ça dépend. Si c'est un casting, on va dans un studio et le client choisit ses mannequins. Il faut être patient. Et on n'est pas toujours choisi!

- **Et si tu es choisi?**

Slimane: C'est super, mais c'est fatigant aussi. Pendant les vacances, par exemple, je travaille six ou sept heures par jour. Il fait chaud, sous les projecteurs! Mais tout le monde est très sympa.

- **Et ton avenir?**

Slimane: Certainement pas mannequin ... J'adore la mode, c'est vrai, mais plus tard, je voudrais devenir styliste.

mannequin	*model*
les panneaux	*billboards*
tout le monde	*everybody*
styliste	*fashion designer*

 1 **Answer the questions in English.**

- **a** What is Slimane's job?
- **b** What was he interested in around the age of nine?
- **c** Why does he say that he needs a lot of patience?
- **d** How do you know he enjoys what he does?

 2 **In English, describe a typical day for Slimane.**

 3 **What positive phrases does Slimane use to talk about his interests and his job?**

Exemple: absolument ...

 4 **Correct the following statements.**

Exemple: **a** *Slimane est mannequin depuis l'âge de onze ans.*

- **a** Slimane est mannequin depuis l'âge de neuf ans.
- **b** Slimane travaille comme mannequin du mercredi au samedi.
- **c** Les castings ne durent pas longtemps.
- **d** Dans les studios, il y a des radiateurs et il ne fait pas froid.
- **e** Plus tard, Slimane veut travailler comme mannequin adulte.

6.8 *Vidéo*

Le quizz

Regarde l'épisode 6. Qui utilise ces vêtements? Attention: quelquefois, il y a *deux* bonnes réponses.
Who uses the following as part of their activities? There might be two correct answers.

Exemple: **a** *Basile*

a un anorak	**g** un jogging
b des baskets	**h** une jupe
c un bonnet	**i** des lunettes
d des gants	**j** un pantalon spécial
e un imperméable	**k** une robe
f un jean	

Qui fait quoi? Recopie et remplis la grille.
Who does what?

	aller en ville	boxe	Internet	jeux vidéo	ski
Zaied		✔			
Diakouba					
Basile					
Jules					
Clarisse					

Complète les phrases.

Zaied Je pratique cette activité une fois par semaine, *le samedi après-midi*.
Diakouba Tu as gagné. Je joue sur la console de jeux vidéo ▒▒▒.
Basile Non, c'est impossible de faire cette activité quand ▒▒▒ . Je fais cette activité en hiver.
Jules Oui, je surfe sur Internet ▒▒▒ .
Clarisse Quand ▒▒▒ , je porte un imperméable.

👥 À quelle personne ressembles-tu? Que portes-tu pour ton activité préférée?
Which character from the video are you most like? What do you wear for your favourite occupation?
Exemple: Zaied – Moi aussi, je porte un short quand je joue au foot.

6.9 Test

1 Listen to Anaïs, Émilie and Nicolas. What do they do on Saturdays?
Copy and complete the grid. (See pages 98–101.)

	getting up time	am	pm	evening	bedtime
1 Anaïs	7am				
2 Émilie			basketball		
3 Nicolas					

2 Talk about your clothes and hobbies. Prepare a short presentation giving
the following information. (See pages 94–101.)
- what clothes you wear: *Je porte …*
- what clothing style you like and why: *J'aime le look … parce que …*
- what you do at the weekend: *Le week-end, je vais en ville/je fais du sport …*
- what time you get up/go to bed: *Je me lève …/Je me couche …*

3 Read Charlotte's email
and answer the questions
below in English.
(See pages 94–101.)

Exemple: **a** *She always
does sport.*

> Sujet: Mes activités
>
> Le dimanche matin, je fais toujours du sport pendant deux heures.
> L'après-midi, je discute avec mes copains sur Internet et quelquefois
> je télécharge de la musique. Je joue aussi au basket deux fois par
> semaine et quelquefois on a des matchs le samedi. Ce week-end,
> je n'ai pas de match donc je vais à une fête chez Hamel. C'est son
> anniversaire et je vais porter ma robe bleue parce qu'elle est super chic.

a What does Charlotte do on Sunday mornings?
b What does she do in the afternoon?
c When does she play basketball?

d What sometimes happens on Saturdays?
e Where is she going this weekend?
f What is she going to wear and why?

4 Describe what you do when … Use the pictures for ideas. (See pages 94–101.)

Exemple: **a** *Quand il pleut, je vais au cinéma avec mes copains.*

a Qu'est-ce que tu fais quand il pleut?
b Qu'est-ce que tu fais quand il fait froid?
c Qu'est-ce que tu fais quand il fait chaud?
d Qu'est-ce que tu portes quand …
- tu vas en ville?
- tu vas à une fête?
- tu fais du sport?

Exemple: *Quand je vais en ville, je porte mon jean slim.*

To improve your work, remember to develop
your sentences. Use time expressions,
a future tense, and
give opinions.

Simple detail.

For example:
Je joue au basket.

More detail.

For example:
*Quand il fait beau,
je joue au basket.*

Even more detail.

For example:
*Quand il fait beau,
je joue au basket
avec mes copains.
J'adore ça.*

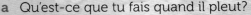

Vocabulaire

Clothes

Qu'est-ce que tu portes?	*What do you wear?*
je porte	*I wear*
j'aime porter	*I like to wear*
des baskets	*trainers*
un blouson	*bomber jacket*
un bonnet	*woolly hat*
des bottes	*boots*
une casquette	*cap*
des chaussures	*shoes*
une chemise	*shirt*
en cuir	*(made of) leather*
une écharpe	*scarf*
des gants	*gloves*
un imper(méable)	*raincoat*
un jean	*pair of jeans*
une jupe	*skirt*
des lunettes (de soleil)	*(sun) glasses*
un maillot de bain	*bathing costume*
un pantalon	*pair of trousers*
un parapluie	*umbrella*
une robe	*dress*
un short	*pair of shorts*
un sweat	*sweatshirt*
un survêtement	*tracksuit*
un T-shirt	*T-shirt*
à talons	*high-heel*
une veste	*jacket*
des vêtements de marque	*designer clothes*

Weather

Quel temps fait-il?	*What is the weather like?*
il fait chaud	*it is hot*
il fait froid	*it is cold*
il fait du vent	*it is windy*
il gèle	*it is freezing*
il neige	*it is snowing*
il pleut	*it is raining*
il y a de l'orage	*there is a (thunder)storm*
il y a du soleil	*it is sunny*

Expressions of frequency

Tu en fais souvent?	*Do you do it often?*
souvent	*often*
quelquefois	*sometimes*
une fois par jour	*once a day*
deux fois	*twice*
toujours	*always*
tous les jours	*every day*
tous les soirs	*every evening*
le week-end	*at the weekend*
le samedi soir	*on Saturday evenings*
le dimanche après-midi	*on Sunday afternoons*
le jeudi	*on Thursdays*

dimanche	*on Sunday*
pendant	*during/for*

Telling the time and weekend activities

Quelle heure est-il?	*What time is it?*
Il est ...	*It is ...*
quand	*when*
midi	*midday*
minuit	*midnight*
une heure	*one o'clock*
une heure dix	*ten past one*
une heure et quart	*a quarter past one*
une heure et demie	*half past one*
une heure moins le quart	*a quarter to one*
une heure moins dix	*ten to one*
J'écoute de la musique.	*I listen to music.*
Je joue sur ma console de jeux vidéo.	*I play on my games console.*
Je reste à la maison.	*I stay at home.*
Je surfe sur Internet.	*I surf the net.*
Je télécharge de la musique.	*I download music.*
Je vais en ville.	*I go to town.*
bloguer	*to blog*
envoyer	*to send*
partager	*to share*
passer	*to spend*
se coucher	*to go to bed*
s'entraîner	*to train, practise*
se lever	*to get up*
surfer	*to surf*
tchater	*to chat*

Opinions about clothes

à la mode	*fashionable*
classe	*classy*
incroyable	*unbelievable*
indispensable	*essential*
pratique	*practical*
top	*brilliant*

◎ Grammar and skills: I can...

- ◉ use *porter* and *j'aime porter*
- ◉ use *son/sa/ses*
- ◉ use *faire* and *jouer* with activities
- ◉ tell the time
- ◉ use simple reflexive verbs
- ◉ re-use language in different contexts
- ◉ use time expressions to build longer sentences
- ◉ use listening strategies
- ◉ use strategies to memorise grammar

7.1 Je vais en vacances

- Vocabulary: talk about usual holidays and preferred holidays
- Grammar: use *choisir* and *finir* in the present tense
- Skills: adapt texts

1 On finit le travail cette semaine. On va où cette année? Vous avez le choix: la mer, la campagne ou la montagne. Pierre, qu'est-ce que tu choisis?

2 Moi, je choisis la mer, en Espagne, parce qu'il fait très chaud et parce qu'il y a du soleil. C'est super quand il fait chaud!

Oh non, je préfère aller à la campagne! Moi, je voudrais aller à la campagne en Allemagne et faire du vélo. Je veux être active!

3 Faire du vélo? Je n'aime pas ça.

Où veux-tu aller, Maman?

4 Moi aussi, je choisis la campagne, mais j'aimerais aller dans un gîte en France. C'est très relaxant.

5 Papa, qu'est-ce que tu choisis, la campagne ou la mer?

Je choisis d'aller à la montagne aux États-Unis. J'adore quand il fait froid, et on peut faire des randonnées. C'est très amusant.

6 Ah non!

Si, je n'aime pas quand il fait chaud.

ÉCOUTER 1

Écoute et lis le texte. Qui parle? Maman, Papa, Pierre ou Mélissa?

Exemple: **a** *Pierre*

a J'aime aller à la plage.
b Je préfère partir en vacances en hiver.
c J'adore les vacances relaxantes.
d J'aime faire beaucoup de sport en vacances.
e Je n'aime pas faire du vélo.
f J'aimerais visiter l'Amérique.
g J'aimerais partir en vacances à la campagne.

Grammaire
p. 168–169
WB p.32–33

Finir and *choisir*

Finir (to finish) and *choisir* (to choose) are both examples of regular *-ir* verbs.

	finir	choisir
je	fini**s**	choisi**s**
tu	fini**s**	choisi**s**
il/elle/on	fini**t**	choisi**t**

ÉCOUTER 2

Écoute (1–7). C'est quelle image?

Exemple: **1** *b*

a

b

c

d

e

f

g

Lis avec un(e) partenaire.
Using correct pronunciation, read the texts aloud.

> D'habitude, je vais en vacances **avec ma famille. Je vais en Espagne** ou en Allemagne et **je fais du camping.** J'aime le camping parce que c'est amusant mais **je préfère aller à l'hôtel** parce que c'est plus relaxant.
>
> Audrey

> D'habitude, je vais en vacances avec mon frère et ma mère et **on va dans un gîte à la campagne.** J'aime aller à la montagne en Italie ou en Allemagne et j'aime dormir en auberge de jeunesse.
>
> Karim

> Moi, d'habitude, je vais en vacances sur la côte d'Azur, où il fait très chaud. Je pars **avec ma tante** et mes cousins mais je préfère partir avec mes parents. **On va dans une villa** et c'est super.
>
> Julie

Vrai, faux ou pas mentionné?
Exemple: **a** *vrai*

a Audrey usually stays on a campsite.
b Karim prefers to stay in a youth hostel with his friends.
c Julie usually goes on holiday to hot places.
d Audrey finds hotels more fun than campsites.
e Karim likes walking in the mountains.
f Julie prefers going on holiday with her parents rather than her aunt.

◎ **Correct any false information in a–f.**

Écris.
Change the information in **bold** in activity 3 to create your own personal responses. Where will you go on holiday this year? You can make up your answers!

- D'habitude, tu vas en vacances avec qui?
- Où vas-tu en vacances?
- Tu préfères aller à l'hôtel ou dans un camping?
- Où veux-tu aller en vacances cette année?
- Tu vas en vacances avec qui cette année?

Adapte la conversation de l'activité 1.
Create a role-play between four friends choosing where to go on holiday together. See page 123 for speaking strategies.

Où vas-tu en vacances?	
je vais/on va	à l'hôtel dans une villa dans un gîte chez mes grands-parents
je dors/on dort	dans une auberge de jeunesse
je fais/on fait	du camping
je voyage	sur un bateau de croisière

à la montagne	en France
à la campagne	en Espagne
à la mer	au Maroc
en ville	aux États-Unis

Plenary

Review your work on activity 6. How much better are you at <u>adapting</u> and <u>building</u> texts than you were six months ago? Think very carefully about <u>text type</u> and your progress in this particular area of your learning.

Now, choose a text from activity 3 and adapt it further.

 Change some of the words.

 Link your sentences together and add opinions.

➕ Create more complex sentences, adding reasons and opinions.

- Vocabulary: talk about items you take on holiday
- Grammar: use *prendre* in the present tense; use the near future tense
- Skills: develop dictionary skills

 Relie les images et les mots. Qu'est-ce que tu prends quand tu vas en vacances?

D'habitude, je prends 1) **un bon livre** et mon portable. Cette fois, je vais aussi prendre 2) **mon maquillage!**

Moi, d'habitude, je prends 3) **mes lunettes de soleil**, mais ce week-end, je vais prendre 4) **ma batte de cricket** et 5) **mes BD.**

D'habitude, je prends 6) **de la crème solaire** et 7) **mon frisbee**, mais cette fois, je vais aussi prendre 8) **mon lecteur MP4.**

D'habitude, je prends 9) **mon jean préféré**, mais ce week-end, je vais prendre 10) **ma casquette** et mon maillot de bain.

a  b  c  d  e

f  g  h 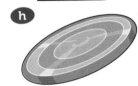 i  j

 Écoute. Recopie la grille et note en français. Qu'est-ce qu'ils vont prendre?

Max	frisbee, ...
Flore	
Leïla	

d'habitude
cette fois
cette année
ce week-end

 **Sondage.**
Take a survey of the class to find out people's essential holiday item, from the texts in activity 1.
Tally the results.

Exemple: **A** *Pour toi, quel est l'objet essentiel?*
B *Je vais prendre ...*

 Cherche dans le dictionnaire.
Use a dictionary to find five more objects that you would take on holiday. Compare your words with your partner.

Using a dictionary

When you are looking for something in the dictionary, always check first that you have the correct spelling in English, e.g 'there' or 'their'.

In activity 4 you are looking for <u>objects</u>, so remember that you are looking for <u>nouns</u>.

When you find a word, make sure you have found the right type of word: 'break', for example, could be *casser* (verb, as in 'to break a glass') or *la pause* (noun, as in 'coffee break'). There will usually be the word *noun* written next to the word, or *nm* (masculine noun), *nf* (feminine noun) or *npl* (plural noun).

5 **Lis les textes. Recopie et remplis la grille.**
Read the texts and write out each person's packing list and activity plan in English.

En vacances   Accueil   Profil   Compte

Je pars en vacances à la mer et je vais prendre un maillot de bain, de la crème solaire et des lunettes de soleil parce qu'il fait très chaud. Je vais aller à la plage et je vais me baigner.

Morgane
_____

Cette année, je vais aller à la montagne et je vais prendre des chaussures de randonnée, un imperméable et une carte parce que je vais faire des randonnées et visiter des villages.

Ibrahim
_____

Je pars en vacances à la campagne et je vais prendre des chaussures de randonnée, une bouteille d'eau et une carte parce que je vais faire des randonnées et du vélo. J'adore les vacances actives à la campagne – c'est super.

Léo

> je vais me baigner   *I'm going to swim*
> des chaussures de randonnée   *hiking boots*
> un imperméable   *a waterproof coat*
> une carte   *a map*

	packing list	activity plan
Morgane	*swimming costume, ...*	*go to the beach, ...*
Ibrahim		
Léo		

6 **Utilise un dictionnaire et écris des phrases.**
Use a dictionary to find three words to create sentences similar to activity 5.
Exemple: **A** *Cette année, je vais en Espagne. Je vais prendre **des jumelles** parce que je vais visiter **une réserve naturelle** ...*

a   en Espagne   c   à Paris   e   en Allemagne
b   en Chine   d   au Mexique   f   en Grande-Bretagne

➕ **Choose two more places of your own. Be creative: the moon, the jungle ...**

Grammaire p. 167

Saying 'in' for countries and cities
In Unit 1 you met *en*, *au* or *aux* to say 'in' a country:
*Je vais en vacances **en** France.*
However, to say 'in' a city, you need to use *à*:
*Cette année je vais en vacances **à** Paris.*

Grammaire p. 168–169, WB p. 34–35, WB p. 37, p. 38–39

Using *prendre* and *je vais prendre*

***prendre* – to take**

je prends	I take
tu prends	you take (singular)
il/elle prend on prend	he/she takes we take
nous prenons	we take
vous prenez	you take (plural)
ils/elles prennent	they take

D'habitude, je prends mes BD. – Normally I take my comics.

To form the **near future tense**, use the present tense of the verb *aller* (to go) and an infinitive verb:

I am going	je vais	prendre, manger, jouer ...
you are going	tu vas	
he/she is going	il/elle va	

Je vais prendre mon frisbee. – I am going to take my frisbee.

Plenary

Using reference materials to develop a wide vocabulary <u>effectively</u> is an important skill. Set a 'test' of five new words for holiday items for your partner to find.

⭐ What five items are you going to take with you to a desert island?

◎ Create a desert island list for yourself and for a celebrity then give it to your partner to decide which list belongs to who.

➕ Describe the five items you are going to take to a desert island and why.

- Vocabulary: talk about dream holidays
- Grammar: revise and develop the use of *je voudrais* and *j'aimerais*
- Skills: improve reading skills, apply strategies

LIRE 1

Relie les photos et les descriptions.

Exemple: **1** *e, 2, C*

Je voudrais/J'aimerais....
a faire un safari
b faire une croisière
c faire du trekking
d explorer des planètes
e me détendre sur une île

1 dans la forêt tropicale
2 aux Seychelles
3 dans l'espace
4 aux Caraïbes
5 en Afrique

A dans une cabane dans la forêt
B dans un vaisseau spatial
C dans un hôtel de luxe
D sur un bateau de croisière
E dans une tente

 Work with a partner. Choose two photos and match them with the corresponding phrases.

ÉCOUTER 2

Écoute et vérifie (1–5).

ÉCRIRE 3

Écris des phrases complètes.
Use the matched expressions from activity 1 to write full sentences with *je voudrais* and *j'aimerais*.

Exemple: **1** *Je voudrais me détendre sur une île aux Seychelles et j'aimerais aller dans un hôtel de luxe.*

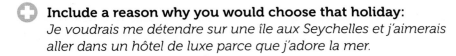 **Include a reason why you would choose that holiday:**
Je voudrais me détendre sur une île aux Seychelles et j'aimerais aller dans un hôtel de luxe parce que j'adore la mer.

Grammaire WB p.42

How to say 'I would like'

je voudrais/j'aimerais + infinitive
– I would like to ...

Je voudrais aller en France. –
I would like to go to France.

J'aimerais aller dans un hôtel de luxe. – I would like to stay in a luxury hotel.

4 **Lis les textes.**

Match each person with an ideal holiday from page 116.

Exemple: **a** 2

a Je voudrais visiter beaucoup de pays différents et j'aime aussi faire beaucoup d'activités. Je n'aime pas aller à l'hôtel mais j'aimerais être au bord de la mer. J'adore les bateaux.

b J'adore la nature et j'aimerais faire de longues randonnées dans la forêt. Je suis très actif et j'adore les singes et les oiseaux colorés.

c Je voudrais aller au bord de la mer et me détendre à la plage. J'aime aller dans les hôtels de luxe — c'est très relaxant.

d J'aimerais bien une grande aventure dans un autre monde parce que j'adore explorer. Je voudrais partir en vacances avec des copains et voyager dans un vaisseau spatial.

e J'adore les animaux et la nature — mon animal préféré, c'est le lion. J'aimerais aussi visiter les pays d'Afrique, mais je ne voudrais pas aller à l'hôtel — je préfère une cabane.

➕ **Translate the texts into English but only allow yourself to look up three words per text.**

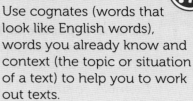
Reading strategies

Use cognates (words that look like English words), words you already know and context (the topic or situation of a text) to help you to work out texts.

For example, in activity 4, you can connect *au bord de la mer* and *les bateaux* with the sea or sailing.

If you still can't work out the meaning, look up key words in a dictionary. This should help you to make sense of the rest of a text without looking up every word.

5 **Parle. A ↔ B.**

Exemple: **A** *Quelles sont tes vacances de rêve?*
B *Je voudrais aller en France/au Mexique ...*
Je voudrais faire du trekking/me détendre sur une île ...
J'aimerais dormir dans un chalet/voyager sur un bateau de croisière ...

◎ **Give reasons for your choices:** *parce que j'adore ...*

 6 **Écoute. Recopie et remplis la grille.**

	Jules	Éva
usual holiday destination	Morocco	
usual holiday companions		
preferred holiday companions		
dream destination		

 7 **Décris tes vacances de rêve.**
Write a paragraph describing your dream holiday, using the texts in activities 1 and 4 to give you some ideas.

Exemple: **A** *Je voudrais faire un safari et dormir ...*

➕ **Justify all your choices, use connectives and more than one tense.**

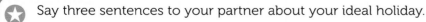
Plenary

⭐ Say three sentences to your partner about your ideal holiday.

◎ Say five sentences about your ideal holiday without using your notes. Use *parce que* to justify your choices.

➕ Talk for one minute about your ideal holiday. You mustn't hesitate or repeat yourself. Get your partner to time you.

Give each other feedback. Take note of the hints, make any changes you need to and then record your sentences for your teacher.

- Vocabulary: understand and describe activities that happened in the past
- Grammar: form and use the perfect tense with *avoir*
- Skills: work out grammar patterns; transcribe sentences

 LIRE 1 **Lis la carte postale de Mathieu et trouve les verbes.**
Read Mathieu's postcard and find the verbs (there are 12 in total).
What do you notice about them? Can you recall the grammar rules?

Exemple: je suis, …

Salut! Je suis en vacances à New York, aux États-Unis et c'est super! Hier, j'ai visité la Statue de la Liberté et j'ai acheté des souvenirs. J'ai acheté une statue miniature et des cartes postales. Après, j'ai joué au basket et j'ai mangé un hamburger avec des frites. J'ai aussi bu un coca. Ensuite, j'ai trouvé un ballon de foot à Central Park. Puis, j'ai visité Times Square et j'ai vu un taxi jaune. C'était une journée géniale.

À bientôt!

Mathieu

Working out grammar patterns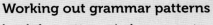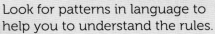

Look for patterns in language to help you to understand the rules.

Remember the grammar memorisation strategies on page 105? Which one might help you remember the pattern below?

j'ai visité   *j'ai acheté*   *j'ai voyagé*

 LIRE 2 **Relis le texte et réponds aux questions en français.**

Exemple: **a** la Statue de la Liberté

a Mathieu a visité quel monument hier?
b Mathieu a acheté quels souvenirs?
c Qu'est-ce qu'il a mangé et bu?
d Qu'est-ce qu'il a trouvé?
e Qu'est-ce qu'il a vu à Times Square?
+ f Mathieu a fait quel sport?

⚙ Grammaire p. 168–169 WB p.40

Talking about the past

The perfect tense in French is usually formed with the present tense of *avoir* and the past participle of the verb, for example *visiter – visité*.
j'ai visité – I have visited/I visited

j'ai		I have	
tu as	joué	you have (singular)	played
il/elle a on a	visité trouvé	he/she has we have	visited found
nous avons	acheté mangé	we have	bought eaten
vous avez	fait …	you have (plural)	done …
ils/elles ont		they have	

The imperfect tense is used to describe what something *was* like: *c'était* – it was

Lis les textes et regarde les photos. C'est quel jour?
Match the place to the day that Alice visited it.

Exemple: lundi d, Sydney

Le tour du monde en une semaine

Lundi: J'ai visité la place de l'Opéra et j'ai vu le grand pont. C'est magnifique! Ensuite, j'ai joué au beach-volley et j'ai mangé une glace au chocolat – elle était délicieuse.

Mardi: J'ai fait une longue promenade dans Green Park puis j'ai fait du shopping à Covent Garden. J'ai acheté un T-shirt et un bus rouge miniature.

Mercredi: J'ai mangé un hot-dog et j'ai visité le Centre Rockefeller – c'est énorme! Puis, j'ai fait du skate au parc. C'était génial.

Jeudi: J'ai vu le Christ Rédempteur et j'ai dansé la samba – c'était extraordinaire! Je suis aussi allée à la plage. J'ai encore joué au beach-volley et j'ai nagé. C'était cool.

Vendredi: J'ai visité le Colisée et le Panthéon. C'est magnifique! Après, j'ai mangé un pain au chocolat. Miam miam, délicieux!

 Écoute. Louis a visité Paris. Recopie des phrases.
Listen to Louis and write down some complete sentences from the conversation.

Exemple: Tout d'abord, j'ai fait une promenade ...

 Parle avec un(e) partenaire.
Using the correct sequence, say sentences to describe Louis' day.

Exemple: **A** *D'abord, Louis a fait une promenade.*
B *Ensuite, il a vu la tour Eiffel.*

hier	j'ai visité le parc/un musée/la tour Eiffel
(tout) d'abord	j'ai acheté des souvenirs/des cartes postales
puis	j'ai joué au foot/au beach-volley/au basket
après	j'ai mangé une glace/un hamburger/des frites
ensuite	j'ai bu de la limonade/du coca/de l'eau
pour finir	j'ai vu le Colisée/la tour Eiffel/un taxi jaune
	j'ai fait une promenade

 Imagine que tu as fait le tour du monde, comme Alice. Écris des phrases.

Exemple: Hier, j'ai visité la grande pyramide et j'ai vu le sphinx ...

Plenary

Can you transcribe words you hear more accurately now and then use them in your work? Challenge yourself as you write a travel journal for a celebrity or a sports personality.

⭐ Describe the activities that they did on each day.

◎ Write a postcard from the person to another celebrity describing their visit. Use sequencing words and connectives to create a paragraph.

➕ Write a column for a travel magazine describing your visit. Include opinions and reasons to extend and improve your work.

- Vocabulary: talk about festivals; use time expressions with tenses
- Grammar: practise the perfect tense of *aller*
- Skills: use time expressions to work out tenses; combine three tenses; read a longer text

 LIRE 1

Lis les textes. C'est Thomas ou Anaïs?

Exemple: **a** *Thomas*

a Je regarde les feux d'artifice à la télévision.
b Je mange au restaurant avec ma famille.
c Je suis allé à Paris.
d Je vais faire un pique-nique avec mes copains.

e Je vais aller chez ma grand-mère.
f J'ai mangé au restaurant.
g Je regarde les défilés dans la rue.

1

Salut! Je m'appelle Thomas et j'habite à Toulouse, en France. En France, la fête nationale, c'est le 14 juillet. Nous célébrons ça avec des feux d'artifice. Il y a toujours un grand spectacle à Paris. D'habitude, je regarde le feu d'artifice à la télévision avec ma famille mais l'année dernière, je suis allé à Paris et j'ai regardé le spectacle dans la rue. Il y avait beaucoup de monde. C'était super!

D'habitude, ma mère fait un bon dîner pour toute la famille et nous mangeons ensemble à la maison mais cette année, je suis allé au restaurant avec des copains. C'était sympa!

L'année prochaine, je vais encore aller à Paris, mais avec des copains cette fois. Ça va être super! Je vais faire un pique-nique dans un parc et regarder les feux d'artifice avec mes copains parce que c'est plus amusant.

la fête nationale *Bastille Day*
le feu d'artifice *fireworks*
le spectacle *show*

2

Salut! Je m'appelle Anaïs et j'habite à Port-Louis, à l'île Maurice. À l'île Maurice, la fête nationale, c'est le 12 mars. Il y a un grand spectacle qu'on peut regarder à la télévision et il y a aussi des défilés militaires dans la rue. Je vais toujours dans la rue pour regarder les défilés avec mes copains. Cette année, nous avons aussi fait un pique-nique dans un parc. C'était trop cool.

D'habitude, je vais au restaurant avec toute ma famille et nous faisons un grand repas ensemble mais l'année dernière, je suis allée chez ma copine et j'ai mangé avec sa famille.

L'année prochaine, je vais probablement regarder le spectacle culturel à la télévision avec ma grand-mère parce qu'elle adore ça. Je veux aussi regarder les défilés dans la rue avec mes copains. C'est un choix difficile!

le défilé *parade*

2 **Écoute et mets les six activités dans le bon ordre.**
Exemple: c, ...

a going to the beach
b eating out with her grandparents
c going for a walk
d watching the fireworks display
e chatting with her friends
f playing volleyball

Grammaire p. 168–169
WB p.41

Perfect tense of *aller*

You have met the perfect tense with
avoir in Unit 3 and on pages 118–119:
j'ai mangé – I ate
j'ai joué – I played
j'ai visité – I visited
To say 'I went', you form the perfect tense
with *être* and the past participle of *aller*:
je suis allé – I went (masculine)
je suis allée – I went (feminine)

3 **Relis les textes de l'activité 1. Les phrases a–f sont au passé, au présent ou au futur?**
Read the texts in activity 1 again carefully. Are the events below in the past, the present or the future?
Exemple: **a** *passé*

a Thomas: 'Je suis allé à Paris.'
b Thomas: 'Nous mangeons ensemble à la maison.'
c Anaïs: 'Je vais toujours dans la rue pour regarder les défilés.'
d Anaïs: 'J'ai mangé avec sa famille.'

e Thomas: 'Je vais faire un pique-nique dans un parc.'
f Anaïs: 'Je vais probablement regarder le spectacle culturel.'

⭐ **Find two verbs in the present tense and two verbs in the perfect tense in the texts. Write their meanings in English.**

4 **Écris un paragraphe.**
Use the texts on page 120 to help you to write a description of a special day or event.

⭐ **Use one tense.**

◎ **Use two tenses.**

✚ **Combine three tenses.**

D'habitude,	je vais je regarde je joue je mange		c'est ...
L'année dernière,	je suis allé(e) j'ai regardé j'ai joué j'ai mangé	J'aime/Je n'aime pas parce que	c'était ...
L'année prochaine,	je voudrais + *verb* j'aimerais + *verb* je vais + *verb*		ça va être ...

Plenary

Work in small groups on a cartoon strip including some 'top tips' for switching confidently between the tenses. Share this with another group before you start the medal task.

⭐ Write a description of what you did last year at a festival or special day where you live.

◎ Write a blog entry for a tourist who visited last year. What did they do at your festival compared to what they normally do?

✚ You are on the organising committee for the festival. Write three paragraphs describing what you usually do at the festival, what happened last year and what you would like to include next year. Be creative!

Using time expressions

You can often work out the tense by looking at the time expressions being used.

D'habitude means 'normally' and you would expect to see the present tense.

L'année dernière means 'last year' and so you would expect to see the past tense.

7.6 Labo-langue

Finir and *choisir*

1 **Complete the verb with the correct ending.**

a Quand je fin _is_ l'école à la fin du mois de juin, j'aime aller en vacances avec ma famille.

b Par contre, mon frère ne fin _____ pas l'école avant début juillet.

c Mes parents fin _____ le travail fin juillet.

d Camping ou hôtel? En général, nous chois _____ l'hôtel.

e La montagne ou la mer? D'habitude, je chois _____ le bord de la mer, parce que j'aime nager.

f Par contre, mes parents chois _____ d'aller sur la côte d'Azur cette année et mon frère et moi, nous allons chez nos grands-parents.

> You have met the present tense of regular -er verbs such as *jouer*, 'to play' (see pages 43 and 50, for example).
>
> *Finir* (to finish) and *choisir* (to choose) are both examples of regular -ir verbs.
>
> | | finir | choisir |
> |---|---|---|
> | je | fin**is** | chois**is** |
> | tu | fin**is** | chois**is** |
> | il/elle/on | fin**it** | chois**it** |
> | nous | fin**issons** | chois**issons** |
> | vous | fin**issez** | chois**issez** |
> | ils/elles | fin**issent** | chois**issent** |

Talking about the past

2 **Complete the sentences with the correct verb. Not all the verbs are used.**

a Éva, tu es *allée* à la piscine samedi?

b Non, je suis _____ en ville avec mon frère Jules.

c D'abord, j'ai _____ un film au cinéma.

d Ensuite, nous avons _____ un sandwich et nous avons _____ un coca.

e Puis j'ai _____ au foot et Jules a _____ du vélo.

f Après ça, nous avons _____ le petit zoo dans le parc.

g Puis Jules est _____ au petit café du parc.

h Il a _____ deux glaces au chocolat. C'était très bon.

i Pour finir, nous avons _____ de la musique sur mon lecteur MP4.

> joué ~~allée~~ visité trouvé allé acheté
> mangé fait allé bu voyagé allée
> écouté regardé

> The perfect tense (*le passé composé*) in French is usually formed with the present tense of *avoir* and the past participle of the verb, for example *visiter – visité*.
>
> *j'ai visité* – I have visited/I visited
>
> | j'ai | | I have | |
> |---|---|---|---|
> | tu as | joué | you have (singular) | played |
> | il/elle a on a | visité trouvé | he/she has we have | visited found |
> | nous avons | acheté mangé | we have | bought eaten |
> | vous avez | fait ... | you have (plural) | done ... |
> | ils/elles ont | | they have | |
>
> The imperfect tense (*l'imparfait*) is used to describe what something *was* like: *c'était* – it was
>
> Some verbs form the perfect tense with *être* (to be) and the past participle. For these verbs the past participle must agree with the gender of the people doing the action:
>
> je suis allé
> je suis allé**e** — I went/I have been
>
> tu es allé
> tu es allé**e** — you went/you have been

Speaking strategies

Use these strategies with activity 6, page 113.

Speaking tasks in French can seem quite daunting, and sometimes you can get a bit tongue tied. Here are some strategies you can try for conversations in pairs or groups.

Plan what you want to say **before** you begin:

- **Use the texts** to help you find the words you might have forgotten, e.g. *randonnée*. Don't forget about the questions: it is important to ask for, as well to as give information.
- **Make a cue card** (key words or pictures) to help you remember what to say.
- If you want to say something but don't know how (e.g. 'I would like to stay with my aunt in a cottage in the Welsh valleys'), **say something else** (e.g. 'I would like to stay with my aunt in a house in Wales'), or **look it up** in the book or dictionary. **It is OK to make it up!**

- If you are worried about asking a question (e.g. *Qu'est-ce que tu choisis?*), try **answering the question instead** and then asking *et toi?* (e.g. *Moi, je choisis le camping. Et toi?*).

While you're speaking:

- Give yourself time to think by **using hesitation words** like *ah bon, eh bien, alors …* (right, so, well …)
- **Ask others for help** if you get stuck or forget a word, e.g. *Comment dit-on* 'seaside' *en français?*
- **Show you are listening** and keep the conversation going by responding to other people, using phrases like the ones on pages 25–26, e.g. *C'est intéressant, moi aussi, moi, je déteste ça.*

Pronunciation: liaison after *s*

3 **Do these phrases require liaison or not? Listen to check.**

a dans un camping – *yes*
b dans mon sac
c dans une auberge de jeunesse
d dans la salle de classe
e dans une villa
f dans ma chambre
g dans un gîte
h dans ma ville
i dans le désert
j dans un jardin
k dans une cabane dans les arbres

Usually in French you don't pronounce the consonant at the end of words.

However, when the word that follows starts with a vowel you can pronounce the consonant *s* as it makes it sound smoother. Joining the sound of one word onto the sound of another in this way is called *liaison*. It makes *dans un camping* sound like *dans **zun** camping.*

- Vocabulary: revise holiday language
- Grammar: use the perfect tense
- Skills: read for detail

1 **ÉCRIRE**
Fill in the gaps.

a à la m▢▢▢ ▢▢ ag▢▢ ▢▢
b à ▢▢ c▢▢▢ p▢▢▢▢ e
c ▢▢ la ▢▢▢▢ ▢▢▢

d sur ▢▢ b▢▢ e▢▢ ▢▢ de c▢▢▢ ▢▢ siè▢▢ ▢▢
e e▢ v▢▢▢▢ ▢▢
f dans l'e▢▢ ▢▢▢▢ ▢▢▢

2 **LIRE**
Which is the odd one out?

a	il fait beau	IL Y A DU SOLEIL	il neige	IL FAIT CHAUD
b	au Portugal	en Espagne	en France	aux Pays-Bas
c	à la montagne	en ville	à la campagne	dans la forêt
d	faire du ski	faire du trekking	faire une croisière	faire un safari
e	relaxant	AMUSANT	génial	super

3 **LIRE**
Read the texts and match the statements with each person.

Exemple: **a** *Magali*

Philippe: J'adore aller sur la côte d'Azur parce qu'il fait très chaud et j'aime me détendre à la mer.

Magali: D'habitude, je vais en vacances en Allemagne parce que j'aime bien faire des randonnées et j'aime la nature.

Camille: J'aime voyager dans beaucoup de pays différents, mais j'aime aller à la mer en France.

Paul: D'habitude, je pars en vacances en hiver parce que j'aime beaucoup faire du ski.

a I like going hiking when I am on holiday.
b I tend to go on holiday in winter.
c I like to visit lots of different places when I am on holiday.
d I like to relax by the sea.
e I enjoy the countryside when I am holiday.

4 **ÉCRIRE**
Imagine these pictures represent your holiday. Describe it using the pictures and key verbs to help you.

- Where did you go? *D'abord, je suis allé(e) ...*
- What did you do? *Puis j'ai visité/j'ai fait ...*
- What did you eat and drink? *Après, j'ai mangé/j'ai bu ...*
- Did you buy anything? *Aussi, j'ai acheté ...*

- Vocabulary: revise holiday language
- Grammar: correct common errors; combine three tenses
- Skills: develop dictionary skills; read for detail

ECRIRE 1 **Cherche dans le dictionnaire.**

Use your dictionary to find ...

- five new adjectives to describe a holiday
- four new activities you can do on holiday
- three new places where you can stay
- two new countries

LIRE 2 **Corrige les erreurs et puis tradius les phrases en anglais.**

There is one mistake in each sentence. Correct the error and write out the full sentence. Then translate into English.

Exemple: **a** *D'habitude, je vais en vacances ~~au~~ en France –*
Normally I go on holiday to France with my family.

a D'habitude, je vais en vacances au France avec ma famille.
b Ma copine Sarah préfère aller en États-Unis parce qu'elle adore voyager.
c Hier, je visité la tour Eiffel et j'ai acheté des souvenirs.
d J'ai aussi mangé dans un restaurant. C'été délicieux.
e L'année dernière, j'ai allé en vacances en Espagne.
f Par contre, l'année prochaine, je vouloir aller en vacances en Chine avec ma copine Sarah.
g Bretagne ou côte d'Azur? Je choisi la Bretagne.

LIRE 3 **Lis le texte et réponds aux questions.**
Vrai, faux ou pas mentionné?
Exemple: **a** *faux*

a Leïla usually goes on holiday to Morocco. *F*
b She usually goes on holiday with her family.
c Leïla finds staying in a hotel boring.
d She would prefer to stay in a villa with a swimming pool.
e She usually does watersports at the beach.
f Last year they went to Paris.
g She prefers the seaside because it is cooler.
h Next year she is going to Greece with her friends.

Mes vacances   Accueil   Profil   Compte

Salut! Je m'appelle Leïla et j'habite au Maroc. D'habitude, je pars en vacances avec ma famille et nous allons à la mer en Grèce. Nous allons dans un hôtel et c'est très relaxant, mais je préfère une villa avec une piscine parce que c'est plus amusant. J'adore aller à la plage et nager, mais j'aime aussi lire un bon livre.

L'année dernière, je suis allée en France, à Paris et j'ai visité beaucoup de monuments historiques et touristiques. C'était super mais je préfère aller à la mer. Il fait très chaud en ville et j'aime quand il y a du vent à la mer. L'année prochaine, je vais encore aller en Grèce, mais avec mon oncle et ma tante cette fois. Je voudrais aller dans une villa mais nous allons encore à l'hôtel – c'est bien aussi!

LIRE 4 **Traduis le texte en anglais.**

Exemple: *Hi! My name is Leïla and I live in Morocco ...*

ECRIRE 5 **Utilise le texte de Leïla pour décrire les vacances d'Antoine.**

Exemple: *Bonjour! Je m'appelle Antoine et ...*

Le blog de Lucie   Accueil   Profil   Compte

Une grande fête en Belgique: le carnaval de Binche

Au mois de mars, j'ai visité la Belgique et je suis allée au carnaval de Binche. C'est un spectacle extraordinaire. Le festival dure trois jours.

Le premier jour, le dimanche, les Gilles (des habitants de Binche) défilent dans les rues, avec des tambours. Les Gilles portent des costumes spectaculaires. Il y a beaucoup de monde dans les rues. Moi aussi, j'ai dansé.

Le deuxième jour, le lundi, les enfants et les jeunes se déguisent et défilent. J'ai vu des batailles de confettis dans les cafés et dans les rues. Moi aussi, j'ai jeté des confettis. Le soir, j'ai regardé le feu d'artifice. Quand on est rentrés à l'hôtel, vers minuit, on a trouvé des confettis partout, dans nos cheveux, dans nos chaussures…

Le troisième jour, c'est le Mardi Gras, et le jour le plus important du festival. Les Gilles sont masqués et portent d'énormes chapeaux à plumes. Ils dansent et ils jettent des oranges. J'ai attrapé une orange et je l'ai mangée! Pour finir, il y a un magnifique feu d'artifice sur la place.

J'ai adoré ce festival, parce qu'il est très original.

les Gilles	*entertainers at the Binche carnival*
défilent	*march*
les tambours	*drums*
se déguisent	*dress up*
j'ai jeté	*I threw*
Mardi Gras	*Shrove Tuesday*
des chapeaux à plumes	*feathered hats*
ils jettent	*they throw*
j'ai attrapé	*I caught*

1   **Read Lucie's blog entry. She describes her visit to the Binche carnival, and also what she did there. Can you list all the verbs in the perfect tense?**

Exemple: j'ai visité, …

2   **Read Lucie's blog again. Put the actions below in the order in which they happened.**

Exemple: **h** *I went to the carnival, …*

a The entertainers were masked and wore feathered headgear.
b I ate an orange.
c I threw confetti.
d There was a superb fireworks display.
e I got hold of an orange.
f The entertainers threw oranges.
g Young people dressed up and marched.
h I went to the carnival.
i We found confetti in our hair.

Reading skills: cognates

When you read texts about unfamiliar subjects, look for cognates, words that are similar in French and in English, and so easy to guess. How many can you find in this text?

3   **Choose a paragraph in the text and translate it into English.**

Le tour du monde

Regarde l'épisode 7.
Where are Basile and Noura going?
What are they going to do? Answer in English.

Qui emporte quoi?

Exemple: Basile: un appareil photo, ...
Noura: une bouteille d'eau, ...

a un appareil photo
b de l'argent
c une bouteille d'eau
d un casque
e du chocolat
f une couverture
g de la crème solaire
h un jean

i un maillot de bain
j des pantoufles
k un passeport
l du pop-corn
m un pull
n un pyjama
o un sweat
p une veste

Vrai ou faux?
Correct the wrong sentences. Add a detail in English if you can.

Exemple: b C'est faux. Noura ne va pas emporter son maillot de bain.
She will take her pyjamas.

a Pendant son tour du monde, Noura va visiter beaucoup de pays.
b Noura va emporter son maillot de bain.
c Le voyage de Basile, c'est un cadeau d'anniversaire.
d Millau, c'est loin de Montpellier.
e Basile va faire un saut en parachute.
f Basile va emporter des lunettes de soleil.
g Basile va sauter en parachute avec une autre personne.
h Pour son voyage, Noura emporte son passeport.
i Noura va mettre des photos dans la capsule.

Quelles vacances préfères-tu, celles de Basile ou de Noura? Pourquoi?

Exemple: Je préfère les vacances de ... parce que ...

ECOUTER 1 Listen. Copy and fill in the grid. (See pages 112–119.)

	where	who with	type	activities	opinion	ideal holiday
1 Claire	*Spain*	*parents*	*luxury hotel*			
2 Loïc						
3 Julie						
4 Audrey						

PARLER 2 Give a presentation about your holidays. (See pages 112–119.)

You could include:

- where you usually go on holiday:
  D'habitude, je vais en/à/aux/chez …
- where you stay: *On va … On dort …*
- what you like to do on holiday:
  J'aime jouer/faire/visiter …
- where you went last year: *L'année dernière, j'ai visité … je suis allé(e) …*
- what you did: *J'ai visité … J'ai fait … J'ai joué …*
- your opinion: *C'était …*
- where you will/would like go on holiday next year: *L'année prochaine, je vais aller en/au/aux/chez …*

Je m'appelle Morgane et j'habite en France. D'habitude, je vais en vacances au mois de juillet avec ma famille. On part quand je finis l'école et nous allons à la mer en Espagne ou au Portugal pendant deux semaines. C'est vraiment amusant et d'habitude, il fait très chaud et il y a beaucoup de soleil. Nous allons dans une villa avec une piscine et je nage tous les jours. Par contre, je préfère le camping parce qu'on peut jouer au volley-ball et au foot. L'année dernière, j'ai fait beaucoup de randonnée et j'ai aussi fait du vélo. C'était super parce que j'adore le sport! Mes vacances de rêve? J'aimerais aller dans un hôtel de luxe en Espagne. Ça serait très relaxant.

LIRE 3 Read the text and answer the questions in English. (See pages 112–119.)

Exemple: **a** *in July*

- **a** When does Morgane usually go on holiday?
- **b** How long does she go on holiday for?
- **c** What activity does she do every day?
- **d** Why does she prefer staying on a campsite?
- **e** What activities did she do last year?
- **f** Why did she enjoy it?
- **g** Where would she stay on her dream holiday?

ECRIRE 4 Write a letter to your partner school in France describing your holidays. (See pages 112–119.) Aim to include three paragraphs:

- your usual holidays and opinions
- an account of your last holiday
- a description of your ideal holiday

Use the prompts in activity 3.

Develop your answer as much as you can.

Some connectives. → Connectives and time expressions. → Reasons and opinions.

Vocabulaire

Going on holiday

Où vas-tu en vacances?	Where do you go on holiday?
à la campagne	in/to the countryside
à la mer/au bord de la mer	by/to the seaside
à la montagne	in/to the mountains
chez mes grands-parents	at my grandparents' house
en ville	in town
une auberge de jeunesse	a youth hostel
un bateau de croisière	a cruise ship
un camping	a campsite
un gîte	holiday cottage
un hôtel	a hotel
une villa	a villa
se baigner/nager	to swim
choisir	to choose
dormir	to stay overnight
faire des randonnées	to go hiking
faire du vélo	to go cycling
finir	to end, finish

Holiday essentials

Qu'est-ce que tu vas prendre?	What are you going to take?
un ballon	ball
ma batte de cricket	my cricket bat
mes BD	my comics
un bon livre	a good book
une carte	a map
une carte postale	a postcard
ma casquette	my baseball cap
de la crème solaire	sun cream
mon frisbee	my frisbee
mon jean préféré	my favourite jeans
mon lecteur MP4	my MP4 player
mes lunettes de soleil	my sunglasses
mon maillot de bain	my swimming costume/ swimming trunks
mon maquillage	my make-up
mon portable	my mobile phone

Dream holidays

Quelles sont tes vacances de rêve?	What is your dream holiday?
explorer des planètes	to explore planets
faire une croisière	to go on a cruise
faire un safari	to go on a safari
faire du trekking	to go trekking
me détendre sur une île	to relax on an island
dans la forêt tropicale	in a tropical rainforest
dans l'espace	in space
dans une cabane dans la forêt	in a forest cabin

aux Caraïbes	in the Caribbean
aux États-Unis	in the USA
aux Seychelles	in the Seychelles
en Afrique	in Africa
un vaisseau spatial	spaceship

Activities in the past

Qu'est-ce que tu as fait?	What did you do?
j'ai acheté	I bought
j'ai bu	I drank
j'ai fait	I did
j'ai joué	I played
j'ai mangé	I ate
j'ai trouvé	I found
j'ai visité	I visited
j'ai voyagé	I travelled
j'ai vu	I saw
je suis allé(e)	I went
je suis rentré(e)	I came back home
c'était	it was

Sequencing words

d'habitude	usually
hier	yesterday
(tout) d'abord	first of all
puis	then
ensuite	then
après	after
pour finir	finally

◉ Grammar and skills: I can…

- ◉ use *choisir*, *finir* and *prendre*
- ◉ use the near future
- ◉ use *je voudrais* and *j'aimerais*
- ◉ form and use the perfect tense with *avoir*
- ◉ use *aller* in the perfect tense
- ◉ use time expressions and work out tenses
- ◉ use strategies to improve reading skills
- ◉ work out grammar patterns

8.1 Tu aimes le sport?

- Vocabulary: talk about sports you like and do
- Grammar: practise *jouer* and *faire* with different activities; use *depuis*
- Skills: remember grammar rules; use reading skills

 1 Écoute les phrases (1–10). Mets les images dans l'ordre.

Exemple: **1** e

a
Je joue au tennis.

b
Je fais du skate.

c
Je fais de la voile.

d
Je joue au hand.

e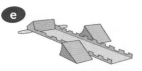
Je fais de l'athlétisme.

f
Je fais de la planche à voile.

g
Je joue au hockey sur glace.

h
Je fais du VTT.

i
Je joue au basket.

j
Je ne fais pas de sport.

 2 Réponds aux questions. A↔B.

Exemple: Tu joues (au foot)? – Oui, je joue (au foot).
Tu fais (de la natation)? – Non, je ne fais pas (de natation).

◎ Can you add a reason?

 3 Écoute. Quels sports fais-tu? Recopie et
remplis la grille.

	Karen 🇬🇧	Luke 🇬🇧	Aïsha	Brice
netball	✓			
swimming				
basketball				
athletics				
badminton				
hockey				
handball				
tennis				
➕ extra details	netball: at school with friends			

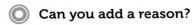

ne ... ni ... ni   *neither ... nor*

Grammaire p. 168–169

Jouer or faire?

When you talk about sports, use *jouer* for sports using a ball or *faire* for all other sports.

je joue tu joues il/elle/on joue	(à + le) → **au**	tennis
	(à + la) → **à la**	pétanque
	(à + les) → **aux**	boules
je fais tu fais il/elle/on fait	(de + le) → **du**	canoë
	(de + la) → **de la**	natation
	(de + l') → **de l'**	équitation

Remembering grammar rules

A Venn diagram can help to highlight the differences and similarities between grammatical structures.

du / de l' / de la
au / à l' / à la

Copy out this diagram, then write the names of sports in the correct part.

See page 105 for grammar memorisation strategies.

Lis et traduis les expressions soulignées.
Exemple: je suis canadien – I am Canadian

Les jeunes et le sport

Bonjour! Je m'appelle Kévin <u>et je suis canadien</u>. Le hockey sur glace, <u>c'est ma passion</u>. Je fais du hockey <u>depuis l'âge de six ans</u>. Je joue pour l'équipe de Québec City! <u>Mon équipe préférée</u>, c'est Montréal Canadiens. En plus, je joue au basket le lundi soir avec des copains.

Je m'appelle Cristina et <u>je ne suis pas sportive</u>. Je n'aime ni le basket ni le foot, je déteste tous les sports. Au collège, <u>j'ai deux heures de sport</u> par semaine mais c'est fatigant et j'ai horreur de ça. Le sport, c'est nul!

Je suis Mackenzie et je suis fan de foot. <u>Mon joueur préféré</u>, c'est David Beckham. <u>Je joue pour l'équipe du collège</u>. J'ai un entraînement tous les mercredis après-midi et <u>on a des matchs le week-end</u>. Je fais aussi de l'athlétisme et du tennis. C'est super et passionnant!

un joueur *player*
une équipe *team*
fatigant *tiring*
un entraînement *training session*

Je joue	au tennis/foot/rugby/handball/ basket/cricket/hockey/ badminton/golf	une/deux fois par semaine/mois. depuis deux ans.
Je ne joue pas/jamais		
Je fais	du surf/skate/karaté de la natation/voile/planche à voile de l'athlétisme/escalade	toutes les semaines.
Je ne fais pas de skate/de voile. Je ne fais pas de sport.		
J'ai	un entraînement	tous les jours/soirs/ mercredis.

⚙ Grammaire WB p.29

Depuis

Depuis means 'for' or 'since'. The verb is in the <u>present tense</u>:
*Je <u>joue</u> au hand **depuis** deux ans.* – I have been playing handball **for** two years.
*Je <u>fais</u> de la voile **depuis** l'âge de cinq ans.* – I have been sailing **since** the age of five.

 Écris un paragraphe sur les sports que tu fais. Utilise les expressions de l'activité 4.
Exemple: Je joue au … , c'est ma passion. J'ai un entraînement le jeudi.

You must include:
• how long you have been doing it
• when you train
• whether you play for a team
• which team or players you like.

◎ **Use opinions, reasons, connectives and time expressions.**

✚ **Can you include more than one tense?**

Plenary

Work in pairs. A chooses a sport, B makes a sentence. Swap over.

⭐ Make a simple sentence.
◎ Include a time expression.
✚ Include a time expression and extra details.

Comment on your partner's performance:
• Are they using *jouer* and *faire* correctly?
• Are they adding extra details?
• Are they speaking without hesitation?
• Do they have a good French accent?

8.2 Sports d'été ou sports d'hiver?

- Vocabulary: talk about winter and summer sports
- Grammar: use *je voudrais/j'aimerais*
- Skills: recycle language in a different context; answer questions

f
du canoë-kayak

1

C'est un sport d'hiver ou un sport d'été? Écoute et vérifie.

Exemple: sports d'hiver *: a, ... sports d'été* *: ...*

J'aime faire ...

a

du ski acrobatique

b

du canyoning

c

du patin à glace

d

du quad

e

de la plongée

g

du VTT

h

du snowboard

2

Écoute (1-5). Recopie et remplis la grille.

			sports	other details
1 Jaouen	✓		skiing	with family every year
2 Inès				

3

Répète le dialogue avec ton/ta partenaire. Change les mots **en *italique*.**

Exemple: **A** Tu aimes les sports *d'hiver*?
B *Oui, j'adore faire du ski.*
A Quels sports *d'hiver* tu préfères?
B Je préfère *faire du ski mais j'aime aussi le snowboard.*
A Pourquoi?
B Parce que *c'est passionnant/j'aime la neige!*
A Tu fais souvent *du ski*?
B Oui, je fais *du ski tous les hivers avec ma famille.*

J'aime/Je préfère ... parce que	c'est cool/intéressant/différent. j'adore la mer/les poissons.	
J'aime faire du/de la/de l' ...		
Je fais ...	toutes les semaines/tous les étés	au collège/avec mes copines/avec ma sœur.

Answering questions

Give as much detail as you can when answering questions in speech or writing.

- Use connectives, time expressions and opinions with reasons to extend your sentences.
- Include different tenses.
- Ask a question back: *Et toi?* – And you?

See pages 51 and 123 for further strategies and Workbook, page 27.

4 **Lis le mail de Maxence et réponds aux questions.**

Exemple: **a** *3 days*

Sujet: Sports d'hiver

Salut!

Je suis dans les Alpes depuis trois jours. <u>La neige est super bonne</u>. J'adore les sports d'hiver et je fais du ski <u>toute la journée</u>. J'adore skier sur les pistes rouges. C'est cool et passionnant! Demain, je voudrais faire une piste noire <u>avec mon moniteur</u>. <u>J'ai un peu peur</u> mais je suis très excité. Le soir, on mange au resto ou on va au ciné. <u>Je me couche tôt</u> parce que je suis fatigué. <u>Ce week-end</u>, je voudrais faire du snowboard et de la motoneige avec mon père!

> passionnant   *exciting*
> un moniteur   *(skiing) instructor*
> une motoneige   *snowmobile*

a How long has Maxence been in the Alps?
b Which colour piste does he normally use?
c What is he going to do tomorrow?
d How does he feel about it?
e What does he do in the evening?
f Which sports would he like to do?

 Translate the underlined phrases.

Grammaire WB p.42

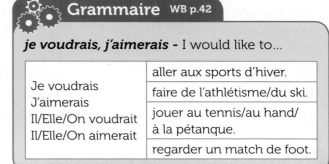

je voudrais, j'aimerais - I would like to...

	aller aux sports d'hiver.
Je voudrais	faire de l'athlétisme/du ski.
J'aimerais	jouer au tennis/au hand/
Il/Elle/On voudrait	à la pétanque.
Il/Elle/On aimerait	regarder un match de foot.

5 **Écoute. Recopie et remplis la grille (1–5). Que fait chaque personne? Que voudrait faire chaque personne?**

	★ what activity they do now	◉ what they would like to do	✚ other details
1	*dance, ...*	*hip-hop ...*	
2			

6 **Choisis deux personnes de l'activité 5 et écris un paragraphe.**

Exemple: *Je m'appelle Axelle, je fais de la danse mais je voudrais faire du hip-hop.*

★ **Describe what you do and would like to do:** *Je fais ...* *Je voudrais faire ...*

◉ **Add connectives, opinions and reasons:** *C'est cool, parce que ...*

✚ **Add time expressions and other tenses:** *Ce week-end, je vais ...*

Plenary

Evaluate your use of reading strategies in activity 4. Did you use language that you knew already to work out the meaning of new sentences?

★ Say a sport you like or don't like. Say if it is a winter/summer sport.

◉ Add a reason.

✚ Add what you would like to do.

- Vocabulary: describe leisure activities and talk about active holidays
- Grammar: practise using *aller* in the perfect tense
- Skills: develop confidence in using different tenses

Vacances actives

Le centre aéré est ouvert tous les jours (sauf le week-end) pendant les vacances.

Tu aimes bouger? Tu veux essayer une nouvelle activité, faire un stage sportif? Le centre aéré est pour toi!

De 10h à 11h30 et de 14h à 17h

Prix: 10€ par jour

Des vacances actives, c'est super!

	Matin	Après-midi
Lundi	10h zumba	14h danse hip-hop
Mardi	10h tir à l'arc	14h course d'orientation
Mercredi	10h à 17h course au trésor (pique-nique compris)	
Jeudi	10h balle aux prisonniers	14h atelier de dessin
Vendredi	10h atelier théâtre	14h yoga

1 Lis la brochure. Vrai, faux ou pas mentionné?

ouvert	*open*	compris	*included*
essayer	*to try*	un atelier	*workshop*

Exemple: **a** *faux*

a Le centre aéré est ouvert le samedi matin.
b Le hip-hop, c'est le lundi matin.
c La course au trésor est le mercredi matin et après-midi.
d Il y a un feu de camp le jeudi.

e Le centre est ouvert à midi le lundi.
f C'est douze euros par jour.
g Il y a un atelier musique.
h Le yoga, c'est le vendredi matin.

◎ **Translate the sentences a–h into English.**

✚ **Correct the sentences: a** *Le centre n'est pas ouvert le samedi matin.*

2 Regarde la brochure. C'est quand? A↔B.

Exemple: **A** *La zumba, c'est quel jour?*
B *C'est le lundi.*
A *À quelle heure?*
B *À dix heures.*

3 Écoute. Quelles activités font-ils? Recopie la grille et réponds en anglais.

	Monday	Tuesday	Wednesday	Thursday	Friday	other details
Maeva		archery				difficult but brilliant
Thomas						
Justine						
Bastien						

◎ **Choose a speaker and transcribe what they say:**
Maeva – Je vais au centre aéré et je …

Lis les messages et réponds aux questions en anglais.

Exemple: **a** *two weeks*

a How long is Oliver's course?
b What do they do in the morning?
c Where did he go last year?
d What did he do?
e Who did he see?
f How long is Morgane's camp?
g Name two activities she does.
h What did she do last week?

Qu'est-ce que tu fais pendant les vacances?   Accueil   Profil   Compte

Salut! Cette année, pendant les vacances, je vais dans un centre aéré. Je fais un stage de baseball pendant deux semaines. C'est génial. On a deux heures d'entraînement le matin et l'après-midi, on a des matchs. L'année dernière, je suis allé à Montréal et j'ai fait un stage de hockey sur glace. J'ai vu l'équipe des Canadiens, c'était fantastique!

Oliver, Québec, Canada

Moi, je vais en colonie de vacances en Bretagne pendant un mois. Mon frère va en colonie aussi mais il va en Provence! La Bretagne, c'est super. On va à la plage, on fait des feux de camp, on fait des courses au trésor, on joue à la balle aux prisonniers. La semaine dernière, on est allés à la plage et on a fait de la voile avec les moniteurs. C'était super difficile mais j'ai adoré.

Morgane, France

un stage   *course*
une colonie de vacances
summer camp

 Écris un paragraphe sur tes vacances de cette année et de l'année dernière.

Write a paragraph about your holidays this year and last year. See page 141 for strategies to check written work.

Exemple: *Cette année, je fais un stage de tennis.*
L'année dernière, je suis allé(e) au centre aéré ...

D'habitude, Toutes les semaines, Tous les mardis, Tous les week-ends, Tous les étés/hivers,	je vais ... je fais ... je joue ...
L'année dernière, Hier, L'été/L'hiver dernier, La semaine dernière,	je suis allé(e) ... j'ai fait ... j'ai joué ...

Plenary

Prepare a short presentation on sports and leisure.

⭐ Say the sports you do at school.
◎ Add what you did last summer.
➕ Add what you would like to do later on.

Now listen to your partner's presentation and assess his/her performance. Listen for:
• a good French accent
• tenses used well
• a good variety of vocabulary.

8.4 Aïe, j'ai mal!

- Vocabulary: name parts of the body and talk about injuries caused by sporting activities
- Grammar: use *j'ai mal* + parts of the body; use *je peux/je ne peux pas*
- Skills: use correct pronunciation; build longer sentences using *parce que* and *donc*

Écoute et trouve la phrase.

Exemple: **1** *f*

Qu'est-ce que tu as?
Utilise les phrases de l'activité 1. A↔B.

Exemple: **A** *Qu'est-ce que tu as?*
B *J'ai mal à la tête.*
A *C'est a!*

Pronouncing vowels

Watch out for vowel sounds when pronouncing the parts of the body. Look back at page 13 to help you.

Lis le texte. Qui a quoi?
Who's got what?

Exemple: **a** *Mum*

- **a** a headache
- **b** a bad arm
- **c** a backache
- **d** a bad knee
- **e** a bad foot
- **f** nothing wrong

a J'ai mal à la tête.

b J'ai mal à l'épaule.

c J'ai mal au bras.

d J'ai mal à la jambe.

h J'ai mal au dos.

g J'ai mal au genou.

f J'ai mal à la cheville.

e J'ai mal au pied.

La famille Catastrophe

Oh là là, quelle catastrophe! Toute ma famille va mal: mon père a mal au dos parce qu'il joue beaucoup à la pétanque! Mon petit frère a mal au pied depuis son match de football, ma demi-sœur a mal au genou (elle fait du hip-hop) et moi, j'ai mal au bras depuis deux jours après mon match de badminton. Maintenant, ma mère a vraiment mal à la tête mais … mon chien Youpi va très bien!

Jules

Can you find two reasons for their injuries?
How long has Jules been in pain for?

Écoute les interviews (1–6). Recopie et remplis la grille.

	sport	injury	since when?
1	rugby	bad foot	for 3 days
2			

Nathan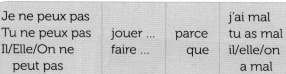

> Je ne peux pas jouer au rugby parce que j'ai mal au pied depuis trois jours.

 Lis et choisis la bonne réponse.

a Lilou goes to aerobics on a <u>Monday</u>/Tuesday/Saturday.
b Her teacher has *a bad ankle/a bad back/a bad knee*.
c Sophie has had a bad knee for *two days/three days/two weeks*.
d Lilou went to taekwondo on *Friday afternoon/Friday evening/Thursday evening*.
e She has a bad *shoulder/arm/leg*.
f She has a tennis match on *Friday/Saturday/Sunday*.

> Ma semaine catastrophe!
> <u>Le lundi</u>, d'habitude, j'ai <u>une heure d'aérobic</u>. Malheureusement, le prof était absent parce qu'il a <u>mal au dos</u>! Ma copine Sophie a <u>mal au genou</u> depuis <u>trois jours</u> donc on ne peut pas <u>jouer au tennis</u>! <u>Vendredi soir</u>, j'ai fait <u>deux heures de taekwondo</u> et maintenant, j'ai <u>mal au bras</u>. J'ai <u>un match de tennis dimanche</u> mais je ne peux pas jouer parce que j'ai trop mal! C'est nul!
> Lilou

 Grammaire p. 168

Pouvoir

je peux aller – I can go
tu peux jouer – you can play
il/elle/on peut faire – he/she/we can do
To make a sentence like this negative, you wrap *ne ... pas* around *peux/peut*:
*Je **ne** peux **pas** jouer au badminton demain.* – I cannot play badminton tomorrow.

 Imagine une 'semaine catastrophe'.
Use the text in activity 5 but change the underlined expressions.

Je ne peux pas Tu ne peux pas Il/Elle/On ne peut pas	jouer ... faire ...	parce que	j'ai mal tu as mal il/elle/on a mal	au dos/pied. à la tête. à l'épaule.

J'ai mal Tu as mal Il/Elle/On a mal	donc	je ne peux pas tu ne peux pas il/elle/on ne peut pas	jouer ... faire ...

 Lis ton texte de l'activité 6 tout haut. A↔B.
Read your text aloud to each other. Assess each other's performance:
• Good accent?
• Used *je peux* and *je ne peux pas*?
• Spoke fluently?

Plenary

In pairs, create sentences. Say them aloud to each other. Assess your performances.

⭐ Make a simple sentence: *J'ai mal au pied.*

◉ Add a reason: *Je ne peux pas faire de natation parce que j'ai mal au bras.*

➕ Include a past tense: *Hier, j'ai joué ... et maintenant, j'ai mal au pied.*

Décris les problèmes de Paul et Marie Catastrophe.
Exemple: Paul a mal au bras, ...
Il ne peut pas ...

◉ **Add a time phrase, a connective or an opinion:**
Il a mal au bras depuis deux jours./Il a mal au bras, donc il ne peut pas jouer au rugby.

➕ **Add a reason in the perfect tense:** *Il a mal au bras depuis deux jours parce qu'il a joué au tennis.*

8.5 *Les stars du sport*

- Vocabulary: talk about sports personalities and international events
- Grammar: practise using *il/elle* with different verbs
- Skills: read for detail

 1 **Lis l'article et réponds aux questions.**

Exemple: **a** *Spanish*

a What nationality is Nadal?
b Which sports does he enjoy? (three details)
c When did he win his first title?
d Where was Bolt born?

e When did he start athletics?
f What other sports does he like?
g What nationality is Jessica's mother?
h When did she start athletics?

Les stars du sport

Rafaël Nadal est espagnol. Il est né le 3 juin 1986. Il a une sœur qui s'appelle Maria. Il aime le football et le basket mais son sport préféré, c'est le tennis. À treize ans, il gagne le championnat du monde des 13–14 ans! Maintenant, c'est un grand champion de tennis.

Usain Bolt est né le 21 août 1986 en Jamaïque. Il commence l'athlétisme à six ans. Il joue aussi au football et au cricket. Il a gagné 16 médailles aux Jeux olympiques de Londres de 2012.

Jessica Ennis-Hill est née le 28 janvier 1986 à Sheffield, en Angleterre. Sa mère est anglaise et son père est jamaïcain. Elle fait de l'athlétisme depuis l'âge de dix ans. Elle a participé aux Jeux olympiques de 2012 et elle a gagné la médaille d'or de l'heptathlon (sept épreuves).

une épreuve   *event*

⭐ **Pair work. A names a celebrity and B gives one detail:**

Exemple: **A** *Nadal.*
B *Il est espagnol.*

◎ **Give two or three details:** *Il est espagnol et il adore le tennis.*

➕ **Give more than three details:** *Il est espagnol. Il adore le tennis. Il est né en 1986. Il aime le foot.*

PARLER 2

C'est vrai ou c'est faux? A↔B.
Using the text in activity 1, make up a statement.
Your partner decides if it is true or false.

Exemple: **A** *Nadal est anglais.*
B *Non, c'est faux.*

Give the right answer: *Non, il est espagnol.*

ECRIRE 3

Écris un article sur Andy Murray. Fais des recherches sur Internet.
See page 141 for strategies to check written work.

Il/Elle est né(e)	le ... en ... à ...
Il/Elle a	X frère(s)/sœur(s) qui s'appelle(nt) ...
Il/Elle commence à	faire/jouer ...
Il/Elle aime	le rugby ...
Il/Elle a gagné	un tournoi/une médaille ...

Can you add your own opinion on Murray? *J'adore Murray parce que c'est un super joueur de tennis.*

Choose your favourite sportsperson, research their life and prepare a short presentation.

ECOUTER 4

Écoute et trouve les mots.

Les Jeux paralympiques sont des Jeux **1** *olympiques* pour les athlètes handicapés. C'est tous les **2** ______ ans comme les Jeux olympiques. C'est un évènement très **3** ______ . Il y a des **4** ______ en fauteuils roulants **5** ______ jouent au basket, au tennis, des **6** ______ malvoyantes ou malentendantes qui **7** ______ de l'athlétisme ou du foot. C'est incroyable. Ils sont excellents et très **8** ______ !

un fauteuil roulant *wheelchair*
malvoyant *visually impaired*
malentendant *hard of hearing*

courageux font ~~olympiques~~ important
personnes quatre qui sportifs

With a partner translate the article above into English.

Plenary

In a group of four, choose a famous sportsperson to describe. Each student describes a different aspect. Then have a discussion to check that group work skills are continually improving.

- Describe him/her: nationality ...
- Add what he/she likes.
- Add what he/she has done.

8.6 Labo-langue

Depuis

1 **Put the words in the right order then translate the sentences into English.**

Exemple: **a** *Ma sœur fait de la danse depuis quatre ans.*

a sœur fait ans ma la danse depuis de quatre.
b fais dernière de natation je depuis l'année la.
c jouent foot ils depuis minutes au vingt.
d copain fait de depuis mon athlétisme mois deux l'.
e fait un la voile depuis de mois on.
f frère au mon depuis joue rugby 2012.

> *Depuis* is always used with the present tense:
> *Je joue au foot depuis un an.* – I have been playing football for a year.
> *Je vais au centre aéré depuis lundi.* – I have been going to the youth centre since Monday.
>
> *depuis mardi* – since Tuesday
> *depuis deux jours* – for two days

Je voudrais, j'aimerais

2 **Translate the following sentences.**

Exemple: **a** *Je voudrais faire du ski./J'aimerais faire du ski.*

a I would like to go skiing.
b He would like to go to a summer camp.
c Would you like to play tennis?
d I would like to go ice skating.
e My dad would like to play badminton with me.
f Nadal would like to play football.

> *Je voudrais* and *j'aimerais* are both followed by the infinitive of the verb:
>
> *J'aimerais faire du karaté./Je voudrais faire du karaté.* – I would like to do karate.
>
> | j'aimerais | aller, faire, jouer, visiter |
> | il/elle/on aimerait | ... |
>
> To ask a question, say *Tu voudrais/Tu aimerais ... regarder un match de hockey?*

Aller in the present and in the perfect

3 **Fill in with the present tense.**

a Elle ___*va*___ au tournoi de tennis.
b Je _____ au match de foot.
c Vous _____ au stage de rugby?
d Mon frère _____ en colonie.
e Ils _____ au tournoi de hand.
f Tu _____ au centre aéré?

4 **Fill in with the perfect tense.**

a Marie et Max sont _____ au centre aéré.
b Mon frère est _____ en colonie.
c Mes sœurs sont _____ au stade.
d Mes amis sont _____ à Rome.
e Léa et Laura, vous êtes _____ à la mer?

> *Aller* (to go) is an irregular verb.
>
> It forms its perfect tense with the **present tense of *être* + the past participle**.
>
> With *être*, the past participle agrees with the gender (masculine/feminine) and number (singular/plural) of the subject.

	present	perfect	
		masculine	feminine
sing.	je vais	je suis allé	je suis allée
	tu vas	tu es allé	tu es allée
	il/elle va	il est allé	elle est allée
pl.	on va	on est allés	on est allées
	nous allons	nous sommes allés	nous sommes allées
	vous allez	vous êtes allés	vous êtes allées
	ils/elles vont	ils sont allés	elles sont allées

Describing aches and pains

5 **What is wrong? Write sentences.**

Exemple: **a** *J'ai mal au genou.*

a Je …

b Tu … ?

c Elle …

d Il …

e Ils …

f Elles …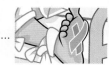

You use *avoir mal* to describe aches and pains.

j'ai tu as il/elle/on a nous avons vous avez ils/elles ont	mal	**au** dos
		au pied
		au bras
		au genou
		à la tête
		à la cheville
		à l'épaule
		aux dents

J'ai mal au pied. – My foot hurts.

Samuel a mal à la tête. – Samuel has got a headache.

Tu as mal au genou? – Have you got a sore knee?

Strategies for checking written work

Use these strategies with activity 3, page 139.

Now you've written about Andy Murray, try writing a new draft, checking your work afterwards just like you do in English lessons.

How do you go about checking your work in French? How many strategies can your class come up with? Which of the following does the class already use?

1 **Take a break** after you've written your text, then **come back** and **look at it again** fresh.

2 **Read it through** a few times, each time concentrating on something different:

- **Does it make sense**? *Andy j'aime le foot* doesn't make sense in French. Translate it back again into English to check.
- Does the **spelling** look right? Is it *sœur* or *souer*?
- Does it **sound right**, for example *Il a une frère*?

3 Pay attention to the mistakes you tend to make a lot, for example is it *grand* or *grande*, *il* or *elle*?

4 Try to spot what you may have got wrong, and look it up, using the dictionary strategies on page 114 and the grammar in the Labo-langue sections.

Pronunciation: distinguishing between present and perfect

6 **You have to listen carefully to distinguish between the present and the perfect tense. Try to pronounce these verbs, then listen and repeat.**

a je joue; j'ai joué
b je danse; j'ai dansé
c je regarde; j'ai regardé
d je gagne; j'ai gagné

7 **Listen (a–f): present tense or perfect tense?**

Exemple: **a** *perfect*

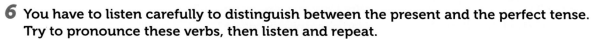

8.7 Extra Star

- Vocabulary: practise using vocabulary related to sports
- Grammar: use the correct verb with sports, *jouer* or *faire*
- Skills: use a reading text as a basis for writing

1 Fill in the missing letters and find 12 words for sports.

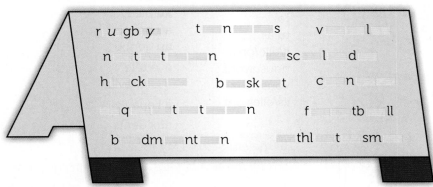

r u gb y   t n   s   v   l
n   t   t   n   sc   l   d
h   ck   b   sk   t   c   n
    q   t   t   n   f   tb   ll
    b   dm   nt   n   thl   t   sm

2 Read and fill in the correct prepositions from the box.

a Je fais _de_ _la_ natation.
b Je joue _____ badminton.
c Il fait _____ _____ escalade.
d Je fais _____ _____ planche à voile.

e Je fais _____ _____ danse.
f Je fais _____ ski.
g Je joue _____ hand.
h Je joue _____ _____ pétanque.

> au   à la   du
> de l'   de la

3 Read Léa's email and answer the questions in English.

Exemple: **a** in a summer camp in the Alps

> colo = colonie de vacances
> *summer camp*
> plein   *loads*

Sujet: Super, la colo!

Bonjour! Je suis en colo dans les Alpes depuis une semaine.
On fait plein d'activités! On fait de l'escalade, de la voile
sur le lac, de l'équitation. C'est génial.
Hier, j'ai fait du canyoning! C'était la première fois.
Aïe aïe aïe, c'était effrayant ☺. J'ai aussi joué au
badminton avec mon copain Youssef. C'est vraiment
top, la colo, j'adore ça.

Bisous, Léa

a Where is Léa?
b How long has she been there?
c Name two sports they do.

d What did she do yesterday?
e Had she done it before?
f What other sport did she do?

4 Imagine you are in a summer camp. Write an email to your family. Change the underlined expressions in Léa's email.

Exemple: Je suis en colo <u>dans le Kent</u> depuis <u>trois jours</u> …

- Vocabulary: practise using vocabulary related to sports
- Grammar: use the correct verb with sports, *jouer* or *faire*
- Skills: understand longer passages; appreciate cultural differences

1 **Complète les phrases avec *joue* ou *fais*.**

a Je … au tennis.   c Je … à la pétanque.   e Je … de la natation.   g Je … aux boules.

b Je … de l'escalade.   d Je … de la danse.   f Je … de la voile.   h Je … du karaté.

2 **Lis. Recopie et remplis la grille en anglais.**

| le saut à l'élastique | bungee jumping |
| le parapente | paragliding |

Alisée

J'habite à Genève, en Suisse. Je suis très sportive. Je joue au hand tous les mardis soirs et je fais de la danse depuis l'âge de six ans. L'été dernier, je suis allée en colonie pendant un mois et on a fait du saut à l'élastique. C'était incroyable! J'aimerais bien aller aux sports d'hiver et faire du ski l'année prochaine!

Noah

Je suis de la Guadeloupe. J'aimerais beaucoup faire du ski mais ici, c'est impossible parce qu'il fait trop chaud! Je joue souvent au foot avec mes copains et comme j'habite au bord de la mer, on fait aussi de la plongée. Hier, j'ai joué au beach-volley sur la plage avec mes copains.

Lucy

Je suis canadienne. Ici, on peut faire beaucoup de sports d'hiver comme le ski, le patin à glace, le hockey. Je joue au hockey toutes les semaines dans l'équipe du collège. L'été dernier, j'ai fait du parapente avec mon père. C'était génial. J'aimerais faire de l'équitation parce que j'adore les chevaux.

	sports they do	sport they did	sport they would like to do
Alisée	*handball*		
Lucy			
Noah			

3 **Écris un mail. Utilise le vocabulaire de l'activité 2.**

Exemple: Je m'appelle Yannick, j'ai 13 ans … Aujourd'hui, je …
Hier, j'ai … J'aimerais …

	Yannick colonie de vacances Biarritz, France	Aujourd'hui	
Hier		J'aimerais …	

Léa Romain

En juin 2013, Léa Romain a gagné le championnat de France de tennis des 13–14 ans à Roland-Garros. Portrait d'une apprentie championne.

Léa Romain joue au tennis depuis qu'elle est petite. Son père, Florent, est professeur de tennis. Dès son plus jeune âge, Florent a emmené sa fille sur les courts de tennis. Comme elle aimait ça, elle a continué.

Léa s'entraîne beaucoup et en avril 2013, elle gagne plusieurs matches dans le tournoi Tennis Europe. Elle est parmi les 100 meilleures joueuses au monde. En juin 2013, Léa remporte le championnat de France de tennis des 13–14 ans.

Le secret du succès? Le père de Léa pense qu'il faut du talent, mais aussi beaucoup d'autres choses. Il faut de la ténacité et beaucoup de travail. Il faut aussi une famille qui aide et qui soutient. Il faut bien sûr un bon entraîneur.

Alors Léa travaille très dur. Elle s'entraîne tous les jours avec son père, plusieurs heures par jour. Elle dit: "Mon père est un entraîneur exigeant, mais il est aussi super gentil!"

Par contre, Léa ne va pas au collège, elle étudie par correspondance. Elle veut améliorer son anglais, pour pouvoir parler avec d'autres joueurs.

Pour se détendre, Léa collectionne les peluches, elle lit et elle aime bien regarder les séries télévisées. Elle passe du temps avec sa famille, par exemple son frère Rémi et sa petite cousine Inès. Inès aussi joue bien au tennis! Une autre future championne dans la famille?

emmener	*to take*
le tournoi	*tournament*
remporter	*to win*
le championnat	*championship*
la ténacité	*persistence*
qui aide	*who helps*
qui soutient	*who supports*
étudier par correspondance	
to do distance-learning	

Read the article about Léa. True or false? Correct the false statements.

Exemple: **a** *false – Léa has been playing tennis since she was small.*

a Léa started playing tennis at the age of 10.
b In June 2013, she won a very important match.
c Léa's father is also her coach.
d Léa also plays tennis at school.
e Léa learns English to be able to read books and magazines.
f At home, Léa keeps many toys.
g Léa's brother and sister are called Rémi and Inès.

Find the matching phrase or sentence.

Exemple: **a** *depuis qu'elle est petite*

a since she was small
b from her youngest age
c as she liked that, she carried on
d you need persistence

e she wants to improve
f to be able to speak with other players
g collects soft toys
h she spends time with her family

Le hockey sur glace

 Regarde l'épisode 8.
Where are Zaied and Clarisse?
Who is Geoffrey? Answer in English.

 Qui fait quelle activité?

Exemple: **a** *Zaied*

a les sports d'hiver
b le hockey sur glace
c le football
d la boxe
e la danse
f le jogging
g l'entraînement au gymnase

 Choisis la bonne réponse.

a Zaied joue au foot <u>tous les soirs</u>/tous les samedis/tous les week-ends.
b Son sport préféré, c'est le foot/la boxe/les sports d'hiver.
c Clarisse fait de la danse depuis trois ans/quatre ans/quatre mois.
d Geoffrey aime le hockey parce que c'est dangereux/un sport sur glace/très rapide.
e Il joue souvent le samedi/le dimanche/pendant la semaine.
f Son ambition, c'est de voyager en avion/jouer pour l'équipe nationale/entraîner d'autres joueurs.
g Il s'entraîne deux jours par semaine/cinq jours par semaine/tous les jours.
h Zaied invite Geoffrey à jouer au foot/faire du judo/faire un jogging.

 Qui parle, Zaied, Clarisse ou Geoffrey? Attention: quelquefois, il y a deux bonnes réponses.
Exemple: **a** *Zaied*
a Mon sport préféré, c'est la boxe.
b Je n'ai pas le temps de jouer au foot.
c Le hockey sur glace, c'est dangereux.
d Je voudrais essayer le hockey.
e Je pratique mon sport depuis quatre ans.
f Les matchs, c'est surtout l'hiver.

 Tu aimes les sports rapides comme les sports d'hiver ou le hockey? Tu préfères les sports moins dangereux, comme la natation ou le jogging? Discute en groupe.
Exemple: Je préfère ...

ECOUTER 1 Listen to the four speakers. Copy and fill in the grid in English. (See pages 130–137.)

	Mathias	Karim	Sabrina	Yasmina
Sports	*basketball*			
When/How often?				
What would they like to do?				
Other details				

PARLER 2 Discuss your favourite sports with a partner. A↔B. (See pages 130–137.)

- Quels sports fais-tu d'habitude? *Je joue/Je fais …*
- Tu fais … depuis quand? *Je fais … depuis …*
- Quel sport aimerais-tu faire? *J'aimerais/Je voudrais …*
- Qui est ton sportif préféré? *J'aime … parce qu'il/elle est …*
- Quel sport as-tu fait hier/la semaine dernière? *J'ai fait/joué … Je suis allé(e) …*

LIRE 3 Read Aziz's mail and answer the questions in English. (See pages 130–137.)

Exemple: **a** *2 weeks*

Sujet: Stage sportif

Salut! Je suis en stage sportif en Suisse depuis deux semaines. C'est super parce qu'on joue au volley ou au basket tous les matins et l'après-midi, on va au lac et on fait de la voile ou de la planche à voile! Mon copain Paul ne peut pas faire de sport en ce moment parce qu'il a mal au genou depuis deux jours. C'est nul! Le soir, on fait des feux de camp ou des courses au trésor, c'est vraiment génial. La semaine prochaine, on va regarder le Tour de France. Je voudrais voir le champion 2013, Chris Froome, il est fantastique!

Aziz

a How long has Aziz been at his sports camp?
b What activities do they do in the afternoons?
c What is wrong with Paul?
d What do they do in the evenings?
e What would Aziz like to do next week?
f What does Aziz think of Chris Froome?

ECRIRE 4 Imagine you are staying at a summer camp. Write an email describing your activities. (See pages 130–137.) Include:

- what activities you do during the day
- what you do in the evenings
- what you prefer: winter or summer sports
- which sport you would like to do
- who is your favourite sports personality

Remember, the more you can develop your answers, the better your work will be.

Sports and dance

Quels sports tu préfères?	*What sports do you prefer?*
je préfère	*I prefer*
c'est ma passion	*I'm passionate about it*
les boules	*bowls*
la danse	*dance, ballet*
l'équitation	*horse-riding*
l'escalade	*rock climbing*
le hand(ball)	*handball*
la natation	*swimming*
la pétanque	*petanque*
la planche à voile	*windsurfing*
le roller	*rollerskating*
le skate	*skateboarding*
le surf	*surfing*
le vélo	*cycling*
la voile	*sailing*
le VTT	*mountain bike*

Summer and winter sports

les sports d'été/d'hiver	*summer/winter sports*
les sports extrêmes	*extreme sports*
je fais du/de la/de l' ...	*I do/play ...*
je joue au/à la/aux ...	*I play ... (+ ball game)*
la motoneige	*snowmobile*
la plongée	*scuba diving*
le patin à glace	*ice skating*
le parapente	*paragliding*
la randonnée	*hiking*
le saut à l'élastique	*bungee jumping*
le ski	*skiing*
le snowboard	*snowboarding*

Active holidays and summer camps

un atelier	*workshop*
la balle aux prisonniers	*dodgeball*
un centre aéré	*after school centre*
une chasse/course au trésor	*treasure hunt*
les claquettes	*tap dancing*
une colonie de vacances	*summer camp*
la course d'orientation	*orienteering*
un feu de camp	*a camp fire*
un(e) moniteur(trice)	*instructor*
un stage (sportif)	*short (sports) course*
le tir à l'arc	*archery*

Parts of the body and injuries

Qu'est-ce qui ne va pas?	*What is wrong?*
J'ai mal au/à la/à l'/aux ...	*my ... hurts, I have a sore ...*
le bras	*arm*
la cheville	*ankle*
les dents	*teeth*
le dos	*back*
l'épaule	*shoulder*
le genou	*knee*
la jambe	*leg*
le pied	*foot*
la tête	*head*

Time expressions and connectives

cet été	*this summer*
cet hiver	*this winter*
depuis	*since/for*
donc	*so*
mais	*but*
ou	*or*
parce que	*because*
pendant	*during*
tous les lundis	*every Monday*

Useful words and phrases

j'ai commencé	*I started*
j'ai fait	*I did*
j'ai joué	*I played*
je m'entraîne	*I train*
je ne peux pas faire	*I cannot do*
je suis allé(e)	*I went*
je voudrais/j'aimerais	*I would like*
bouger	*to move/to be active*
un championnat	*championship*
une équipe	*team*
essayer	*to try*
fatigant	*tiring*
un joueur	*player*
une médaille	*medal*
un tournoi	*tournament*

◎ Grammar and skills: I can...

- ◉ use *aller, jouer* and *faire* with sports, in the present and the perfect tenses
- ◉ use *je voudrais/j'aimerais*
- ◉ use *j'ai mal* with parts of the body
- ◉ use *je peux/je ne peux pas*
- ◉ use verbs with *il/elle*
- ◉ use reading skills
- ◉ recycle language in a different context
- ◉ answer questions
- ◉ build longer sentences using *parce que* and *donc*
- ◉ use formal and informal language with confidence
- ◉ use strategies to check written work

9.1 Mon pays

- Vocabulary: talk about where you live
- Grammar: compare places using *plus* and *moins*
- Skills: use transferable structures; identify key points in a text

Écoute (1–6). C'est quel endroit, Montpellier ou Amantan?
Which place is being described?

Exemple: 1 *Montpellier*

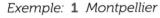

Amantan

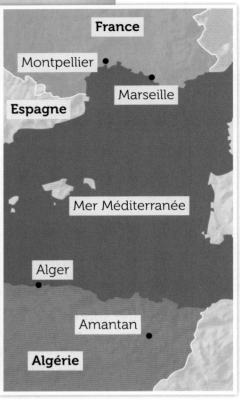

France

Montpellier

Marseille

Espagne

Mer Méditerranée

Alger

Amantan

Algérie

Travaille avec un dictionnaire. Regroupe les contraires.
Use a dictionary. Pair up the opposites.

Exemple: moderne – historique

~~moderne~~ ~~historique~~ plat moche
pittoresque rural propre montagneux
urbanisé bruyant pollué tranquille
vivant désert ennuyeux peuplé

 Add your own pair of opposites describing a place.

Parle de l'endroit où tu habites.
Fais la comparaison. A ↔ B.
Talk about where you live and compare it to
another place.

Exemple: **A** *Vas-y!*
B *OK. Oxford, c'est plus tranquille que Londres.*
Londres, c'est moins tranquille. Vas-y, à toi!
A *D'accord. Oxford, c'est moins vivant que*
Londres. Londres, c'est plus vivant. Vas-y
encore une fois!
B *Watford, c'est ...*

Grammaire p. 167 WB p.12

Comparisons

Use *plus* (more) and *moins* (less) *que*
(than) to make comparisons.
*C'est **plus** tranquille **que** Londres.* –
It's quieter (more quiet) than London.
*C'est **moins** tranquille **qu'**Oxford.* –
It's less quiet/It's noisier than Oxford.
C'est plus tranquille. – It's quieter.
C'est moins tranquille. – It's noisier.

Transferable structures

Some phrases can be used over
and over again:

vas-y – go on/your go

vas-y, à toi – you go on

vas-y encore une fois – go on/
your go again

4 **Lis les textes. Recopie et remplis la grille.**

En ce moment, j'habite dans le sud de la France, à Saint-Martin près de Montpellier. Saint-Martin, c'est assez rural et très calme mais c'est un peu ennuyeux. Plus tard, je vais habiter à Dakar, dans l'ouest du Sénégal. Dakar est plus bruyant que Saint-Martin et c'est moins pittoresque, mais c'est plus vivant et moins ennuyeux.
Solène

Grammaire p. 168

Near future (going to)
j'habite – I live
je vais habiter – I am going to live

En ce moment, j'habite dans le nord-est de l'Algérie, à Amantan. Amantan, c'est pittoresque et montagneux mais c'est un peu trop calme. Plus tard, je vais habiter à Marseille, dans le sud de la France. C'est très différent de chez moi! Marseille, c'est plus vivant et plus urbanisé qu'Amantan. Amantan, c'est moins bruyant et moins pollué.
Samir

	now	description	later	description
Solène	*Saint-Martin*			
Samir				

5 **Vrai ou faux? Lis et décide.**

Exemple: **a** *vrai*

a En ce moment, Solène habite à Saint-Martin, près de Montpellier.
b Plus tard, elle va habiter en France.
c Saint-Martin, c'est plus calme que Dakar.
d Samir habite en Algérie, dans le nord-est, à Amantan.
e Plus tard, il va habiter à Amantan, dans le nord-est de l'Algérie.
f Amantan est plus vivant que Marseille mais Marseille est moins pollué.

◎ **Correct the wrong sentences.**

6 **Tu vas habiter où plus tard? Discute en groupe.**

Exemple: **A** *Tu vas habiter où plus tard?*
B *Je vais habiter à Oxford.*

◎ **Extend and justify. Look at how you can 'grow' your answer:**

Exemple: **B** *J'habite à Londres mais plus tard, je vais habiter à Oxford.*
B *J'habite à Londres mais plus tard, je vais habiter à Oxford. C'est moins bruyant que Londres.*

7 **Où habites-tu? Où vas-tu habiter plus tard? Écris un paragraphe.**
Where do you live and where are you going to live in the future?

En ce moment, j'habite Plus tard, je vais habiter	à Dakar à Paris etc.	dans le nord/ sud/est/ouest	de la France. du Sénégal. etc.	C'est ... C'est plus/moins ... que ...

Plenary

★ In one sentence, say where you live and where that place is.

◎ Describe your town using *plus* and *moins*.

✚ Make up sentences saying where you live now and where you are going to live in the future.

You have been reflecting on similarities and differences between life here and in other francophone countries. Discuss with your partner why it is a useful skill to 'compare and contrast'.

Ma journée

- Vocabulary: talk about your daily routine
- Grammar: use reflexive verbs
- Skills: improve your speaking and writing; use the 24-hour clock

 1 **Écoute, lis et relie.**
Exemple: **1** *b*

 a
 b
 c
 d
 e

 f
 g
 h
 i
 j

1 Je me réveille.
2 Je me brosse les dents.
3 Je me lève.
4 Je quitte la maison.

5 Je me lave.
6 Je vais au collège.
7 Je prends mon petit déjeuner.

8 Je rentre chez moi.
9 Je m'habille.
10 Je fais mes devoirs.

 2 **Écoute et mets les images dans le bon ordre (1–8).**
Exemple: *b, …*

Avant midi　　　midi/minuit
onze heures cinquante-cinq　　　une heure cinq
dix heures cinquante　　　deux heures dix
neuf heures quarante-cinq　　　trois heures quinze
huit heures quarante　　　quatre heures vingt
sept heures trente-cinq　　　cinq heures vingt-cinq
six heures trente

Après midi　　　douze heures/zéro heure
vingt-trois heures　　　treize heures
vingt-deux heures　　　quatorze heures
vingt et une heures　　　quinze heures
vingt heures　　　seize heures
dix-neuf heures　　　dix-sept heures
dix-huit heures

Grammaire p. 168–169 WB p.43

Reflexive verbs

Reflexive verbs are used when the person or thing doing the action is doing it to themselves. These verbs have an extra pronoun to show this:
*je **me** lave* – I wash myself

je **me** lave	je **m'**habille
tu **te** laves	tu **t'**habilles
il/elle **se** lave	il/elle **s'**habille

3 **Écoute et relie (1–6).**
Exemple: **1** *b*

a 16:30　　d 07:40
b 07:30　　e 21:00
c 08:00　　f 18:00

je me couche　*I go to bed*

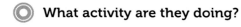
What activity are they doing?

Sondage: 'Tu te couches à quelle heure?'

Class survey. What time do you go to bed?

Exemple: **A** *Tu te couches à quelle heure?*
B *Je me couche à vingt-deux heures. Et toi?*
A *Je me couche à vingt-deux heures trente.*

 Give extra detail in your answer:
D'abord, je me douche à vingt heures trente, puis je ... pour finir, je ... Et toi?

5 **Lis et réponds aux questions.**

Exemple: **a** *Janjak wakes up and ...*

je m'occupe de   I look after/take care of

Ma vie en Haïti: Une journée typique

Salut! Je m'appelle Janjak et j'ai treize ans. À six heures, je me réveille et je me lève. D'abord, je me lave et je m'habille. Ensuite, je me brosse les dents. À sept heures et demie, je quitte la maison et je vais à l'école, mais je ne prends pas de petit déjeuner. L'école finit à midi, alors je rentre à la maison. Je mange à treize heures puis je travaille dans le jardin et je m'occupe des animaux. À vingt heures, je me couche. Je suis toujours très fatigué.

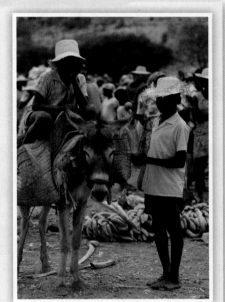

a What happens at six o'clock?
b List all the things Janjak does after getting up and before going to school.
c What doesn't he do?
d What happens at half past seven?
e What time does school finish? What does he do then?
f What does he do at home?
g What time does he go to bed and why?

6 **Écris un paragraphe. Décris ta journée typique.**
Describe your daily routine.

Exemple: *D'abord, je me réveille à sept heures trente et ...*

 Compare your routine with Janjak's: *Je me réveille à sept heures trente, mais Janjak, il se réveille à six heures.*

> **Improving your speaking and writing**
>
> How long a sentence can you make using these sequencers to describe your morning routine?
>
> *d'abord* – firstly   *après* – after
> *puis* – then/next   *après ça* – after that
> *ensuite* – then/next   *pour finir* – finally

Plenary

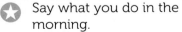 Say what you do in the morning.
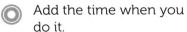 Add the time when you do it.
Use sequencers to make the sequence clear.

Think about the lives of children your age in other countries. Can you **compare** your daily routines? Do you think it is fair that some children have to work long hours and cannot go to school? **Imagine** you are a teacher planning this lesson for future pupils. **Write down** three things you think younger pupils would find interesting. How and when did _you_ learn this information?

9.3 Où es-tu allé?

- Vocabulary: talk about what you did yesterday
- Grammar: use the perfect tense with *être*
- Skills: use connectives for contrast; use speaking strategies

 ÉCOUTER 1

Écoute Anthony, de la Guadeloupe, et Caroline, de Paris (1–6). C'est quelle image?

Exemple: **1** *b*

a Je suis partie de la maison. `08:00`

b Je suis parti de la maison. `07:30`

c Je suis allée au collège à pied.

d Je suis allé au collège en bus.

e Je suis arrivée au collège. `08:20`

f Je suis arrivé au collège. `07:50`

➕ **Explain your answers in French:** *Le numéro un, je pense que c'est b!*

 PARLER 2

 Interviewe trois personnes. Pose trois questions et note les réponses.

Exemple: **A** *Tu es parti(e) à quelle heure, hier?*
B *Je suis parti(e)* ***à huit heures***.
A *Tu es allé(e) au collège comment?*
B *Je suis allé(e) au collège* ***en voiture***.
A *Tu es arrivé(e) à quelle heure?*
B *Je suis arrivé(e)* ***à huit heures quinze***.

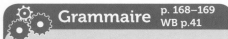

Grammaire
p. 168–169
WB p.41

Perfect tense with *être*

In Units 7 and 8, you saw that *aller* (to go) takes *être* to form the perfect tense. So do *partir* (to leave), *arriver* (to arrive), and a few others The verbs that take *être* are sometimes called 'verbs of motion'.

	masculine	feminine
singular	je suis arrivé	je suis arrivé**e**
	tu es arrivé	tu es arrivé**e**
	il est arrivé	elle est arrivé**e**
plural	on est arrivé**s**	on est arrivé**es**
	nous sommes arrivé**s**	nous sommes arrivé**es**
	vous êtes arrivé**s**	vous êtes arrivé**es**
	ils sont arrivé**s**	elles sont arrivé**es**

Speaking strategies: using your senses 🔧

Try giving full answers when you are practising your spoken French. When you become more confident you can just give the necessary information. In activity 2, you could have answered the questions with just the phrases in **bold**.

- Say (or sing) aloud (or in your head) what you are doing/have done or what you can see: *je suis allé(e) au parc à pied*
- repeat aloud (or in your head) useful expressions you hear
- exaggerate the sound (and use a facial expression): *je suis parti* (eeeeeee), etc.

3 **Lis et décide. C'est qui, Caroline ou Anthony?**

Exemple: **a** *Caroline*

Je suis partie de la maison à huit heures.
Je suis allée au collège à pied.
Je suis arrivée au collège à huit heures vingt.
Je suis entrée à huit heures trente.
Je suis rentrée à la maison à seize heures trente.
Je suis allée au cinéma à dix-neuf heures.

Je suis parti de la maison à sept heures trente.
Je suis allé au collège en bus.
Je suis arrivé au collège à sept heures cinquante.
Je suis entré à huit heures.
Je suis allé au club de foot à quinze heures.
Je suis rentré à la maison à seize heures.

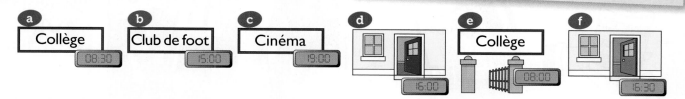

a	b	c	d	e	f
Collège 08:30	Club de foot 15:00	Cinéma 19:00	16:00	Collège 08:00	16:30

➕ **Explain your answers in French. If you're not sure, guess:** *Je devine … c'est Anthony?*

4 **Compare et trouve les différences. A↔B.**

Exemple: *Caroline est partie à huit heures mais Anthony est parti à sept heures trente.*

5 **Écoute (1–5). Recopie et remplis la grille.**
What do they normally do? What did they do yesterday?

	d'habitude	hier
1	leave house at 8	left at 7.30
2		

sept heures et demie	sept heures quarante-cinq	huit heures et demie	trois heures trente-cinq	deux heures trente
7.30	7.45	8.30	3.35	2.30

6 **Parle de ta journée d'hier et écris une comparaison.** 🖱
Compare what you did yesterday with what Caroline did in activity 3.

Exemple: *Moi, je suis parti(e) de la maison à sept heures, mais elle est partie à huit heures.*

➕ **Include at least four activities.**

Using connectives to contrast 🔧
Certain connectives words signal contrast or contradiction. One you have already used is *mais* (but). There are lots of other interesting connectives:

pourtant – however

cependant – however

par contre – on the other hand

Plenary

⭐ Write down some 24-hour clock times (p.m.) and say them to your partner.

◎ Say what you did yesterday and at what time.

➕ Compare this to what you normally do.

Building on your learning from previous units, how many countries can you name in French in 60 seconds, and are these words in your long-term memory? What time zone are those countries in? Apply your understanding of the 24-hour clock to work out what the time is now in one of these places.

9.4 Engagez-vous!

- Vocabulary: talk about what you are going to do to help others
- Grammar: use the near future
- Skills: identify and combine different tenses

 1 **Lis et relie.** *Je m'engage pour changer le monde. Je vais …*

Exemple: **a** 4

a   b   c   d   e

1 *faire* du travail bénévole
2 *donner* des vieux vêtements à la friperie
3 *organiser* une vente de gâteaux
4 *collecter* de l'argent pour une association caritative
5 *participer* à un évènement sponsorisé

 2 **Lis et écoute. Recopie et remplis la grille.**

	activity	extra details
Sylvain	e	loves to cook
Magali		
Dylan		
Miriam		
Florian		

 3 **Traduis ces expressions en anglais et décide: présent, passé ou futur?**

Exemple: le week-end dernier –
last weekend, passé

le week-end dernier   le week-end prochain
maintenant   l'année prochaine
l'année dernière   hier   demain

 Can you add some of your own with the help of a dictionary?

Grammaire p. 168 WB p.38–39

Near future – *aller* + infinitive

When you talk about what you are *going to do*, you use the immediate future formed with *aller* + infinitive.

Je vais organiser une vente de gâteaux. – I am going to organise a cake stall.
Tu vas faire du travail bénévole? – Are you going to do voluntary work?
Nous allons collecter de l'argent. – We are going to collect money.

 Lis le texte.

Make notes in English. What did Ricky do? What is he doing at the moment? What is he going to do?

> **Ricky Rosco, chanteur: « Mes gestes pour changer le monde »**
>
> L'année dernière, j'ai gagné un concours à la télé, 'La France a du talent'. Après, je suis devenu une star! J'ai décidé d'utiliser ma célébrité pour aider les autres. Alors, j'ai commencé à faire du travail bénévole. Par exemple, j'ai fait un spot publicitaire pour une association caritative en Haïti. L'association collecte des fonds pour reconstruire les écoles détruites pendant le tremblement de terre de 2010. Actuellement, je ne fais pas grand-chose parce que je travaille beaucoup, mais le week-end prochain, je vais participer à un évènement sponsorisé (un marathon à Paris) et l'année prochaine, je vais aller en Haïti.

> actuellement
> *at the moment*

 Écoute les interviews (1–4). Recopie et remplis la grille.

	past	present	future	➕ extra détails
1	I organised a cake sale			
2				

 Écris un article pour le blog d'une école.

On a French school blog, write about your charity work.

➕ ◎ **Build in extra detail with two tenses for silver and three tenses for gold.**

 Lis ton article de l'activité 6 tout haut. A↔B

You are recording your article as a podcast. Practise reading it aloud with a partner first.

Plenary

In a group, discuss the success criteria for the task below. What medal are you aspiring to achieve? Can the roles you play in the group help all of you to achieve more? Which member of your group seems to understand the three tenses well? Nominate him/her to answer questions if anyone needs help.

⭐ Say what you are going to do to help others.

◎ Add what you are doing at the moment.

➕ Add what you did last year.

 Tenses

Expressions of time help you to work out what tense is being used in a text. Showing that you can understand and use different tenses helps you to improve your work.

⭐ Confident use of one tense.

Try to use at least two different verbs, expressions of time and connectives.

◎ Confident use of two tenses.

Try to use at least two different verbs for each tense, expressions of time and connectives.

➕ Confident use of three tenses.

Try to use at least two different verbs for each tense, expressions of time and connectives.

L'année dernière,	En ce moment,	L'année prochaine,
j'ai participé à ...	je participe à ...	je vais participer à ...
j'ai organisé ...	j'organise ...	je vais organiser ...
j'ai fait ...	je fais ...	je vais faire ...
j'ai donné ...	je donne ...	je vais donner ...
j'ai collecté ...	je collecte ...	je vais collecter ...

- Vocabulary: identify and locate francophone countries; talk about Africa
- Grammar: use expressions with *avoir* (*avoir faim*)
- Skills: use transferable structures to discuss answers

le nord
l'ouest — l'est
le sud

Écoute et décide (1–5). C'est quel pays?
Which country is it?

Exemple: **1** b, le Maroc

Choisis un pays. Fais des dialogues. A↔B.
Choose a country. Talk in pairs.

Exemple: **A** *C'est un pays en Afrique du Nord.*
B *OK. Je devine ... c'est le Cameroun?*
A *Non.*
B *C'est ... le Maroc?*
A *Oui.*

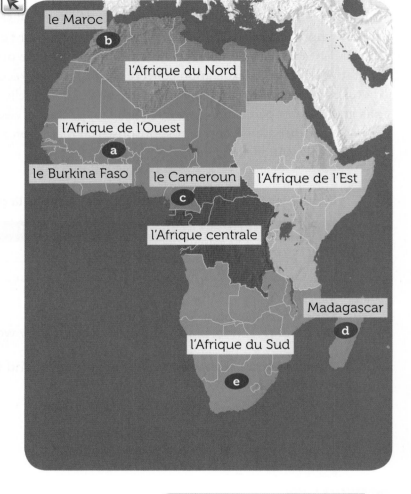

le Maroc
b
l'Afrique du Nord
l'Afrique de l'Ouest
a
le Burkina Faso   le Cameroun   l'Afrique de l'Est
c
l'Afrique centrale
Madagascar
d
l'Afrique du Sud
e

➕ **Use other phrases from the box to develop the conversation further.**

Discussing answers
Use these phrases to discuss your answers:
Je devine. – I'm guessing.
Essaie encore une fois. – Try again.
J'ai deviné juste? – Did I guess right?
Tu as deviné juste. – You guessed right.

Écoute et remplis les blancs.

Un pays francophone est un pays où on parle **1** *français* . Un ou une francophone est une **2** _____ qui parle français. Il y a environ 96,2 millions de **3** _____ en **4** _____ . Dans l'ensemble des pays francophones, environ 200 **5** _____ de personnes parlent français. On parle français dans **6** _____ pays et sur **7** _____ continents. Le français est une langue très **8** _____ !

> 33   ~~français~~   importante   millions   Afrique
> personne   cinq   francophones

Decimal points
In French, the comma is used as a decimal point. For example, 'there are around **96.2** million French speakers in Africa' but *il y a environ **96,2** millions de francophones en Afrique.*

Watch out for words like *environ* ('around' or 'about') which can have an effect on numbers.

◎ **Can you fill in the blanks with the words covered up?**

LIRE 4 Lis. Recopie et remplis la grille.

L'Afrique, terre de contrastes

L'Afrique est un continent vaste et très divers. Dans certains pays, il y a la famine et la sécheresse, donc on a faim et on a soif, mais dans d'autres pays, il y a une abondance d'eau et de nourriture. Dans certaines régions, c'est très rural et désert. Par contre, dans d'autres régions, c'est urbanisé et très peuplé. C'est un continent où il y a beaucoup de pauvreté et beaucoup de richesse. C'est aussi un continent de conflit et de paix.

la sécheresse *drought*
la nourriture *food*
la pauvreté *poverty*
le conflit *conflict*
la paix *peace*

L'Afrique, terre de contrastes	
une abondance de nourriture	*la famine*
...	...

Grammaire p. 168

Expressions with *avoir*

There are lots of expressions that take *avoir* (to have) in French. You already know *avoir* ___ *ans* (to be ___ years old). Here are some more:

j'ai faim – I **am** hungry
j'ai de la chance – I **am** lucky
j'ai soif – I **am** thirsty
j'ai peur – I **am** scared
j'ai confiance – I **am** confident
on a faim – we **are** hungry
on a peur – we **are** scared

LIRE 5 Lis et décide.

a Dans mon pays, il y a la famine ... donc *j'ai faim*/j'ai soif.
b Dans mon pays, il y a la sécheresse ... donc j'ai faim/j'ai soif.
c Dans mon pays, il y a une abondance d'eau ... donc je n'ai pas soif/j'ai soif.
d Dans mon pays, il y a une abondance de nourriture ... donc je n'ai pas faim/j'ai faim.
e Dans mon pays, il y a un conflit ... donc j'ai de la chance/j'ai peur.
f Dans mon pays, il n'y a pas de famine, pas de sécheresse et pas de conflit ... donc j'ai de la chance/j'ai peur.

ÉCRIRE 6 Dessine un poster: L'Afrique, terre de contrastes.
Design a poster using the expressions with *avoir* above.
Exemple: J'ai soif. J'ai ...

➕ **Can you take ideas and language from activity 4?**
Dans mon pays, il y a un conflit. J'ai peur.

Dans mon pays, il y a la famine et la sécheresse. J'ai ...

Plenary

⭐ Name some francophone countries or explain the meaning of the word 'francophone'.
◎ List some idiomatic expressions using *avoir*.
➕ Explain why Africa is a land of contrasts.

The headteacher at your partner school in France has asked for suggestions for fundraising. Applying persuasive writing skills learnt in English and any other techniques you know to your learning of French, spend two minutes drafting a bid for funds to go to an area in Africa.

Dans mon pays, il y a l'abondance. J'ai de la chance. Je n'ai pas soif, je n'ai pas ...

Reflexive verbs

1 Complete the sentences below.

a Tu _te_ lèves à quelle heure?
b Je _____ lève à huit heures.
c Mon père, il _____ lève à cinq heures.
d Ma mère, elle _____ lève à six heures et demie.
e Vous _____ levez à quelle heure, le week-end?
f Mes amis, ils _____ lèvent à onze heures!

Reflexive verbs have subject pronouns (like *je, tu, il/elle*) but they also need a **reflexive** pronoun to show that the subject and the object are the same: *Je me lave* – I wash (**myself**).

se réveiller – to wake (**oneself**) up			
je	**me** réveille	nous	**nous** réveillons
tu	**te** réveilles	vous	**vous** réveillez
il/elle/on	**se** réveille	ils/elles	**se** réveillent

Perfect tense with *avoir* and *être*

2 Rewrite Lucie's story, inserting the correct agreements after each past participle.

Je suis **1** ~~parti~~ _partie_ de la maison à huit heures ... nous sommes tous **2** parti _____ de la maison à huit heures! Maman, elle est **3** allé _____ au travail en voiture. Papa, il est **4** allé _____ en ville en bus. Mon frère et moi, nous sommes **5** allé _____ à l'école à pied et nous sommes **6** arrivé _____ à huit heures et demie. Mon frère est **7** entré _____ à huit heures trente-cinq. Moi, je suis **8** entré _____ à huit heures quarante, à la sonnerie. Nous sommes **9** rentré _____ à seize heures. Maman et papa sont **10** arrivé _____ peu après. Maman et moi, nous sommes **11** sorti _____ à dix-neuf heures pour aller au cinéma.

To form the perfect tense, you need an **auxiliary verb** and a **past participle** (see Units 3, 7 and 8). With most verbs, the auxiliary verb is *avoir*.

avoir	+ past participle		
j'**ai**			
tu **as**			
il/elle/on **a**	joué	played	
nous **avons**	répondu	replied	
vous **avez**	fini	finished	
ils/elles **ont**			

With verbs of motion, or movement, such as *aller* (to go), *partir* (to leave), *arriver* (to arrive), *entrer* (to come in) and a few others, you form the perfect tense with *être*.

When you form the perfect tense with *être*, the past participle has to 'agree' with the person or thing doing the action.

	masculine	feminine
singular	je suis arriv**é**	je suis arriv**ée**
	tu es arriv**é**	tu es arriv**ée**
	il est arriv**é**	elle est arriv**ée**
plural	on est arriv**és**	on est arriv**ées**
	nous sommes arriv**és**	nous sommes arriv**ées**
	vous êtes arriv**és**	vous êtes arriv**ées**
	ils sont arriv**és**	elles sont arriv**ées**

Near future

3 **Write sentences for these future plans.**

a Tu  *Tu vas organiser une vente de gâteaux.*

b Il   **e** Vous ?

c Nous **f** Elles

d Je

The near future is used to talk about what is **going to** happen. You form it with the present tense of *aller* (to go) followed by the **infinitive** of the verb.

present tense of *aller*	+ infinitive		
je **vais**		I am going	
tu **vas**		you are going	
il/elle **va**		he/she is going	
on **va**	**organiser** ...	we are going	to organise ...
nous **allons**			
vous **allez**		you are going	
ils/elles **vont**		they are going	

Thinking strategies: preparing for a test

When preparing for a test, think back to all the strategies you've used throughout this book, to see if they can help.

Whatever the skill, or whatever the task, you may have noticed that there are certain key strategies which come up again and again, for example:

- **Using what you already know:** cognates, common sense
- **Using your senses:** images, sounds, movements
- **Planning and predicting:** what to say/write/ listen out for/look for
- **Noticing and noting patterns:** spidergrams, Venn diagrams, mind maps, grammar structures.

Before a listening test, think about the listening strategies you have used before, and use the symbols below to assess how effective they were. Then do the same before speaking, reading and writing tests.

- ☺ tried it, worked well
- ☹ tried it, didn't help
- → not tried it yet, will give it a go

After your tests, think about whether using strategies has helped you improve your French, and your test scores. Identify changes you will make next time you have a test or similar task.

Bonne chance!

Pronunciation *ll*

4 **Listen to the words below. Is the sound 'luh' or 'yuh'?**

Example: **a** *'yuh'*

a famille **e** se réveiller **i** mille
b fille **f** billet **j** million
c ville **g** belle
d Lille **h** s'habiller

Double *l* (*ll*) can be pronounced 'luh' or 'yuh' depending on what comes before it. If double *l* (*ll*) comes after the letters *a*, *e*, *o* or *u*, then the sound is 'luh' (for example, *elle*) but if it comes after the letter *i*, the sound is 'yuh' (for example, *famille*, *réveille*, etc.). There are a few exceptions to this rule, such as *ville* (where *ll* is sounded 'luh').

9.7 Extra Star

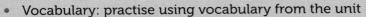

- Vocabulary: practise using vocabulary from the unit
- Grammar: use reflexive verbs
- Skills: use and understand 24-hour clock time

 Write the following 24-hour clock times in digits.

Exemple: **a** 17.15

a dix-sept heures quinze
b neuf heures dix
c vingt heures trente
d vingt et une heures quarante-cinq
e vingt-deux heures cinquante
f vingt-trois heures

 Read the paragraph and answer the questions.

Exemple: **a** Martha Koundé, volunteer ...

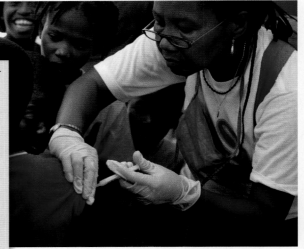

Bonjour, je m'appelle Martha Koundé. Je suis médecin bénévole pour une association caritative qui s'appelle *Médecins sans Frontières*.

Mon travail, il est parfois difficile mais il est très satisfaisant. Le matin, je me lève à six heures. D'abord, je me douche puis je m'habille. Je prends le petit déjeuner à six heures et quart et ensuite, je me brosse les dents. Je quitte la maison à six heures trente et je vais à l'hôpital à pied. Je commence le travail à sept heures et je termine à midi (je rentre à la maison pour déjeuner).

Je retourne à l'hôpital à quatorze heures et je travaille jusqu'à vingt heures, puis je rentre à la maison. Je dîne, je me déshabille et finalement, je me couche. D'habitude, je suis très fatiguée quand je me couche. Voilà ma journée typique.

a Who is speaking and what do they do? (2 answers)
b Who does she work for and what does she say about her work? (3 answers)
c Describe her morning routine before she goes to work. (7 answers)
d How many hours does she work? (1 answer)
e Describe her evening routine. (3 answers)

 Imagine that you work for *Infirmiers et Infirmières sans Frontières*. Describe your daily routine.

Exemple: **a** *Je me lève à six heures quinze.*

Bonjour, je m'appelle Didier Raymond et je suis bénévole pour *Infirmiers et Infirmières sans Frontières*. Mon travail est varié et très intéressant mais parfois un peu stressant.

9.7 *Extra Plus*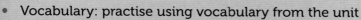

- Vocabulary: practise using vocabulary from the unit
- Grammar: use the perfect past tense with *être*
- Skills: identify tenses; use appropriate expressions of time

 Lucie a fait quoi? Et à quelle heure?

Exemple: **a** 2

Alors … je vais parler des endroits où je suis allée hier. Le matin, je suis partie de la maison à sept heures quarante-cinq. Je suis allée à l'école en bus (le bus est arrivé à huit heures). Je suis arrivée au collège à huit heures vingt et je suis entrée à huit heures trente. Je suis rentrée à la maison à quinze heures trente mais je suis sortie à dix-neuf heures pour aller au cinéma.

 Décris ta journée. Adapte le texte de l'activité 1: Tu as fait quoi? Et à quelle heure?

Exemple: *Je suis parti(e) de la maison à … heures …*

 Lis l'histoire de Thomas. Recopie et remplis la grille.

> être à l'heure — *to be on time*
> être en retard — *to be late*

Ma journée désastreuse!

Quelle catastrophe! Ce matin, mon réveil n'a pas sonné … D'habitude, je quitte la maison à sept heures trente, mais ce matin, je suis parti de la maison à huit heures. Et d'habitude, je vais au collège en bus, pourtant ce matin, j'y suis allé à pied (le bus était parti). D'habitude, j'arrive au collège à huit heures, mais ce matin, je suis arrivé à huit heures quarante-cinq. D'habitude, j'entre dans le collège à huit heures trente, mais ce matin, je suis entré à huit heures cinquante. D'habitude, je suis à l'heure, mais aujourd'hui, j'étais en retard!

		normally …	today …
a	Leaves house at …	7.30	
b	Goes to school by …		
c	Arrives at …		
d	Goes in at …		

 Récris le texte en utilisant les expressions appropriées.
Rewrite the text using the appropriate expressions of time.

Exemple: **1** **L'année dernière**, … j'ai organisé une vente de gâteaux …

> l'année dernière   hier
> le week-end prochain
>   actuellement
> l'année prochaine   plus tard

J'habite à Nantes, dans l'ouest de la France.
1 *L'année dernière* , dans mon collège à Nantes, j'ai organisé une vente de gâteaux et j'ai participé à un évènement sponsorisé mais **2**   ,
je ne fais pas grand-chose car j'ai beaucoup de travail. Alors **3**   , j'ai pris une résolution.
4   , je vais donner des vieux vêtements à la friperie. Puis **5**   , après mes examens en été, je vais commencer à faire du travail bénévole dans une des friperies de Nantes. Et je vais aussi participer à un marathon sponsorisé.
6   , je vais faire du travail bénévole à l'étranger.

Madagascar – Fiche info

1

Madagascar est une très grande île au sud-est de l'Afrique. On l'appelle "l'île-continent", "la Grande Île", ou aussi "l'île rouge", parce que la terre est rouge.

2

Dans cette "Grande Île", les paysages sont variés. L'île a développé des espèces de plantes et d'animaux uniques au monde, comme les lémuriens.

3

Les habitants s'appellent les Malgaches et la langue nationale est le malagasy; 20 pour cent de la population utilisent aussi le français.

4

À Madagascar, on mange beaucoup de riz. On consomme aussi des bananes, des noix de coco, du poisson et des fruits de mer, comme la langouste. Il existe des spécialités d'origine indienne, comme le samoussa, en forme de triangle.

5

C'est un pays agricole: Madagascar est le premier producteur mondial de vanille. C'est aussi un pays pauvre: un Malgache ordinaire a cinq euros par jour. Mais c'est une population chaleureuse, un pays magnifique, et le tourisme va peut-être se développer.

> la terre *soil*
> les paysages *landscape*
> utilisent *use*
> la langouste *lobster*
> chaleureuse *warm and friendly*

1 **Match the headings with the paragraphs in the text.**

Exemple: paragraph 1, Où?

- Et la nature?
- Où?
- Qu'est-ce qu'on parle?
- Quel avenir pour Madagascar?
- Quelle cuisine?

2 **Answer the questions about Madagascar and its people in English.**

Exemple: **a** *l'île-continent (continent island), …*

a What are the three nicknames used for Madagascar?
b What is unique about natural life in Madagascar?
c What is their first language?
d What typical food do they share with India?
e What do they produce more than any other country in the world?
f How much does an average person live on?
g What do they hope to develop?

3 **Translate paragraph 5 into English.**

Exemple: What future for Madagascar? It is a farming country …

Sénégalais à Montpellier

Regarde l'épisode 9. C'est Montpellier, le Sénégal ou les deux?
Exemple: Montpellier: **a**, ...
          le Sénégal:

a C'est dans le sud de la France.
b C'est en Afrique de l'Ouest.
c On y parle français.
d La capitale, c'est Dakar.
e Ce n'est pas très grand, mais c'est moderne.
f Le tambour, c'est l'instrument de musique typique.

Lis le résumé. Complète avec les mots.
Exemple: **a** *reportage*
          b ...

Diakouba et ses amis font un **a**   sur L'Afrique. Ils vont faire un film et mettre le film dans la **b**   . À Montpellier, c'est facile: il y a beaucoup de gens de **c**   différents, souvent de pays africains et **d**   . Les amis rencontrent Paco, un **e**   de Dakar, la **f**   du Sénégal. Avec Paco et AfricaTala, Diakouba et ses **g**   apprennent une danse, la **h**   . Ils s'amusent bien, mais Basile préfère essayer le **i**   . Clarisse danse beaucoup et elle oublie de filmer. **j**   recommencer.

amis   capitale   capsule témoin   danseur
   Djamba Dour   francophones   Il faut
      pays   ~~reportage~~   tambour

 Que penses-tu de la danse sénégalaise? Et des tambours?
Tu préfères la musique ou la danse?

Exemple: J'aime bien la musique sénégalaise. Je préfère ...

ECOUTER 1

Listen (1–6). Which topics from the list below is Nicolas discussing? (See pages 148–155.)

Exemple: 1 c

a Maintenant, j'habite …
b Plus tard, je vais habiter …
c Ma journée typique.
d Ma journée d'hier.
e Le monde francophone.
f Je m'engage pour changer le monde.

 PARLER 2

Prepare a presentation and include the following information. (See pages 148–155.)

- Where you live: *Actuellement, j'habite …*
- Where you are going to live: *Plus tard, je vais habiter …*
- Your morning routine: *Je me réveille à …*
- Your journey to school yesterday: *Hier, je suis parti(e) de la maison à …*
- How you are going to help others: *Je m'engage pour changer le monde. Par exemple …*

LIRE 3

Read the text and answer the questions a–f. (See pages 148–155.)

Exemple: **a** *Sainte-Anne, …*

> Sujet: Salut!
>
> Salut! Je m'appelle Élodie Lafont. J'habite en Martinique à Sainte-Anne. Sainte-Anne, c'est très pittoresque. Plus tard, je vais habiter en France, à Paris. Paris, c'est beaucoup plus urbanisé et vivant que Sainte-Anne mais je préfère Sainte-Anne. C'est normal, c'est ma ville!
>
> Ma journée? Je me lève tard (à onze heures d'habitude) parce que je me couche tard. Hier, je suis partie de la maison à vingt heures pour aller à un concert (pour collecter de l'argent pour une association caritative). Je suis arrivée au concert à vingt et une heures et je suis rentrée à la maison à minuit!
>
>

a Where does Élodie live?
b What does she think of where she lives?
c Where is she going to live in the future?
d What does she say about the time she gets up and goes to bed?
e Where did she go yesterday and why?
f What time did she arrive and what time did she get home?

 ECRIRE 4

Write a profile for your own web page. (See pages 148–155.)

Remember, the more you can develop your answers, the better your work will be.

Qui je suis	Accueil Profil Compte

Salut! Je m'appelle … Je suis …

Moi, j'habite …

Mais j'habite aussi …

Plus tard, je vais habiter …

C'est beaucoup plus/moins …

Ma journée? Je me …

Hier, je suis parti(e) …

Pour changer le monde, je …

Vocabulaire

Where I live

j'habite	I live
je vais habiter	I am going to live
dans le nord/le sud/l'ouest/ l'est	in the north/south/west/ east
dans le centre	in the centre
C'est (plus/moins) …	It's (more/less) …
bruyant/tranquille	noisy/peaceful
désert/peuplé	sparsely-populated/ densely-populated
moderne/historique	modern/historic
pittoresque/moche	picturesque/unattractive
plat/montagneux	flat/mountainous
propre/sale	clean/dirty
urbanisé/rural	built-up/rural
vivant/ennuyeux	lively/boring

Daily routine and time (24 hour clock)

je me réveille	I wake up
je me lève	I get up
je me douche	I have a shower
je me lave	I wash
je m'habille	I get dressed
je prends le petit déjeuner	I have breakfast
je me brosse les dents	I brush my teeth
je quitte la maison	I leave the house
je vais au collège	I go to school
je rentre à la maison	I go home
je mange	I eat
je travaille dans le jardin	I work in the garden
je m'occupe des animaux	I look after the animals
je me couche	I go to bed
je quitte le collège	I leave school
je fais du sport	I do sport
je fais mes devoirs	I do my homework
je regarde la télévision	I watch television
je vais au lit	I go to bed
je m'endors	I go to sleep
Tu te couches à quelle heure?	What time do you go to bed?
Je me couche à …	I go to bed at …
à treize heures	at 1 p.m./13.00
à quatorze heures	at 2 p.m./14.00
à quinze heures	at 3 p.m./15.00
à seize heures	at 4 p.m./16.00
à dix-sept heures	at 5 p.m./17.00
à dix-huit heures	at 6 p.m./18.00
à dix-neuf heures	at 7 p.m./19.00
à vingt heures	at 8 p.m./20.00
à vingt et une heures	at 9 p.m./21.00
à vingt-deux heures	at 10 p.m./22.00
à vingt-trois heures	at 11 p.m./23.00
à minuit	at midnight

What did you do?

je suis parti(e)	I left
je suis arrivé(e)	I arrived
je suis allé(e)	I went
pourtant/cependant	and yet

Getting involved

Je vais …	I am going to …
participer à un événement. sponsorisé	take part in a sponsored event.
collecter de l'argent pour une association caritative.	collect money for a charity.
faire du travail bénévole.	do voluntary work.
organiser une vente de gâteaux.	organise a cake sale.
donner des vieux vêtements à la friperie.	give old clothes to the charity shop.

Turn-taking phrases

Vas-y!	Go on!
Vas-y encore une fois.	Go again.
OK/D'accord.	OK.
Je devine.	I'm guessing.
Essaie encore une fois.	Try again.
J'ai deviné juste?	Did I guess right?
Tu as deviné juste.	You guessed right.
Je suis prêt(e).	I'm ready.
Je ne suis pas prêt(e).	I'm not ready.
Attends!	Wait!

◉ Grammar and skills: I can…

- ◉ make comparisons with *plus* and *moins*
- ◉ use reflexive verbs to talk about daily routine
- ◉ use the 24-hour clock
- ◉ use the perfect tense with *être*
- ◉ use the near future
- ◉ identify and combine tenses
- ◉ use expressions with *avoir*
- ◉ use transferable structures to discuss answers
- ◉ identify key points in a text
- ◉ use strategies to improve my speaking and writing
- ◉ use connectives for contrast

Grammaire

Nouns and articles

All French nouns are either masculine or feminine.

Le/La are **definite articles**. They mean 'the'.
le portable – the mobile phone
la voiture – the car

Un/Une are **indefinite articles**. They mean 'a (or 'an').
un portable – a mobile phone
une voiture – a car

In the plural (more than one), the definite article is *les* and the indefinite article is *des*. You cannot omit *des*.
les portables – the mobile phones
Elle a des cartes postales. – She's got (some) postcards.

	masculine	feminine	plural
definite article	le portable	la voiture	les portables les voitures
indefinite article	un portable	une voiture	des portables des voitures

Le or *la* in front of a vowel loses a letter.
l'objet – the object

Partitive articles

You use the partitive articles *du, de la, de l'* or *des* to talk about unspecified quantities, for example with food.

	masculine	feminine
singular	du pain	de la salade
plural	des œufs	des chips

Use *de l'* for a singular word starting with a vowel: *de l'eau*.

You often use the partitive article after *faire*.
Je fais de la voile, du VTT et de l'athlétisme. – I go sailing, mountain biking and I do athletics.

After a negative verb, use *de* (*d'* in front of a vowel).
Je ne fais pas de voile. – I don't go sailing.
Je ne mange pas d'œufs. – I don't eat eggs.

Direct object pronouns

You can use the definite articles *le, la, l', les* (the) as direct object pronouns, meaning 'him', 'her', 'it' or 'them'. They go in front of the verb.

Ma copine Marion? Je la connais depuis deux ans. – My friend Marion? I have known **her** for two years.

Le prof de maths? Je le déteste. – The maths teacher? I can't stand **him**.

Ma petite sœur? Je l'adore. – My little sister? I love **her**.

Adjectives – position

Adjectives describe nouns. They normally go <u>after</u> the noun.
un chat gris – a **grey** cat

Some adjectives, often short ones such as *beau, joli, jeune, vieux, petit, grand, gros, nouveau*, go <u>before</u> the noun.
une grande maison – a large house
un petit chien – a small dog

Adjectives – agreement

Most adjectives agree with the noun. Their sound and spelling change according to whether the noun they describe is masculine or feminine, singular or plural. They add an *-e* in the feminine and an *-s* in the plural.

	masculine	feminine
singular	un petit chien	une petite maison
plural	deux petits chiens	deux petites maisons

If an adjective already ends in *-s*, it doesn't change in the masculine plural. This often happens with adjectives of nationality.
deux garçons français – two French boys

If an adjective already ends in *-e*, it doesn't change in the feminine singular.
une maison rouge – a red house

Some adjectives follow different rules when they agree.

masculine	feminine	masc. plural	fem. plural
actif	active	actifs	actives
courageux	courageuse	courageux	courageuses
travailleur	travailleuse	travailleurs	travailleuses
gentil	gentille	gentils	gentilles
long	longue	long(s)	longues
gros	grosse	gros	grosses
national	nationale	nationaux	nationales
roux	rousse	roux	rousses
beau	belle	beaux	belles

Some common adjectives have irregular agreements.

masculine	feminine	masc. plural	fem. plural
blanc	blanche	blancs	blanches
vieux	vieille	vieux	vieilles

Some adjectives, such as *marron, orange, sympa, cool*, do not agree at all: they are invariable.
Mes copines sont cool. – My (girl) friends are cool.

Compound adjectives (made of two adjectives) are also invariable.

*des yeux **bleu foncé*** – dark blue eyes

Adjectives: comparison

You use *plus ... que* (more ... than) or *moins ... que* (less ... than) in front of adjectives to make comparisons.

*Le français est **plus** intéressant **que** la géographie.* – French is more interesting than geography.

*Océane est **moins** travailleuse **que** Manon.* – Océane is less hard-working than Manon.

*Mes copines sont **plus** amusantes **que** mes parents.* – My (girl) friends are more fun than my parents.

Possessive adjectives

In French, possessive adjectives (the words for 'my', 'your', 'his/her', 'its') agree with the noun. It does not matter if you are talking about a girl or a boy (a woman or a man). What matters is the noun that follows.

		my	your	his/her
masc. (or starting with vowel)	un T-shirt une écharpe	mon T-shirt mon écharpe	ton T-shirt ton écharpe	son T-shirt son écharpe
fem.	une console	ma console	ta console	sa console
plural	les parents	mes parents	tes parents	ses parents

*Pierre dort chez moi. **Sa** mère est en vacances.* – Pierre is staying at my house. **His** mother is on holiday.

*Léa joue bien au tennis. **Son** père est prof de tennis.* – Léa plays tennis well. **Her** father is a tennis teacher.

Prepositions

You use *en* with names of countries that are feminine or start with a vowel.

J'habite en Angleterre. – I live in England.

Je vais en France. – I'm going to France.

You use *au/aux* with names of countries that are masculine.

J'habite au pays de Galles. – I live in Wales.

Je vais aux États-Unis. – I'm going to the States.

You use *à* with names of towns and cities.

J'habite à Londres. – I live in London.

Je vais à Paris. – I'm going to Paris.

You use *au/à la/à l'* with places in town.

masculine		au cinéma.
feminine	Je suis/Je vais	à la piscine.
noun starting with a vowel		à l'église.

Other useful prepositions include:

dans	in, inside
devant	in front of
derrière	behind
entre	between
à côté de	next to
en face de	opposite
à gauche de	left of
à droite de	right of

masculine	à côté du cinéma
feminine	en face de la piscine
noun starting with a vowel	à gauche de l'église
plural	à droite des magasins

Negatives

To make a sentence negative, you put *ne ... pas* either side of the verb.

*Je **ne** vais **pas** au parc.* – I'm not going to the park.

After a negative, the indefinite or partitive article becomes *de*.

*Je mange **de la** viande.* – I eat (some) meat.

*Je ne mange pas **de** viande.* – I don't eat (any) meat.

*Il y a **des** girafes au zoo.* – There are (some) giraffes at the zoo.

*Il n'y a pas **de** girafes au zoo.* – There aren't any giraffes at the zoo.

With a reflexive verb, *ne ... pas* goes around the pronoun + verb phrase.

*Je **ne me lève pas** à six heures.* – I don't get up at 6am.

With the perfect or near future tenses, *ne ... pas* goes either side of the auxiliary verb (*être, avoir* or *aller*).

*Je **ne suis pas** allé à Paris.* – I didn't go to Paris.

*Je **n'ai pas** visité la tour Eiffel.* – I didn't visit the Eiffel Tower.

*Je **ne vais pas** jouer au foot demain.* – I am not going to play football tomorrow.

With modal verbs, *ne ... pas* goes around the modal verb.

*Je **ne veux pas** sortir demain.* – I don't want to go out tomorrow.

Grammaire

Verbs: the present tense

There is only one present tense in French.
Je joue au foot. – I play football.
Je joue sur mon ordi. – I am playing on my computer.
The pronoun *je* in front of a vowel is shortened to *j'*.
J'aime les fraises. – I love strawberries.

Regular *-er*, *-ir* and *-re* verbs

To form the present tense of regular *-er* verbs, replace *-er* with the correct ending.
With verbs such as *préférer* you also have to change the accent.

There are a few small exceptions:

manger (to eat) – *nous mangeons*
commencer (to start) – *nous commençons*

To form the present tense of regular *-ir* verbs, replace *-r* with the correct ending.
To form the present tense of regular *-re* verbs such as *répondre*, replace *-r* with the correct ending.

Irregular verbs

There are many irregular verbs, for example *avoir* (to have), *être* (to be), *faire* (to do, make), *aller* (to go), *prendre* (to take), *sortir* (to go out).
Je suis français. – I am French.
J'ai faim. – I'm hungry.

Reflexive verbs

You use reflexive verbs to talk about an action you do to yourself. Reflexive verbs have an extra pronoun.
Je me couche. – I go to bed. (I take **myself** to bed.)
The pronouns *me*, *te* and *se* in front of a vowel are shortened to *m'*, *t'* and *s'*.
Je m'habille. – I get dressed.

Modal verbs: *pouvoir, vouloir*

Modal verbs are normally followed by a verb in the infinitive.
Le samedi, je peux aller au cinéma. – On Saturdays, I can go to the cinema.
Je veux jouer au tennis. – I want to play tennis.

Verbs: past tenses

To talk about an action in the past, you use the **perfect tense.**
With most verbs, you form the perfect tense with the auxiliary *avoir* (in the present tense) and the past participle of the verb.
*J'ai **joué** au foot.* – I played football.
With some verbs, normally verbs of movement, you use the auxiliary *être* + past participle.
*Je **suis allé** au parc et j'ai joué au foot.* – I went to the park and I played football.

With the auxiliary *être*, the past participle has to agree with the subject.
*Sophie et Anna **sont allées** à la piscine.* – Sophie and Anna went to the swimming pool.

masculine singular	feminine singular	masculine plural	feminine plural
je suis allé	je suis allée	on est allés nous sommes allés	on est allées nous sommes allées
tu es allé	tu es allée	vous êtes allés	vous êtes allées
il est allé	elle est allée	ils sont allés	elles sont allées

To describe the way things used to be in the past, you use the **imperfect tense**.
*Quand j'**étais** petite, je n'**étais** pas sociable.* –
When I was small, I wasn't sociable.
C'était – it was

Verbs: the near future

One way of talking about the future is to use the near future. You form it with the auxiliary *aller* and the infinitive of the verb.
*Ce soir, je **vais faire** mes devoirs.* –
Tonight, I'm going to do my homework.
*Ce week-end, elle **va jouer** au tennis.* –
This weekend, she is going to play tennis.

je vais	
tu vas	
il/elle/on va	
nous allons	+ INF.
vous allez	
ils/elles vont	

Regular verbs

	jouer – to play	*préférer* – to prefer	*finir* – to finish	*répondre* – to answer	*se lever* – to get up	*se coucher* – to go to bed
present	je joue	je préfère	je finis	je réponds	je **me** lève	je **me** couche
	tu jou**es**	tu préfère**s**	tu finis	tu réponds	tu **te** lèves	tu **te** couches
	il/elle/on joue	il/elle/on préfère	il/elle/on finit	il/elle/on répond	il/elle/on **se** lève	il/elle/on **se** couche
	nous jou**ons**	nous préfér**ons**	nous finis**sons**	nous répond**ons**	nous **nous** levons	nous **nous** couchons
	vous jou**ez**	vous préfér**ez**	vous fini**ssez**	vous répond**ez**	vous **vous** levez	vous **vous** couchez
	ils/elles jou**ent**	ils/elles préfèr**ent**	ils/elles fini**ssent**	ils/elles répond**ent**	ils/elles **se** lèvent	ils/elles **se** couchent
perfect	j'ai joué	j'ai préféré	j'ai fini	j'ai répond**u**		

Modal verbs

	pouvoir – to be able to	*vouloir* – to want to
present	je peux	je veux
	tu peux	tu veux
	il/elle/on peut	il/elle/on veut
	nous pouvons	nous voulons
	vous pouvez	vous voulez
	ils/elles peuvent	ils/elles veulent

Irregular verbs

	être – to be	*avoir* – to have
present	je suis	j'ai
	tu es	tu as
	il/elle/on est	il/elle/on a
	nous sommes	nous avons
	vous êtes	vous avez
	ils/elles sont	ils/elles ont
perfect	j'ai été	j'ai eu

Irregular verbs continued

	faire – to do, make	*boire* – to drink	*prendre* – to take	*mettre* – to put	*voir* – to see	*lire* – to read
present	je fais	je bois	je prends	je mets	je vois	je lis
	tu fais	tu bois	tu prends	tu mets	tu vois	tu lis
	il/elle/on fait	il/elle/on boit	il/elle/on prend	il/elle/on met	il/elle/on voit	il/elle/on lit
	nous faisons	nous buvons	nous prenons	nous mettons	nous voyons	nous lisons
	vous faites	vous buvez	vous prenez	vous mettez	vous voyez	vous lisez
	ils/elles font	ils/elles boivent	ils/elles prennent	ils/elles mettent	ils/elles voient	ils/elles lisent
perfect	j'ai fait	j'ai bu	j'ai pris	j'ai mis	j'ai vu	j'ai lu

Verbs of movement

	aller – to go	*venir* – to come	*partir* – to leave	*sortir* – to go out
present	je vais	je viens	je pars	je sors
	tu vas	tu viens	tu pars	tu sors
	il/elle/on va	il/elle/on vient	il/elle/on part	il/elle/on sort
	nous allons	nous venons	nous partons	nous sortons
	vous allez	vous venez	vous partez	vous sortez
	ils/elles vont	ils/elles viennent	ils/elles partent	ils/elles sortent
perfect	je suis allé(e)	je suis venu(e)	je suis parti(e)	je suis sorti(e)

Grammaire

Questions

To ask a closed question (requiring a 'yes/no' answer), you can use a statement and simply raise your voice at the end.
Tu veux jouer au tennis demain? – Do you want to play tennis tomorrow?

You can also use a statement and add *Est-ce que* at the start.
Est-ce que *tu veux jouer au tennis demain?* – Do you want to play tennis tomorrow?

To ask an open question, you need a question word or phrase.
Quel *âge as-tu?* – How old are you?
C'est **quand***, ton anniversaire?* – When is your birthday?
Comment *t'appelles-tu?* – What is your name?
Où *habites-tu?* – Where do you live?
C'est **quoi***?* – What is it?
C'est **qui***?* – Who is it?
Qu'est-ce que *tu portes?* – What do you wear?
Pourquoi *aimes-tu le ski?* – Why do you like skiing?

Instructions (the imperative)

To give an instruction, you use the imperative form. With many verbs, that's the *tu* or the *vous* form of the present tense, without the pronoun.

If the *tu* form ends in *-es*, the imperative form ends in *-e*.
Fais *tes devoirs.* – Do your homework.

Tournez *à gauche.* – Turn left.
Envoie *une carte postale.* – Send a postcard.

Mots utiles

Numbers

un	1	quinze	15
deux	2	seize	16
trois	3	dix-sept	17
quatre	4	dix-huit	18
cinq	5	dix-neuf	19
six	6	vingt	20
sept	7	vint et un	21
huit	8	vingt-deux	22
neuf	9	vingt-trois	23
dix	10	vingt-quatre	24
onze	11	vingt-cinq	25
douze	12	vingt-six	26
treize	13	vingt-sept	27
quatorze	14	vingt-huit	28

vingt-neuf	29	quatre-vingts	80
trente	30	quatre-vingt un	81
quarante	40	quatre-vingt dix	90
quarante et un	41	quatre-vingt onze	91
cinquante	50	cent	100
soixante	60	deux cents	200
soixante-dix	70	trois cents	300
soixante et onze	71		

le premier, la première – the first

Days of the week

lundi
mardi
mercredi
jeudi
vendredi
samedi
dimanche

Months of the year

janvier	juillet
février	août
mars	septembre
avril	octobre
mai	novembre
juin	décembre

Telling the time

12-hour clock		24-hour clock
midi/minuit	midday/midnight	douze heures/zéro heure
une heure	1 o'clock	treize heures
une heure cinq	1.05	treize heures cinq
une heure dix	1.10	treize heures dix
une heure et quart	1.15	treize heures quinze
une heure vingt	1.20	treize heures vingt
une heure vingt-cinq	1.25	treize heures vingt-cinq
une heure et demie	1.30	treize heures trente
deux heures moins vingt-cinq	1.35	treize heures trente-cinq
deux heures moins vingt	1.40	treize heures quarante
deux heures moins le quart	1.45	treize heures quarante-cinq
deux heures moins dix	1.50	treize heures cinquante
deux heures moins cinq	1.55	treize heures cinquante-cinq

For scheduled times, for example railway timetables, etc., you use the 24-hour clock.
Le film passe à **vingt-deux heures trente***.* – The film is showing at 10.30pm (22.30).

A

acheter *v* to buy
l' acteur, l'actrice *n* actor
actuellement at the moment
adorable *adj* lovely
adorer *v* to love
agité *adj* hyperactive
Ah bon? Is that so?
aider *v* to help
aimer (bien) *v* to like, love
l' aire de jeu *nf* play area
ajouter *v* to add
l' Allemagne *nf* Germany
allemand *adj* German
aller *v* to go
aller mal *v* to be unwell
alors so
l' ami(e) *n* friend
amusant *adj* fun, funny
l' an *nm* year
l' âne *nm* donkey
anglais *adj* English
l' Angleterre *nf* England
l' animal domestique *nm* pet
l' année *nf* year
l' anniversaire *nm* birthday
août *nm* August
l' appartement *nm* flat
s' appeler *v* to be called
apporter *v* to bring
après after
l' après-midi *nm* afternoon
l' arabe *nm* Arabic
l' arbre *nm* tree
l' argent *nm* money
les arts plastiques *nm* art
assez rather, quite
l' association caritative *nf* charity
l' atelier *nm* workshop
attention beware
l' auberge de jeunesse *nf* youth hostel
aujourd'hui today
aussi too, as well
l' autoportrait *nm* self-portrait

autre *adj* other
avant before
avec with
à l' avenir in the future
avoir confiance *v* to trust
avoir de la chance *v* to be lucky
avoir faim *v* to be hungry
avoir horreur de *v* to detest
avoir mal *v* to be in pain
avoir peur *v* to be scared
avoir raison *v* to be right
avoir soif *v* to be thirsty
avoir tort *v* to be wrong
avril *nm* April

B

le baby-foot *n* table football
la baguette *n* French stick
se baigner *v* to swim (for relaxation)
la balle aux prisonniers *n* dodgeball
le ballon *n* ball
le banc *n* bench
la bande *n* group
la banlieue *n* suburbs
le basket(ball) *n* basketball
les baskets *nf* trainers
le bateau de croisière *n* cruise ship
la batterie *n* drums
bavard *adj* talkative
bavarder *v* to chat
la BD *n* comic book
beau *adj* beautiful
le beau-père *n* stepfather
beaucoup many, a lot
le bébé *n* baby
belge *adj* Belgian
la Belgique *n* Belgium
la belle-mère *n* stepmother
bénévole *adj* voluntary
berk yuk
le beurre *n* butter
bien good, well

(à) bientôt (see you) soon
la bière *n* beer
le billard *n* snooker
blanc *adj* white
le blanc *n* blank, gap
bleu *adj* blue
blond *adj* fair
le blouson *n* bomber jacket
le bœuf *n* beef
boire *v* to drink
le bois *n* wood
la boisson *n* drink
bon *adj* good; right
bon appétit enjoy your food
bonjour hello
le bonnet *n* woolly hat
le bord de la mer *n* seaside
les bottes *nf* boots
bouclé *adj* curly
bouger *v* to move, be active
la boule *n* scoop
les boules *nf* bowls
le bout du monde *n* the end of the world
la bouteille *n* bottle
le bras *n* arm
la Bretagne *n* Brittany
breton *adj* from Brittany
se brosser les dents *v* to clean one's teeth
brun *adj* brown (hair)
bruyant *adj* noisy

C

c'est *v* it is
C'est à qui? Whose turn is it?
c'est ça that's it
C'est combien? How much is it?
C'est qui? Who is it?
c'est top it's great
C'est tout? Is that all?
c'est tout that's all
c'était *v* it was
ça that
ça marche it works
ça me fait vomir it makes me sick
Ça va? How are you?
ça va (bien) I'm fine
la cabane *n* shed
caché *adj* hidden

le café *n* coffee
le/la camarade *n* mate
la campagne *n* countryside
le camping *n* campsite
le canard *n* duck
la capsule témoin *n* time capsule
car because
les Caraïbes *nf* Caribbean
caramel *adj* toffee
le cari *n* curry
le carré *n* square
la carte *n* map
la carte postale *n* postcard
la casquette *n* cap
le cassis *n* blackcurrant
à cause de because of
ce, cette, ces *adj* this, these
célèbre *adj* famous
célébrer *v* to celebrate
cent one hundred
le centre aéré *n* holiday club
le centre commercial *n* shopping mall
le centre sportif *n* sports centre
cependant however
la chambre *n* bedroom
le champignon *n* mushroom
le championnat *n* championship
changeant *adj* changing
changer *v* to change
le chanteur *n* singer
le chariot *n* trolley
charmant *adj* charming
la chasse *n* hunt
le chat *n* cat
chaud *adj* hot
les chaussures *nf* shoes
le chemin *n* way; path
la chemise *n* shirt
cher *adj* expensive
chercher *v* to look for, look up
le cheval *n* horse
les cheveux *nm* hair
la cheville *n* ankle
chez (moi) at (my) house
le chien *n* dog
les chips *nf* crisps
choisir *v* to choose

Glossaire

le **choix** n choice
le **Christ Rédempteur** n Christ the Redeemer
le **ciné(ma)** n cinema
cinq five
cinquante fifty
la **cinquième** n Year 8
le **citron** n lemon
clair adj light
classer v to sort out
le **club (d'animation)** n (youth) club
le **coca (light)** n coke (lite)
le **cochon** n pig
le **cochon d'Inde** n guinea pig
le **coin** n corner
le **collège** n secondary school
la **colo(nie)** n holiday camp
coloré adj colourful
comme like
commencer v to start
comment how
compléter v to complete
compréhensif adj understanding
compris adj included
le **concours** n competition
la **confiture** n jam
connaître v to know
le **copain, la copine** n mate
le **cornet** n cone
le/la **correspondant(e)** n penfriend
correspondre v to match
corriger v to correct
le **corsaire** n pirate
à **côté de** next to
se **coucher** v to go to bed
coucou hiya
la **coupe** n (ice cream) dish
courageux adj brave
le **cours** n class, lesson
la **course d'orientation** n orienteering
les **courses** nf shopping
court adj short
le **crâne** n skull
créer v to create
la **crème anglaise** n custard

la **crème fraîche** n sour cream
la **crème solaire** n sun cream
la **crêpe** n pancake
la **crêperie** n pancake house
la **critique** n review
je **crois** v I think
la **croisière** n cruise
le **croque-monsieur** n toasted cheese sandwich
la **cuillère** n spoon
le **cuir** n leather
la **cuisine** n cooking
cuisiner v to cook
la **cuisse de grenouille** n frog's leg

D

d'abord first
d'accord OK
d'habitude normally
dangereux adj dangerous
le **débarras** n cupboard
le **début** n start
décrire v to describe
le **défilé** n parade
dégoûtant adj disgusting
le **déjeuner** n lunch
délicieux adj delicious
demain tomorrow
demander v to ask
le **demi-frère** n stepbrother, half-brother
la **demi-sœur** n stepsister, half-sister
la **dent** n tooth
depuis since
dernier(ère) adj last
derrière behind
désert adj sparsely populated
se **déshabiller** v to get undressed
désolé adj sorry
le **dessert** n pudding
le **dessin** n drawing
dessiner v to draw
se **détendre** v to relax
détester v to hate
détruit adj destroyed
deux two
à **deux** in pairs
deuxième adj second

devant in front of
deviner v to guess
la **devise** n motto
les **devoirs** nm homework
le **dictionnaire** n dictionary
différent adj different
difficile adj difficult; fussy
le **dimanche** n Sunday
le **dîner** n dinner
discuter v to discuss
se **disputer** v to have a row
divorcé adj divorced
dix ten
dix-huit eighteen
dix-neuf nineteen
dix-sept seventeen
dommage pity
donc so
donner v to give
dormir v to sleep
le **dos** n back
se **doucher** v to have a shower
douze twelve
à **droite** right
le **DVD** n DVD

E

l' **eau (minérale/du robinet)** nf (mineral/tap) water
l' **écharpe** nf scarf
l' **école** nf school
écossais adj Scottish
l' **Écosse** nf Scotland
écouter v to listen
l' **écran** nm screen
écrire v to write
effrayant adj scary
l' **église** nf church
l' **élève** nmf pupil, student
en in, to
en face de opposite
en fait as a matter of fact
en plus moreover
encore again
l' **endroit** nm place
l' **enfant** nm child
s' **engager** v to commit oneself
ennuyeux adj boring
ensemble together
l' **ensemble** nm the whole
ensuite then

l' **entraînement** nm training, practice
s' **entraîner** v to train, practise
entre between
entrer v to go in
envoyer v to send
l' **épaule** nf shoulder
épicé adj hot, spicy
l' **épreuve** nf event
l' **EPS** nf sport
l' **équipe** nf team
l' **équitation** nf horseriding
l' **erreur** nf mistake
l' **escalade** nf rock-climbing
l' **escargot** nm snail
l' **espace** nm space
l' **Espagne** nf Spain
espagnol adj Spanish
essayer v to try
l' **est** nm East
et and
Et toi? And you?
étaler v to spread
les **États-Unis** nm USA
l' **été** nm summer
expliquer v to explain
l' **expression** nf phrase
extra adj great
l' **extrait** nm extract

F

faire v to do, make
faire cuire v to cook
faire des courses v to go shopping
faire du camping v to go camping
faire peur v to frighten
il **fait chaud** v it is warm/hot
il **fait du vent** v it is windy
il **fait froid** v it is cold
la **famille** n family
la **famine** n hunger
le **fast-food** n fast food restaurant
fatigant adj tiring
fatigué adj tired
il **faut** v you need, you must
le **fauteuil roulant** n wheelchair
faux adj false, wrong
la **ferme** n farm
féroce adj ferocious

la **fête** *n* party
le **feu d'artifice** *n* fireworks
le **feu de camp** *n* campfire
février *nm* February
fidèle *adj* loyal
fille-fille *adj* girly
le **fils/la fille unique** *n* only child
la **fin** *n* end
finir *v* to finish
la **fleur** *n* flower
la **fois** *n* time
foncé *adj* dark
le **foot(ball)** *n* football
le **footballeur** *n* footballer
la **forêt** *n* forest
fort *adj* strong
fou *adj* crazy
le **four** *n* oven
frais *adj* fresh
la **fraise** *n* strawberry
la **framboise** *n* raspberry
français *adj* French
la **France** *n* France
francophone *adj* French-speaking
la **francophonie** *n* French-speaking countries
le **frère** *n* brother
la **friperie** *n* second-hand clothes shop
la **frite** *n* chip
le **fromage** *n* cheese

G

gagner *v* to win
gallois *adj* Welsh
le **gant** *nm* glove
la **gare routière** *n* bus station
le **gâteau** *n* cake
à **gauche** left
la **gaufre Chantilly** *n* waffle with whipped cream
il **gèle** *v* it is freezing
en **général** generally
généreux *adj* generous
génial *adj* great
le **genou** *n* knee
le **genre** *n* kind
gentil *adj* kind
le **geste** *n* gesture
la **girafe** *n* giraffe

le **gîte** *n* holiday cottage
la **glace** *n* ice cream
gore *adj* gory
le **goûter** *n* afternoon snack
goûter *v* to taste
grand *adj* big
la **grand-mère** *n* grandmother
le **grand-parent** *n* grandparent
le **grand-père** *n* grandfather
la **Grande-Bretagne** *n* Great Britain
gratuit *adj* free
la **Grèce** *n* Greece
la **grille** *n* table
grillé *adj* toasted
grincheux *adj* grumpy
gris *adj* grey

H

s' **habiller** *v* to get dressed
habiter *v* to live
haché *adj* chopped
le **hand(ball)** *n* handball
le **haricot vert** *n* green bean
l' **heure** *nf* hour
à **l'heure** on time
heureux *adj* happy
hier yesterday
hindou *adj* Hindu
l' **hippopotame** *nm* hippo
l' **histoire** *nf* history
l' **hiver** *nm* winter
l' **huile** *nf* oil
huit eight

I

s' **identifier à** *v* to identify with
l' **île** *nf* island
l' **image** *nf* picture
l' **imper(méable)** *nm* raincoat
important *adj* important
incroyable *adj* unbelievable
l' **infirmier(ère)** *n* nurse
intéressant *adj* interesting

inutile *adj* useless
inventer *v* to invent
irlandais *adj* Irish
l' **Irlande** *nf* Ireland
en **italique** in italics

J

J'ai X ans. I'm X years old.
jamais never
la **jambe** *n* leg
le **jambon** *n* ham
janvier *nm* January
le **jardin** *n* garden
jaune *adj* yellow
je I
Je t'en prie. You're welcome.
le **jeu de rôles** *n* role-play
le **jeu vidéo** *n* video game
le **jeudi** *n* Thursday
les **jeunes** *nm* young people
les **Jeux Olympiques** *nm* Olympic Games
joli *adj* pretty
jouer *v* to play
le **joueur** *n* player
le **jour** *n* day, date
la **journée** day
joyeux *adj* happy
juillet *nm* July
juin *nm* June
les **jumelles** *nf* binoculars
la **jupe** *n* skirt
le **jus d'orange** *n* orange juice
juste just

L

là où where
là-bas there
le **lac** *n* lake
le **lait** *n* milk
la **langue** *n* language
le **lapin** *n* rabbit
se **laver** *v* to wash oneself
le **lecteur MP4** *n* MP4 player
le **légume (vert)** *n* (green) vegetable
lent *adj* slow
se **lever** *v* to get up
libre *adj* free
en **ligne** online

lire *v* to read
le **livre** *n* book
les **loisirs** *nm* leisure time
le **long de** along
le **lundi** *n* Monday
les **lunettes de soleil** *nf* sunglasses

M

ma *adj* my
le **magasin** *n* shop
le **mail** *n* email
le **maillot de bain** *n* swimming costume
maintenant now
mais but
maison *adj* home-made
la **maison** *n* house
la **maison d'enfance** *n* children's home
la **maison des jeunes** *n* youth club
la **maison individuelle** *n* detached house
la **maison jumelée** *n* semi-detached house
malentendant *adj* hard of hearing
malheureusement unfortunately
malvoyant *adj* visually impaired
maman *n* mum
le **mammifère** *n* mammal
manger *v* to eat
le **maquillage** *n* make-up
le **marché** *n* market
le **mardi** *n* Tuesday
le **Maroc** *n* Morocco
marocain *adj* Moroccan
la **marque** *n* brand
marrant *adj* fun, funny
marron *adj* brown
mars *nm* March
le **match** *n* match, game
la **matière** *n* subject matter
le **matin** *n* morning
mature *adj* mature
méchant *adj* horrible; naughty
la **médaille (d'or)** *n* (gold) medal

Glossaire

le **médecin** *n* doctor
meilleur *adj* best
mélanger *v* to mix
mentionné *adj* mentioned
la **mer** *n* sea(side)
merci (bien/ beaucoup) thank you
le **mercredi** *n* Wednesday
la **mère** *n* mother
mes *adj* my
mettre *v* to put, place
midi *nm* midday
mignon *adj* cute
mi-long *adj* mid-length
minuit midnight
moche *adj* ugly
à la **mode** fashionable
moi me
à **moi** my turn
moins ... que less ... than
le **mois** *n* month
la **moitié** *n* half
mon *adj* my
le **monde** *n* world
le **moniteur** *n* instructor
la **montagne** *n* mountains
montagneux *adj* mountainous
moqueur *adj* mocking
le **morceau** *n* piece
mort *adj* dead
le **mot** *n* word
motivé *adj* motivated
la **motoneige** *n* snowmobile
la **moule** *n* mussel
la **moutarde** *n* mustard
le **mouton** *n* sheep
le **musée** *n* museum
musulman *adj* Muslim

N

nager *v* to swim
la **natation** *n* swimming
natté *adj* braided
né *adj* born
il **neige** *v* it is snowing
noir *adj* black

noisette *adj* hazel(nut)
le **nom** *n* name
le **nord** *n* North
la **note** *n* note; mark
le **nounours** *n* teddy bear
la **nourriture** *n* food
nul *adj* rubbish
le **numéro** *n* number

O

l' **objet** *nm* object
s' **occuper de** *v* to look after
l' **œuf** *nm* egg
l' **oignon** *nm* onion
l' **oiseau** *nm* bird
onze eleven
l' **orage** *nm* thunderstorm
l' **ordi(nateur)** *nm* computer
où where
l' **ouest** *nm* West
ouvert *adj* open

P

le **pain** *n* bread
le **pain au chocolat** *n* chocolate pastry
la **paix** *n* peace
papa *n* dad
le **papier** *n* paper
le **paquet** *n* packet
par contre on the other hand
le **parapente** *n* paragliding
le **parapluie** *m* umbrella
le **parc d'attractions** *n* theme park
le **parc safari** *n* safari park
parce que because
paresseux *adj* lazy
le **parfum** *n* flavour
parler *v* to speak
à **part** apart from
partager *v* to share
le/la **partenaire** *n* partner
participer *v* to take part
partir *v* to leave
pas not
Pas de quoi. You're welcome.
pas grand-chose not much

passer *v* to spend
passionnant *adj* exciting
les **pâtes** *nf* pasta
le **patin sur glace** *n* ice skating
la **patinoire** *n* ice rink
la **pauvreté** *n* poverty
le **pavillon** *n* small detached house
le **pays** *n* country
le **pays de Galles** *n* Wales
la **peinture** *n* painting
la **peluche** *n* soft toy
penser *v* to think
le **père** *n* father
la **personne** *n* person
personnellement personally
la **pétanque** *n* bowls
petit *adj* small
le **petit déjeuner** *n* breakfast
peuplé *adj* populated
le **phasme** *n* stick insect
la **phrase** *n* sentence
le **pied** *n* foot
à **pied** on foot
la **piscine** *n* swimming pool
la **pistache** *n* pistachio
pittoresque *adj* picturesque
la **place** *n* town square; seat
la **plage** *n* beach
la **planche à voile** *n* windsurfing
plat *adj* flat
le **plat** *n* dish
plein de *adj* full of
il **pleut** *v* it is raining
la **plongée** *n* scuba diving
à **plus** see you
plus ... que more ... than
plus tard later
le **poisson** *n* fish
le **poivre** *n* pepper
la **pomme** *n* apple
le **pont** *n* bridge
le **portable** *n* mobile phone
porter *v* to wear
poser *v* to put
poser une question *v* to ask a question
le **pot** *n* tub, pot
le **poulet** *n* chicken

Pour aller ... ? How do I go ... ?
pour finir finally
pourtant however
pouvoir *v* can, to be able to
pratique *adj* practical
préféré *adj* favourite
préférer *v* to prefer
premier(ère) *adj* first
prendre *v* to take
primaire *adj* primary
prochain *adj* next
le/la **prof** *n* teacher
la **promenade** *n* walk, stroll
propre *adj* clean
puis then

Q

Qu'est-ce que c'est? What is it?
quand when
quarante forty
le **quartier** *n* neighbourhood
quatorze fourteen
quatre four
quatre-vingts eighty
quatre-ving dix ninety
la **quatrième** *n* Year 9
que that
quel(le), quel(le)s which, what
Quel âge as-tu? How old are you?
quelqu'un someone
quelqu'un de bien a nice person
quelquefois sometimes
qui who
quinze fifteen
quitter *v* to leave
quoi what

R

raide *adj* straight
la **randonnée** *n* hike
râpé *adj* grated
la **recette** *n* recipe
reconstruire *v* to rebuild
recopier *v* to copy out
regarder *v* to look
relaxant *adj* relaxing
relier *v* to match

Glossaire

la religion *n* religion; religious studies
remettre *v* to put back
remplir *v* to fill in
rentrer *v* to come home
le repas *n* meal
répéter *v* to repeat
répondre *v* to answer
la réponse *n* answer
représenter *v* to represent
rester *v* to stay, remain
le resto *n* restaurant, eatery
en retard late
retourner to return
se retrouver *v* to meet up with
le rêve *n* dream
se réveiller *v* to wake up
rêveur *adj* dreamy
au revoir goodbye
la richesse *n* wealth
ridicule *adj* ridiculous
rien nothing
de rien you're welcome
le riz *n* rice
la robe *n* dress
le roman *n* novel
le rond *n* circle
rose *adj* pink
rouge *adj* red
roux (rousse) *adj* red-haired
la rue *n* street
le ruisseau *n* stream

S

s'il te/vous plaît please
le sac *n* bag
sage *adj* wise
salé *adj* savoury
la salle de classe *n* classroom
salut hello
le samedi *n* Saturday
à sang froid cold blooded
sans without
satisfaisant *adj* satisfying
la saucisse *n* sausage
le saut à l'élastique *n* bungee jumping

sauvage *adj* wild
le/la scientifique *n* scientist
scolaire *adj* school
la sécheresse *n* drought
seize sixteen
le sel *n* salt
sénégalais *adj* Senegalese
séparé *adj* separated
sept seven
ce serait *v* it would be
le shopping *n* shopping (for fun)
si if; yes
le singe *n* monkey
le sirop d'érable *n* maple syrup
la sixième *n* Year 7
le skate *n* skating
la sœur *n* sister
le soir *n* evening
soixante sixty
soixante-dix seventy
le soleil *n* sun
le son *n* sound
le sondage *n* survey
sonner *v* to ring, go off
la sonnerie *n* the bell
la sortie *n* outing
sortir *v* to go out
souligné *adj* underlined
la soupe *n* soup
souvent often
la spécialité *n* specialty
le spectacle *n* show
sportif *adj* sporty
le stage sportif *n* sports course
stressant *adj* stressful
le stylo *n* pen
le sucre *n* sugar
sucré *adj* sweet
le sud *n* South
la Suisse *n* Switzerland
suivre *v* to follow
super *adj* super
le supermarché *n* supermarket
le supplément *n* extra
surfer *v* to surf
le survêtement *n* track-suit
les SVT *nf* science
le sweat *n* sweat-shirt
sympa(thique) *adj* nice

T

à table at table
le tableau *n* blackboard
la tablette *n* tablet; bar
à talons high-heel
la tante *n* aunt
la tartine *n* slice of bread
tchater *v* to chat (on the Net)
la technologie *n* design and technology
la télé *n* TV
télécharger *v* to download
le temps *n* time
de temps en temps from time to time
terminer *v* to finish
le terrain de sport *n* sports ground
la terre *n* land
la tête *n* head
le texto *n* text message
le thé *n* tea
le théâtre *n* drama
le thon *n* tuna
timide *adj* shy
le tir à l'arc *n* archery
le tissu *n* material
toi you
ton/ta/tes *adj* your
la tortue *n* tortoise
toujours always
tourner *v* to turn
le tournoi *n* tournament
tout everything
(tout) d'abord first
tout droit straight on
tout, tous all
la traduction *n* translation
traduire *v* to translate
la tranche *n* slice
tranquille *adj* quiet
le travail *n* work
travailleur *adj* hard-working
traverser *v* to cross
treize thirteen
le tremblement de terre *n* earthquake
trente thirty
très very
le trésor *n* treasure
triste *adj* sad
trois three
la troisième *n* Year 10

trop really
trouver *v* to find
le truc *n* thingy
mon truc my thing

U

un one
un peu a little
utile *adj* useful
utiliser *v* to use

V

les vacances *nf* holidays
la vache *n* cow
le vaisseau spatial *n* spaceship
le véhicule *n* vehicle
le vélo *n* bike
le velours *n* velvet
la vendeuse *n* assistant
le vendredi *n* Friday
la vente *n* sale
vérifier *v* to check
vert *adj* green
la veste *n* jacket
les vêtements *nm* clothes
la viande *n* meat
la vie *n* life
la ville *n* town, city
vingt twenty
violet *adj* purple
vivant *adj* lively, animated
voici here is
la voile *n* sailing
voir *v* to see
la voiture *n* car
je voudrais *v* I would like
vouloir *v* to want
vous you
Vous désirez? What would you like?
voyager *v* to travel
vrai *adj* true
vraiment really
le VTT *n* mountain bike

Y

le yaourt *n* yoghurt
les yeux *nm* eyes

cent soixante-quinze   175

OXFORD
UNIVERSITY PRESS

Great Clarendon Street, Oxford, OX2 6DP, United Kingdom

Oxford University Press is a department of the University of Oxford.
It furthers the University's objective of excellence in research,
scholarship, and education by publishing worldwide. Oxford is a
registered trade mark of Oxford University Press in the UK and in
certain other countries

British Library Cataloguing in Publication Data
Data available

978-0-19-839504-1

20 19 18 17 16 15 14 13 12

Paper used in the production of this book is a natural, recyclable
product made from wood grown in sustainable forests.
The manufacturing process conforms to the environmental regulations
of the country of origin.

Printed in China by Leo Paper Products Ltd

Acknowledgements
The publisher would like to thank the following for permissions to use
their photographs:

Cover illustration by: Claire Rollet

p4: Designpics/ Glow Images; David & Micha Sheldon/ F1 Online/ Corbis;
Digital Vision/ OUP; Jose Luis Pelaez, Inc./ Blend Images/ Corbis; 3bugsmom/
iStockphoto; Fred de Noyelle/ Godong/ Photononstop/ Glow Images; Jorg
Hackemann/ Shutterstock; Weston Colton/ Rubberball/ Glow Images; **p7**: Image
Source/ Glow Images; ostill /Shutterstock; itanistock/ OUP; **p11**: BEPictured/
Shutterstock; **p16**: mimagephotography/ Shutterstock; **p17**: Barry Austin/
Corbis; **p20**: Doug James/ Shutterstock; **p24**: Gurpal Singh Datta/ India Picture/
Glow Images; MBI/ Stockbroker/ Glow Images; Juanmonino/ iStockphoto;
Super Stock/ Glow Images; Maurizio Borsari/ Aflo Score/ Glow Images; Radius
Images/Glow Images; **p25**: Katarina Premfors/ Arabian Eye/ Getty Images; **p28**:
Deborah Kolb / Shutterstock; Jorg Hackemann / Shutterstock; Radius Images/
Glow Images; zhekoss/ Shutterstock; **p30**: Gelpi/ Fotolia; Pavel Davidenko/
Fotolia; **p34**: Pavel Davidenko/ Fotolia; **p35**: Gelpi/ Fotolia; **p36**: Andy Dean
Photography/ Shutterstock; Glenda/ Shutterstock; **p38**: Monkey Business
Images/ Bigstock; **p40**: Franck Guiziou/ Hemis/ Corbis; **p43**: jogyx/ Fotolia;
p45: Elke Van De Velde/ Corbis; **p46**: LeonP/Shutterstock; Vadim Petrakov/
Shutterstock; Johan Swanepoel/Shutterstock; tratong/Shutterstock; Peter
Schwarz/Shutterstock; wimpi/Shutterstock; Gerrit_de_Vries/Shutterstock;
Phattana SangsawangSStock/Shutterstock; **p48**: Masson/ Shutterstock; danielo/
Shutterstock; janecat/ Shutterstock; Netfalls - Remy Musser/ Shutterstock;
Prochasson Frederic/ Shutterstock; Moodboard/ OUP; Eric Isselee/ Shutterstock;
Denisnata/ Pantherstock; **p49**: JONATHAN NACKSTRAND/ AFP/ Getty Images;
p50: Gerrit_de_Vries/Shutterstock; LeonP/Shutterstock; Denisnata/ Pantherstock;
p52: Edyta Pawlowska/ Shutterstock; **p53**: RonaldHope/ iStockphoto; **p56**: OUP/
Tetra Images; **p59**: Regine Mahaux/ Taxi/ Getty Images; **p60**: David Atkinson/
Jetta Productions/ OUP; dacasdo/ Fotolia; Blend Images/ Inti St Clair/ Getty
Images; **p61**: Ron Levine/ Photodisc/ Getty Images; Jörg Hackemann/ Fotolia; **p64**:
maradonna 8888/Shutterstock; OUP/Brent Hofacker/Shutterstock; OUP/Viktor
Fischer; OUP/Martin Wierink; OUP/Ingram; OUP/Alamy Creativity; OUP; **p67**:
Helder Almeida/ Shutterstock; Granger Wootz/ Blend Images/ Corbis; **p70**: Image
Source/ Glow Images; **p71**: maksheb/ Bigstock; **p72**: Amiel/Photo Cuisine/Corbis;

p74: Jeffrey Blackler / Alamy; **p77**: Francesc Muntada/ CORBIS; Guy Thouvenin/
Robert Harding World Imagery/ Corbis; Richard Bowden/ E+/ Getty Images;
Jorg Hackemann/ Shutterstock; **p81**: Masterfile; **p88**: Images22/ TIPS RF/ Glow
Images; **p89**: Slawomir Kruz / Shutterstock; **p90**: Quebec Network of Healthy
Cities and Villages; **p91**: OUP; p95: Shutterstock; Buida Nikita Yourievich/
Shutterstock; Jupiter Images /Photolibrary/ Getty Images; **p102**: Michel Borges/
Fotolia; Alexander Trinitatov/ Fotolia; Alexandre Nunes/ Shutterstock; Masterfile;
Marc Piasecki/ Getty Images Entertainment/ Getty Images; **p103**: Bertrand
Rindoff Petroff/ French Select/ Getty Images; **p107**: Shutterstock; JGI/ Jamie
Grill/ Blend Images/ Getty Images; **p108**: Olivier Renck/Aurora Open/ Corbis
p112: Flashon Studio/Shutterstock; Lee Kennedy/Shutterstock; Quadriga Images/
LOOK-foto/ Glow Images; Chris Hellier/ Alamy; Lautaro/ Alamy; Robert Crum/
Shutterstock; Philippe FARJON/ Demotix/ Corbis; **p116**: Mlenny/ iStockPhoto;
Cruise Ships/ OUP; Paul Harris/ AWL Images/ Getty Images; Pixmann/ ImageZoo/
Glow Images; **p118**: Tatiana Morozova/ Shutterstock; **p119**: Photodisc/ OUP;
QQ7/ Shutterstock; Totajla/ Shutterstock; phant/ Fotolia; **p120**: Etienne Laurent/
Xinhua Press/ Corbis; AFP/ Getty Images; **p124**: Flashon Studio/Shutterstock; Lee
Kennedy/Shutterstock; Quadriga Images/ LOOK-foto/ Glow Images; Pixmann/
ImageZoo/Glow Images; Digital Vision/ OUP; kali9/ iStockPhoto; VisitBritain/
Britain on View/ Getty Images; **p125**: dbimages/Alamy; **p126**: Tracy Whiteside/
Shutterstock; Marc Dozier/ hemis.fr/ Getty Images; **p128**: Fred de Noyelle/
Godong/ Photononstop/ Glow Images; Austrophoto/ F1online/ Glow Images;
p131: Weston Colton/ Rubberball/ Glow Images; Digital Vision/ OUP; **p132**:
mountainpix/ Shutterstock; Aurora Photos/ Alamy; Martin Moxter/ImageBroker/
Glow Images; Dudarev Mikhail/Shutterstock; Rubberball/Jessica Peterson/
Brand X Pictures/ Getty Images; Bob Winsett/ Photolibrary/Getty Images;
Monkey Business/ Fotolia; **p133**: Monkey Business/ Fotolia; **p134**: Able Images/
Iconica/Getty Images; Martin Moxter/ ImageBroker/Glow Images; Deklofenak/
Shutterstock; **p135**: tomprout/ iStockphoto; Erwan Quemere/ Photononstop/
Glow Images; **p138**: MaxiSports/ Dreamstime; Grosremy/ Dreamstime; Leo
Mason/ Corbis; **p139**: Neale Cousland/ Shutterstock; Phil McElhinney/ Demotix/
Corbis; **p142**: aigarsr/ Fotolia; **p143**: Goodluz/Shutterstock; CREATISTA/
Shutterstock; Radius Images/ Glow Images; **p144**: Monsieur Romain Florent et
Madame Schultz Romain Christina; **p146**: Erwan Quemere/ Photononstop/ Glow
Images; **p148**: JeniFoto/ Shutterstock; FAYEZ NURELDINE/ AFP/ Getty Images;
p149: Zurijeta/Shutterstock; Charly Butcher/ iStockphoto; **p155**: Image Source/
OUP; WIS Bernard/ Paris Match Archive / Getty Images; Caro/Alamy; De Agostini/
Getty Images; iStockphoto; **p157**: Anthony Asael/ Art in All of Us/ Corbis; **p160**:
Handout/ Getty Images News / Getty Images; **p162**: Dave Stamboulis/ Alamy;
Henk Bentlage /Shutterstock; **p164**: digitalskillet/iStockphoto.

Background images: Igor Grochev/Shutterstock; WDG Photo/
Shutterstock; Giancarlo Liguori/Shutterstock.

Artwork by: Robin Edmonds, John Hallett, Lisa Hunt, Caron Painter,
Claire Rollet, Martin Sanders, Rory Walker.

The publisher and authors are grateful to the following for permission
to reprint extracts from copyright material: Fondation Maurice Carême
for 'Pour dessiner un bonhomme' from *Fleurs de soleil* by Maurice
Carême, copyright © Fondation Maurice Carême

The publisher and authors would like to thank the following for their
help and advice:

Vee Harris and Kate Scappaticci for writing the language learning
strategies (pages 9, 15, 23, 33, 40, 51, 59, 59, 83, 87, 99, 105, 114, 123,
130, 141, 152 and 159); Liz Black for writing the plenaries.

Geneviève Talon (editor, and author of the *Lire*, *Vidéo* and *Grammaire*
pages); Karine Couly (language consultant); Jackie Coe, Cécile Hughes
and Sally Price (course consultants).

Audio recordings produced by Colette Thomson for Footstep
Productions Ltd; Andrew Garratt (engineer).

Video shot on location in Montpellier, with grateful thanks to Colette
Thomson for Footstep Productions Ltd (producer, director and
scriptwriter); Paul Keating (cameraman); Brian Powell (sound); Agnès
Beligond (location manager); Zaied Ahabri, Basile Dezeuze, Clarisse
Girardet, Oumaïma Helli, Noura Idrissi, Asma Machhouri, Jules
Nguyen, Diakouba Toure (actors), Geoffrey Bergogne and AfricaTala.